MW01324965

J. Elihay

English translation: Carol Sutherland, Susan Fogg

Speaking Arabic

A Course in Conversational
Eastern (Palestinian) Arabic

Book 2
Lessons 16-30

Minerva Publishing House
2009

Minerva Publishing House
P.O.B 7023 Jerusalem 91070, Israel
www.speaking-arabic.com

ISBN 978-965-7397-17-6

Contents

Preface	[7]
Lesson 16	1
Lesson 17	10
Lesson 18	21
Lesson 19	30
Lesson 20	39
Lesson 21	49
Lesson 22	61
Lesson 23	72
Lesson 24	83
Lesson 25	95
Lesson 26	105
Lesson 27	118
Lesson 28	128
Lesson 29	142
Lesson 30	153
Nawāder	163
Key to the Exercises	167
Vocabulary and Rules	187
Rules (indicated by a number inside a square)	197

Preface

Welcome to Book 2!

Before you get to work on Lesson 16, may we suggest that you re-read the sections of the Preface to Book 1 entitled **How to use this course** and **A little more advice.**

Pay special attention to pronunciation, particularly the following points:

– Remember to differentiate between the emphatic consonants (the ones with a dot underneath) and ordinary ones.

– Distinguish carefully between -a and -α (see **Book 1, p. [12]** and the explanation of the emphatic ṣ sound on p. [11]).

– Don't forget to linger over doubled consonants and pronounce them more vigorously than single ones. Bear in mind, however, that the doubling is scarcely audible when a doubled consonant is followed by another consonant, e.g., b**i**(d)dkom.

– Take care to make all long vowels really long (long vowels have a line over the top).

Beware – if you don't pronounce long vowels and doubled consonants properly, or if you get the stress in the wrong place, people will find you hard to understand, and may be unable to suppress a giggle.

Abbreviations and Symbols

We've added two extra symbols to the list in Book 1:

[5] Numbers inside squares indicate which rules apply to the word you're dealing with. You'll find the list of rules at the back of this book, p. 197.

f-2 The letter f + a number between 1 and 10 indicates the verbal Form to which a specific verb belongs; see p. 105. f-2 is short for Form 2, also known as the **fa**^{cc}al Form – see **Lesson 26, p. 107**.

id-dars is-sādes ᶜαšαr – dars sittαᶜš

The Sixteenth Lesson (Lesson Sixteen)

Let's add something new to our knowledge of the comparative adjective:
What happens when the two final root consonants are identical, e.g., ђ-f-f

ђafīf → 'aђaff = *light → lighter*

The two final consonants "crowd up" together so tightly that they have to be pronounced as a double *ff*. The effort of doing this attracts the stress to the end of the word, to the vowel just before the doubled consonant (unlike '**a**kbar, '**a**ḥla, where the stress is on the first syllable).

In the same way: qal**ī**l → 'aq**a**ll (haq**a**ll[1])
(a) little *less*

The word muh**e**mm (*important*), whose root is h-m-m, also belongs to this group of adjectives, and its comparative form is 'ah**a**mm (*more important*).

Vocabulary

ᶜ**i**lbe // ᶜ**u**lbe	tin, can, box	l**u**ġa [luġ**ā**t]	language
[ᶜ**i**lab // ᶜ**u**lab]	tins, cans, boxes	ᶜ**α**rαbi	Arab$^{m\ sing}$; Arabic
ġ**α**ṭα [ġ**u**ṭi]	lid, cover	ᶜαrαb**i**yye	Arab$^{f\ sing}$
z**a**yy	like (prep)	'**a**jnabi ['aj**ā**neb]	foreigner$^{m\ sing}$
ᵉtq**ī**l	heavy	'ajnab**i**yye	foreigner$^{f\ sing}$
'**a**tqal	heavier	ġ**u**rfe[2] [ġ**u**rαf]	room
w**i**seђ (cp:'**a**wsaђ)	dirty	s**a**lle [sl**ā**l]	basket
h**a**yyen	easy^{m}	jār**ū**r // jαrr**ā**r	drawer
h**a**yyne	easy^{f}	[jawār**ī**r]	drawers
'**a**hwan (cp)	easier	ђarb**ā**n	out of order, no good
qy**ā**s	size, measurement[s], dimensions		

1. See **Book 1, p.98, footnote 3**.

2. Don't forget to distinguish between -ġ (which sounds rather like the noise you make when starting to gargle) and -r (an *r* sound rolled on the tip of the tongue, Scots or Spanish style). Try pronouncing this word slowly several times at first: ġu - rᵉ - fe, then try to produce the same sequence of sounds more quickly.

Conversation

– biddi ᶜilab kartōn zayy hādi ᶜišrīn santi ᶜala talātīn.	– I want cardboard boxes like this one, 20 centimeters by 30.
– šūf hadōl.	– Take a look at these <look at these>.
– la', hadōl ḫarbānīn. fīšš ġēr-hom?	– No, these are no good. Don't you have anything else <there are not other-than them>?
– fīʰ hadlāk // hadōlāk[3] fi-l-qurne hunāk, nafs‿il-lōn u-nafs l-ᵉqyās[4], lāken bala ġaṭa.	– There are those in the corner there, the same color and the same size, but without a lid.
– balāš il-ġaṭa ! hāt[5] hadōlāk!	– No need for the lid! Give [me] those!

– iš-šanta hāy‿ᵉtqīle ᶜalēk.	– This suitcase is [too] heavy for you <heavy on you>.
ḫōd[6] is-salle, is-salle ḫafīfe.	Take the basket, the basket's light.
– is-salle 'aḫaff min iš-šanta?	– Is the basket lighter than the suitcase?
– 'ā, ṭabᶜan, iš-šanta 'atqal b-ᵉktīr.	– Yes, of course, the suitcase is **much** heavier <heavier by much>.
hiyye tqīle ᶜa-šān-ha[7] malāne, fī-ha 'awāᶜi ᶜutaq[8].	It's heavy because it's full, it's got old clothes in it <in it [are] old clothes>.

Please note: in the recordings, the Conversation is followed by the sentences marked ■, first those in the Explanations, then those in the footnotes.

3. In northern Galilee (Tarshiha, Fassuta, etc.) you will hear people say hadōk; in Nazareth, Haifa and Acco (Acre): hadlāk; in Jerusalem hadōlāk.

■ 4. As q is pronounced ', the word l-ᵉqyās is pronounced le'... yās. In other words: le + a sudden pause (glottal stop) + yās. Listen carefully to the recording!

5. The word hāt (f: hāti, pl: hātu) means *give! bring! hand [me]......!* This is an isolated word, i.e., it does not form part of a verb conjugation.

6. This is the imperative of the verb 'aḫad (*he took*) which in the past tense conjugates like katab, but is irregular in the other tenses; we'll learn it soon.

7. You can say either ᶜala-šān or ᶜa-šān, as ᶜa- is short for ᶜala. Personal pronouns can be attached to this word, too: ᶜa-šān-ak taᶜbān = *because you're tired.* We can do this with other similar words we know, too: li-ann-ak = li'anno 'inte ...).

8. ᶜatīq (f ᶜatīqa [ᶜutaq / ᶜutoq]) means *old* and is used of inanimate objects only.

qīm il-'awāᶜi min qaleb-ha[9]	Take the clothes out of it <remove the clothes from its inside> and then
u-betṣīr ḫafīfe.	it'll be light <it will become light>.

– hal-banṭalōn[10] ṭawīl ᶜalayy.	– These trousers are too long for me <this [pair of] trousers is long on me>.
fī-š ᶜindek 'iši haqṣar[11] minno?	Don't you[f] have a shorter pair <something shorter than it>?
– hadāk illi fi-l-ḫazāne 'aṭwal kamān. fī-š haqṣar min hāda.	– The ones in the wardrobe / closet are even longer. There's nothing shorter than these <than this>.
– u-biddi kamān ṭaqiyye[12] laš-šuġol, ṭaqiyye‿ndīfe. hādi wisḫa.[13]	– And I want a cap, too, for work. A clean cap, this one's dirty.
– ḫōd hadīk illi fi-l-jārūr (jarrār) hiyye nḍīfe.	– Take that one in the drawer <that [is] in the drawer>, it's clean.
– nḍīfe nḍīfe?	– Really clean <clean clean>?
– yaᶜni… 'anḍaf min hāy.	– Well…. cleaner than this [one].

[This section is not included in the recording]

– kīf il-luġa‿l-ᶜarabiyye, ṣaᶜbe?	– What's Arabic like <how is the Arabic language> – hard?
– 'ā, maᶜlūm, il-ᶜarabi ṣaᶜeb, 'aṣᶜab min il-ᶜubrāni (ᶜibrāni [G])	– Yes, of course <[it's] known>. Arabic's difficult, more difficult than Hebrew.

---

9. The word qalb means *heart* and also *inside* (n); qām [iqīm] means *to remove, take off*, and it conjugates in the same way as the verb jāb. qīm hāda min hōn = *Take that away from here! / Get that out of here!*
qimto means *I took it away*; qimnāh /qimnā-ha = *We took it away / We took it off.*

10) The Arabic for *trousers* is banṭalōn (m sing!), [banāṭlīn[G] // banṭalōnāt[J]], from the French *pantalon.*

11) See **Book 1, p. 98, footnote 3.**

12) The word ṭaqiyye means *cap, beret, skullcap,* etc.

13) The adjective wiseḫ (f wisḫa [wisḫīn]) comes from the same root as the noun wasaḫ, which means *dirt.* The plural form ['awsāḫ] means *pieces of dirt / litter.* Don't confuse this plural with the comparative adjective 'awsaḫ, which means *dirtier.*

– kamān il-ᶜubrāni muš hayyen (muš‿ᵉhwayyen)[G]	– Hebrew's not easy either, <also Hebrew [is] not easy>,
lāken 'ahwan min il-ᶜαrαbi.	but [it's] easier than Arabic.
– kull luġa ṣαᶜbe la-l-'ajāneb,	– Every language is difficult for foreigners.
dars il-luġāt biddo waqt‿u-tamrīn.	Learning languages takes time and practice.
– ṣαḥīḥ ! kull ši biddo	– True! Everything takes <wants / needs>
ṣαbᵉr. ᶜindak‿ᵉktāb‿ᵉmnīḥ,	patience. You've got a good book,
hāda muhemm, bass…	that's important, but…..
iṣ-ṣαbᵉr[14] 'ahamm 'iši.	patience is the most important thing!

– il-ġurfe hādi 'aḥla min hadīk.	– This room is nicer than that one.
u-'αnḍαf kamān.	And cleaner, too.
– mαẓbūṭ, bass hadīk 'αṭwαl	–True, but that one's longer.
fīha maḥall 'aktαr.	It's got <in it> more space.
– bidnā-š maḥall‿ᵉktīr.	– We don't need a lot of space.
hadīk wisḫa,	That one's dirty,
u-hādi 'aḥla ġurfe fi-l-bēt.	and this is the nicest room in the house.
– ṭαyyeb, zayy-ma biddak.	– Fine, whatever you like <as what you like>.

---

14. This word means both *patience* and *prickly pear*, which is a tough and "patient" variety of cactus that can go for a long time without water. The fruit of the prickly pear ■ is called kūz ṣαbᵉr [kwāz] in Arabic. hāt talat‿ᵉkwāz = *Give [me] three prickly pears!*

Explanations

1. Arabic

We've learnt in this lesson that we can say either
il-ᶜarabi or il-luġa‿l-ᶜarabiyye, and, in the same way,
either il-ᶜibrāni (or ᶜubrāni) or il-luġa‿l-ᶜibriyye *Hebrew*,
and also il-'inᵉglīzi / il-luġa l-'inglīziyye *English*.

Even though we haven't learned the verb *to speak* yet, let's learn the following important expression:

■ btiḥki ᶜarabi?	*Do you speak Arabic?*
baḥki šwayy.	*I speak a little.*

2. Centimeter = santi / ṣanti

This form is used for both singular and plural, and it is invariable. When it is preceded by a number between 3 and 10, this number remains "complete," i.e., the final –e /-a is not dropped:

■ talāte santi	*3 centimeters*
ḫamse santi	*5 centimeters*

This is the also case with other foreign words that designate weights and measures: kīlo (*kilogram* or *kilometer*), šēkel (*shekel*), etc.

■ sabᶜa kīlo	*7 kilometers / kilograms*
ᶜašara šēkel	*10 shekels*

We've talked about the numbers between 3 and 10 – but what about 2? The dual ending -ēn is not added to foreign words, and so we say:

■ tnēn santi	*2 centimeters*
tnēn šēkel	*2 shekels*
tnēn kīlo	*2 kilometers*

The form of these foreign words in no way resembles that of any Arabic word. The word mitᵉr (*meter*), on the other hand, looks like an Arabic word (it looks as if it belongs to the same group of words as binᵉt), and so it can assume an Arabic plural form [mtūra / 'amtār]. With a number it behaves just like an ordinary Arabic noun:

■ mitrēn	*2 meters*
tlatt‿ᵉmtūra	*3 meters*

3. bala / balāš

The word *without* translates into Arabic as bala, bidūn or mindūn. From bala we form the word balāš (= bala+ši, i.e., *without [any]thing*). We've already seen how balāš is used to mean *don't; never mind!* It also means *free of charge* (*without anything*, i.e., without money).

■ hāda‿b-balāš — *This is free of charge*
yɑllɑ, yā balāš — *Roll up! It's free!*
(This is what the market vendors shout).

And, last of all: with the attached personal pronouns, bala behaves like wɑrɑ (see **Book 1, p. 69**)

■ balāy — *without me*
balāk — *without you*$^{\text{m sing}}$
balāki — *without you* $^{\text{f sing}}$
balāh — *without him*
balā-ha — *without her* etc.
biddī-š arūḥ balā-kom — *I don't want to go without you*^{pl}.
'iza mumken‿ᵉtrūḥu balāy — *If possible, go*^{pl} *without me*
<if it's possible that you go…>

4. bɑᶜḍ / bɑᶜeḍ

Take care not to confuse this word with baᶜd (*after*), which is written with an **a**, rather than an **ɑ**, and whose final consonant is d, not ḍ. bɑᶜḍ means *some [of]*.

■ bɑᶜḍ‿in-nās — *some people* <some-of the people>
bɑᶜḍ‿il-mɑrrāt — *sometimes*

From here it's only a short step to the Arabic for *each other / one another*:

bizūru bɑᶜḍ-hom il-bɑᶜeḍ — *They visit each other / one another*
(i.e., some of them visit some of the others)

We can say the same thing without repeating the word bɑᶜḍ:

bizūru bɑᶜeḍ — *They visit each other / one another*

It performs a similar function after a preposition:

■ ᶜala bɑᶜeḍ / fōq bɑᶜeḍ — *one on top of the other / above one another*
wɑrɑ bɑᶜeḍ — *one behind the other / one after another*
maᶜ bɑᶜeḍ — *together* <with one another>
jamb bɑᶜeḍ — *side by side* <next to each other>

Note the expressions:

■ talat mɑrrɑ̄t wɑrɑ bɑᶜeḍ — *three times in succession*
<three times one after another>

'arbaᶜ sēᶜāt wɑrɑ bɑᶜeḍ — *four hours on end / four hours in succession / four consecutive hours*

5. That, those:

The final thing we'll learn in this lesson is:

■ *this* (m)	hāda	hadāk	*that* (m)
this (f)	hādi	hadīk	*that* (f)
these	hadōl	hadlāk[G]	*those*
		hadōlāk[J]	

The -k at the end of the words for *that* and *those* conveys the notion of distance (like the -k at the end of the word hunāk). They are used with definite nouns (i.e., nouns preceded by il-) as follows:

hadāk il-bēt / il-bēt hadāk — *that house*

You may also hear: hadīk il-yōm — *that day*[15]
despite the fact that the word yōm is masculine.

---

15. In the sense of *that day [back then]*. If you want to say *on that same day*, you will, of course, say in Arabic fi nafs il-yōm.

Note: As you may have noticed in some of the earlier lessons, English usage sometimes requires the words **hāda** / **hādi** and **hadōl** to be translated as *that / those* rather than as *this / these*.

This lesson has given us a break from the verbs, if nothing else! If you feel it had too much material in it, put it aside for now, then go back and read it tomorrow – or, better still – in a few days' time.

Exercises

A. Translate into English:

1. hal-ᵉktāb malān quṣɑṣ.
2. fīh hōn talat ᶜulab, bikaffi.[16]
3. bass wēn il-ġuṭi?
4. fīh hōn ġɑṭɑ wāḥad, bass wēn il-bāqi?[17]
5. šū‿qyās il-ᶜulbe hāy?
6. qul-li qaddēš‿ᵉqyās il-ġurfe.
7. hōn ma fišš maḥall minšāno.
8. ᵉmbala, fīh maḥall‿ᵉktīr.
9. biddō-š‿irūḥ balāki.
10. 'iza hēk, mᵉnrūḥ balākom.
11. mᵉnzūr // bᵉnzūr bɑᶜᵉḍ.
12. bɑᶜḍ‿il-ᶜilab bala ġɑṭɑ.
13. l-ewlād bifūtu wɑrɑ bɑᶜᵉḍ.

B. Complete the sentences

(Replace the English words with the appropriate expression in Arabic):

14. il-qannīne ([is] full).
15. il-mɑṭbɑḫ ([is] dirty) il-yōm.
16. lōn il-bāb ([is] nicer) min lōn iš-šubbāk.
17. il-yōm il-filᵉm kān (longer) min‿ᵉmbāreḥ.
18. lāzem ijību 'aflām (shorter) minšān l-ewlād.

---

16. Remember this? It's in **Lesson 1**, right at the end of the **Conversation**.
17. See **Book 1**, **Vocabulary, p.63**.

C. Translate into Arabic:

19. I want a bigger room.
20. We want the biggest room.[18]
21. Give (hāt) [me] a smaller box.
22. This is an easy language.
23. There is no [such thing as an] easy language. Every language is difficult for foreigners.
24. Do you speak a foreign language?
25. No, I speak only Arabic.

A word of encouragement: Do you feel that you're drowning in an ocean of new words? Don't worry! Children learn by listening to their parents' conversation. Each day they remember only a portion of what they've heard, but, as the same words recur constantly, eventually they pick them up and make them part of their vocabulary. It's the same with this book: words from previous lessons recur all the time, in both the Conversations and the Exercises. The main thing is to **move forward!**

---

18. Oops, this is a difficult one, isn't it? The word ġurfe is hard enough to pronounce on its own, and here you've got to battle your way through the combination 'akbɑr ġurfe! How do you cope with it? Try splitting the phrase up into syllables and pronouncing them slowly one after another; then repeat the process more quickly tomorrow and the next day. This is the best way to overcome pronunciation difficulties. And if it doesn't work? Well then, you'll just have to make do with a middle-sized room!

The Seventeenth Lesson (Lesson Seventeen)

It's time to go back to the verb. So far we have deliberately ignored the plural forms of t**u**ṭlob, t**i**trek, y**u**ṭlob, y**i**trek.

When we add the ending -u to the verb forms above, the second vowel (e / o) disappears:

y**i**trek *that he leave*	y**i**trk-u	and in actuality	y**i**t^{e}rku *that they leave*
y**u**ṭlob *that he ask (for..)*	y**u**ṭlb-u	and in actuality	y**u**ṭ^{o}lbu *that they ask (for…)*
y**u**ḍrob *that he strike*	y**u**ḍrb-u	and in actuality	y**u**ḍ^{o}rbu *that they strike*

Although some people pronounce these verbs differently, as y**u**ṭl^{o}bu, y**i**tr^{e}ku, etc., most speakers use the forms given in the table above – and we shall use them, too.[1]

It's logical that the same thing should happen before the 2nd person feminine singular ending -i and before the attached personal pronouns -ak, -ek, and -u, i.e., each time we add a suffix that begins with a vowel.

bt**i**trek	*you$^{m\ sing}$ leave*
bt**i**t^{e}rki 'ibnek	*you^{f} sing leave your son*
b^{y}**i**trek	*he leaves*
b^{y}**i**t^{e}rk-ak, b^{y}**i**t^{e}rkek	*he leaves you$^{m/f}$*
b^{y}**u**ḍ^{o}rbak	*he hits you$^{m\ sing}$*

However, when the suffix begins with a consonant, the second vowel of the word is not just retained – it also attracts the stress, in accordance with a rule with which you are already familiar (see **Book 1**, **Lesson 14**, **Explanations 3**). The suffixes -ni, -ha, -na, -ku // -kom and -hen // -hom all begin with a consonant, and so we say:

b^{y}**u**ḍrob	*he hits*
b^{y}uḍr**o**b-ni	*he hits me*

---

1. In Lesson 12 we saw that the vowel -a does not disappear, but is always retained: y**i**dfa^{c} → y**i**dfa^{c}u (*that he pay → that they pay*).

b**a**trek	*I keave*
batr**e**k-ha	*I leave her*

But what happens in the imperative?

First of all, let's recall what happens with verbs of the š**ā**f type: we took the t- off the word t-š**ū**f and were left with š**ū**f ! (*look! see!*).

Here we replace the **ti**- / **tu**- with **'i**- / **'u**-.

	t**i**trek, t**i**tᵉrtku	*that you*$^{\text{m sing}}$ *leave, that you*^{pl} *leave*
■	**'i**trek ! **'i**tᵉrtku !	*Leave*$^{\text{m sing}}$*! Leave*^{pl}*!*
	t**u**skot, t**u**sᵒkti	*that you*$^{\text{m sing}}$ *be quiet, that you*$^{\text{f sing}}$ *be quiet*
	'uskot ! **'u**sᵒkti !	*Be quiet*$^{\text{m sing}}$*! be quiet*$^{\text{f sing}}$*!*

Vocabulary

s**a**baq [y**u**sboq]	to precede / overtake	q**a**wi[4]	strong
q**a**ᶜad [y**u**qᶜod][2]	to sit down	s**u**rᶜa[5]	speed
sayy**ā**rα [sayyār**ā**t]	car, automobile	jn**ū**n	madness, insanity
šuf**ē**r [šufēr**i**yye][3]	driver	ḥ**a**bᵉl ['aḥb**ā**l]	rope
q**ā**m [iq**ī**m]	to remove / take off	ẖ**ē**ṭ [ẖiṭ**ā**n]	thread, cord, string
sand**ū**q [sanādīq]	box, chest; till, cash register, checkout (in a shop, supermarket, etc.)	ḥ**a**mal [yiḥmel][6]	to carry

---

■ 2. The verb q**a**ᶜad [y**u**qᶜod] means *sit down*; *stay, remain. I sat down* = **'a**na q**a**ᶜ**a**dᵉt. *She sat down* = h**i**yye q**a**ᶜdat. *Sit down* (m sing)*!* = **'u**qᶜod / h**u**qᶜod! for reasons similar to those affecting the word **'α**qṣαr (see **Book 1, p.98, footnote 3**). *Sit down* (f sing) = **'u**qᵒᶜdi / h**u**qᵒᶜdi ! These are not easy words for beginners to pronounce. It's best to practice slowly and listen to the recording. Split the word up into separate syllables: h**u** - qoᶜ - di, and gradually increase the speed at which you say it. It may encourage you to learn that people often say h**u**ᶜ -di when they are speaking quickly and carelessly.

3. Or šufar**i**yye. From the French *chauffeur.* The word s**ā**'eq [sā'iq**ī**n#] – from the root s**ū**q – is the formal term used in announcements on the radio, driving lessons, etc. (see the # sign on page [9] at the beginning of **Book 1).** The verb s**ā**q [is**ū**q], on the

■ other hand, is common in everyday speech: *Can you drive?* = btiᶜref‿ᵉts**ū**q? <do you know [how] to drive>? We'll be learning the verb *to know* soon (in Lesson 19).

4, 5, 6. See next page.

Conversation

– f**ī**^{h} wa**rā**k sayy**ā**ra, iš-šuf**ē**r	– There's a car behind you. The <this> driver
h**ā**da b**i**ddo y**u**s^{o}bqak.	wants to overtake you.
– d**ā**yman f**ī**^{h} w**ā**ḥad b**i**ddo[7]	– There's always someone who wants
y**u**sboq it-t**ā**ni.	to overtake somebody else <the second one>.
u-h**ā**da b**i**ddo yusb**o**q-ni?	And this [guy] wants to overtake me?
tf**a**ḍḍal, yā ḥab**ī**bi!	Go ahead, mate / buddy <please, dear>!
– had**ō**l iš-šuf**ē**r**i**yye b**u**s^{o}bqu	– These drivers overtake
b**a**^{ce}ḍ-hom il-b**a**^{ce}ḍ‿eb-s**u**r^{c}a,	one another at [high] speed,
h**ā**da jn**ū**n!	it's madness!

by**u**sboq → b^y**u**sboq / b**u**sboq	He overtakes
busb**o**q-ni; b**u**s^{o}bqak; b**u**s^{o}bqo	He overtakes me; you^m; him

----

– ḫ**ō**d il-ḥ**a**b^{e}l h**ā**da	– Take^m this rope
w-**u**rboṭ is-sand**ū**q.	and tie [up] the box.
'**u**r^{o}bṭo mn**ī**ḥ	Tie it well,
^{c}ala-š**ā**n ik**ū**n q**a**wi.	so that it's strong.
w-**i**nti, j**ī**bi‿l-^{c}**i**lbe had**ī**k…	And you^f, bring [me] that box...
– 'aq**ī**m il-ġ**a**ṭa?	– Should I take the lid off?
– l**a**', ma‿tq**ī**m**ī**-š il-ġ**a**ṭa!	– No, don't take the lid off!

---

4. q**a**wi, f. qaw**i**yye [qaw**ā**ya / '**a**̋qwiya$^{\#}$] means *strong, sturdy.* What is its comparative form? Try to work this out for yourself (think of ḥ**i**lu). You'll find the answer in the Conversation below. Note that the word q**a**wi is also used to mean *full of vitality; headstrong*, etc., e.g., qaw**i**yye h**ā**y! = *She's feisty, that one!*

5. *Quickly* = b-s**u**r^{c}a. Note that b-s**u**r^{c}a indicates the speed at which an action is performed, unlike qaw**ā**m, which means *quickly* in the sense of *immediately, straight away, right now, without delay.*

6. You will sometimes hear this pronounced ḥ**i**mel, especially in Galilee. We'll be learning this verb very soon (in Lesson 18).

7. The word **i**lli (*who, which, that*) is usually dropped after an **indefinite** noun (*someone, a person, a thing*, etc.) We'll discuss this at length in another lesson.

'urobṭi‿l-ᶜilbe b-hal-ḫēṭ	Tie up the box with this [piece of] string.
'urobṭī-ha mnīḥ!	Tie it well!
– kīf yaᶜni?	– How do you mean <how, it means>?
– hāti, 'ana barboṭ-ha.	– Give [it to me]. I'll tie it!
barboṭ, barobṭo, barboṭ-ha	I tie / I'll tie; I tie him; I tie her

----

– šū biddak fīh?	– What do you[m] want from him <in him>?
– ḍarab-ni!	– He hit me!
– maᶜalēš, 'iterko!	– Never mind, leave him [alone]!
hū 'azġar minnak;	He's smaller than you.
muš ᶜēb[8] tuḍrob walad	Aren't you ashamed <[is it] not a disgrace>
'azġar minnak?	to hit a boy smaller than yourself <than you>?
'inte 'aqwa (/ haqwa)	You're stronger than him!
minno, lēš‿ebtuḍorbo?	Why are you hitting him?

– hal-bint‿ebtidfeš	– This girl jostles the other
il-banāt it-tānyīn[9]. ya bint!	girls.You, girl,
lēš‿ebtidefši‿l-banāt hēk?	why do you jostle the girls like that?
muš lāzem tidefšī-hen/-hom.	You mustn't jostle them.
fīh maḥall hōn minšān il-kull.	There's room here for everyone <for all>.

– 'urkoḍ, ya walad! 'urokḍi ya	– Run, boy! Run, girl!
binet! 'urokḍu sawa, ta‿nšūf	Run together so that we can see
mīn busboq it-tāni.	who finishes first <who overtakes the other>!

– šū šuġlek?	– What's your[f] job?

---

8. The word ᶜēb means *shame, disgrace, wrongdoing*, and you will encounter it frequently in contexts like the one above. miš ᶜēb? = *Isn't it a scandal... / Isn't it wrong.../ Aren't you ashamed of yourself?* When people say ᶜēb! by itself in a reproving tone, they mean *Shame on you! / That's wrong!*

9. Remember: tāni doesn't just mean *second*; it also means *other*, and its plural is tānyīn / tānīn.

– 'ana ᶜāmlet[10] sandūq, yaᶜni baqᶜod ᶜala‿s-sandūq fi supermārket.	– I'm a checkout clerk / assistant. In other words <it means> I sit at <on> a cash register in a supermarket.
– illi buqᵒᶜdu ᶜala‿s-sanādīq kīf maᶜāš-hom? 'inti masalan…	– The checkout clerks / assistants – what's their salary like <how's their salary>? You, for example…
– 'ana maᶜāši qalīl, bass fīʰ kamān maᶜāš jōzi u-mᵉndabber ḥālnα[11].	– I don't earn much myself <I, my salary's little>, but there's my husband's salary, too, and we manage <we arrange our situation>.

– bʸiḥmel iš-šanta?	– Can he carry the suitcase <he will carry…>?
– 'ᾱ, bʸiḥmel-ha.	– Yes, he can carry it!
– bʸiḥmel is-sandūq?	– Can he carry the box?
– 'aywa, biḥᵉmlo.	– Yes, he can carry it.
– ana, iš-šanta, baḥmel-ha, bass ma baḥmel-hā-š la-hāli[12].	– I can take the suitcase <I, the suitcase, I'll carry it> But I won't carry it on my own.
– hāt, 'ana baḥmel-ha ᶜannak[13].	– Give [it to me], I'll carry it for you.

– lāzem 'adfaᶜ ᶜala ṭūl?	– Do I have to pay at once?
– 'idfaᶜ hallaq qadd-ma biddak, u-btidfaᶜ il-bāqi ġēr mαrrα. ma tidfaᶜ-š‿il-kull dafᶜa waḥade. balki (ma) maᶜak-š mαṣᾱri.	– **Pay** as much as **you**ᵐ **want** now then **pay** the rest another time. **Don't pay** it all in one go <[in] one payment>. Perhaps **you haven't got** [the] money [on you].

Repeat the section above in the feminine. The five expressions you have to change are marked in bold in the English translation.[14]

– bid-na numroq min hōn.	– We want to go this way <to pass from here>.
– muš mumken tumᵒrqu	– You can't go this way <not possible that

10. This will be explained in Lesson 21.

11. Explained in Lesson 27.

12. See **Book 1, p. 50** for an explanation of the expression la-hāli .

13. See below, in **Explanations**.

14. The feminine forms of these five expressions are provided at the end of the lesson, so that you can check to make sure that you've got them right.

min hōn: fīš ṭarīq!	you go....>. There's no way [through]!
'um^{o}rqu min hunāk / min ġād,	Go that way <pass from there>,
min wara‿l-madrase.	behind the school.

Explanations

1. The imperative

Let's go back over what we said at the beginning of the lesson about the imperative of verbs like **ka**tab:

- To form the imperative, we replace the **ti**- / **tu**- with **'i**- / **'u**-:

■	lāzem titrek[15]	*You've got to leave off.*	'itrek !	*Leave off!*	(m sing)
	lāzem tuṭlob	*You've got to ask.*	'uṭlob !	*Ask!*	(m sing)
	biddek tuṭ^{o}lbi	*You want to ask.*	'uṭ^{o}lbi !	*Ask!*	(f sing)
	biddek tidfa^{c}i	*You want to pay.*	'idfa^{c}i !	*Pay!*	(f sing)

Take good care to distinguish between '**a**trek and '**i**trek.
We've deliberately confused you – now we'll do our best to explain:

lāzem 'atrek	*I've got to leave off.*	'itrek !	*Leave off!*	(m sing)
biddi 'adfa^c	*I want to pay*	'idfa^c !	*Pay!*	(m sing)

However, in negative commands (e.g., *Don't go! / Don't write!*), as we've already said[16], the subjunctive form is used as it stands:

■	(ma tikteb) / ma tikteb-š !	*Don't write!*	(m sing)
	(ma tuṭ^{o}lbu) / ma tuṭ^{o}lbū-š !	*Don't ask!*	(pl)
	(ma tidfa^{c}i) / ma tidfa^{c}ī-š !	*Don't pay!*	(f sing)

There is a more literary and less commonly used way to express negative commands: la + subjunctive:

la tikteb! / la tuktob!	*Don't write!*	(m sing)

This form of negative command is used in the proverb 'uq^{c}od (huq^{c}od) barra wa-la tuq^{c}od ḥadd il-jarra, which means *Sit outside rather than next to the jug*

---

15. The verb tarak means *to leave* (someone); *to leave off / stop* and *to drop / forget about* (a subject, an issue). However, it does not mean *to leave* in the sense of *to depart.*

16. See **Book 1, p. 95, footnote 6**.

(because if you sit next to the jug everyone will ask you to pass it, pour them a glass of water, etc. Better to sit outside).

2. ᶜan

We have already come across the preposition ᶜan (bᶜīd ᶜan bētak; zīḥ il-burdāy ᶜan iš-šubbāk), which is used mainly with actions involving **removal** or **distancing** – unlike the preposition min, which usually indicates an action's **source** or **starting point**. Obviously the two prepositions are not dissimilar, and in some cases ᶜan can be replaced by min and vice versa; nonetheless, there is a subtle difference between the two: ᶜan is closer to the English *away from*, while min is just *from.*

■ ḫōd ᶜanni! *Take [it] away from me* (i.e., off my shoulders, or out of my hands)!

By extension, ᶜan has acquired the additional meaning of *instead of*:

■ baḥmel ᶜannak *I'll carry it for you* (i.e., *I'll take it away from you and carry it instead*).

This means that we can use the expression ḫōd ᶜanni ! to mean *Take over! Replace me!*

– ᶜan is used in a variety of expressions that we'll come across every so often. Here are a couple of examples:

■ ᶜan 'iznak. *With your permission [I'll be on my way].*

'iznak maᶜak! (response to the above) *Your permission is with you!* (i.e., *you are free to decide for yourself*).

It's time to learn a couple more picturesque expressions:

– When mentioning a disaster, an unfortunate incident or anything else unpleasant, people often add, perhaps out of superstition, the expression bᶜīd ᶜannak / ᶜannek / ᶜankom, which means, literally, *[May the thing I've just mentioned be] far from you*, or, in other words, *May this never happen to you* or *Excuse the reference.*

bijību zbāle – bᶜīd ᶜannak – u-birmū-ha[17] ġād.

They bring refuse – excuse the reference – and throw it there.

– When speaking of something upsetting or insulting, people often add the expression l-ᵉbᶜīd or il-baᶜīd#, which means *the distant [one]*, i.e., *the thing or person I have just mentioned or insulted is distant*, i.e., *no aspersions on present company / present company excepted*:

17. We'll learn this verb in Lesson 28.

qult-**i**llo: yā ḥm**ā**r! – l-^{e}b^{c}**ī**d / il-ba^{c}**ī**d# – ...

I said to him, 'you ass' – no aspersions on anyone present...

3. q**a**dd

The original meaning of the word q**a**dd is *quantity, size, extent*, and we've already come across it in the expression qadd**ē**š (qadd + '**ē**š = <quantity what / extent what?>), which means *how much / how many?* The word q**a**dd on its own is also used to mean *the same size / the same quantity*, and, by extension: *as much as; the same as*:

b**a**ḥmal q**a**ddak	*I'm carrying as much as you are / the same quantity as you are.*
'**a**na ṭawī̄l q**a**ddak	*I'm as tall as you.*
q**a**ddi q**a**ddak	*I've got the same amount as you; I've done as much as you have; I'll do as much as you*, etc. <my quantity [is] your quantity>.
k**ū**n qadd ḥ**ā**lak	*Shape up / Rise to the occasion / Show the world what you can do* <be the extent of your situation>!
h**u**mme qadd b**a**^{ce}ḍ-hom	*They're the same size / the same age*, etc. <they [are] equal to one another>
^{c}**i**ndi ġ**u**rfe qadd il-m**a**ṭbaḫ	*I've got a room the size of the kitchen*
hal-q**a**dd / hal-q**a**dde	*that big / small; this big / small; so big / small; so much / so little* <this extent>.

This expression may be accompanied by appropriate hand gestures of the type shown in the illustration overleaf.

All this gives us the expression q**a**dd-ma, which means *as much as*:

q**a**dd-ma bt**u**ṭlob	*as much as you ask for*
q**a**dd-ma b**i**ddak	*as much as you want; as much as you need*

4. Attaching personal pronouns to the preposition fi

We are familiar with the word fi, which means *in / inside*. When we attach personal pronouns to it, its paradigm is as follows:

f**i**yyi / f**i**yye	*in me / inside me*	f**ī**na	*in us*
f**ī**k, f**ī**ki	*in you* (m & f)	f**ī**ku // f**ī**kom	*in you* (pl)
f**i**yyo // f**ī**^{h}	*in him*	f**ī**hen // f**ī**hom	*in them*
f**ī**ha	*in her*		

As you can see, this paradigm includes the word f**ī**^{h}, which means *there is / there are.* The original meaning of f**ī**^{h} (literally: *in it*) has been forgotten, as it has come to be used in a variety of other contexts, and the final -h is not pronounced. If we want to avoid confusing repetitions in sentences like šū fīh fīh (*What's in it?*) we can use the expression b-qalb (*inside / in the heart of*) instead. See p. 3, footnote 9.

šū fīh b-qalbo?	*What's in it* m <in its heart>?
šū fīh b-qaleb-ha?	*What's in it* f ?

For use of the preposition b- instead of fi to mean *in / inside*, please be patient a little longer; we'll explain later.

Does this lesson seem to you to have too much in it? Repeat the summary in the box below several times out loud. Do this again in the coming days, and you can rest assured that you will remember the salient points of the lesson.

lāzem tuṭlob	'uṭlob!
lāzem tuṭolbi	'uṭolbi!
lāzem tit-erku	'iterku!
ḫod canni	baḥmel-ha cannak
'ana tacbān qaddak	qadd-ma biddek
samake hal-qadde	šū fīh‿b-qalbo?

18. samake is a feminine noun (note the feminine ending -e) that means *[a] fish.*

Exercises

A short exercise to start off with:

In the light of what you've learned in this lesson, what do you think happens with the following verbs that we learned earlier?

d**a**ras [y**u**dros] *to study*
s**a**kat [y**u**skot] *to keep quiet*
ġ**a**sal [y**i**ġsel] *to wash*

Complete:

1. '**a**na b**a**ġsel u-**i**nti bt**i**-...
2. '**u**skot '**i**nte u-**i**nti kam**ā**n '**u**s-...
3. ya w**a**lad, l**ā**zem t**u**dros, ya ul**ā**d, l**ā**zem t**u**d-...

And now for our traditional exercises:

A. Translate into English:

4. '**u**ṭlob q**a**dd-ma b**i**ddak.
5. ya ul**ā**d, '**i**k^{e}tbu‿d-d**a**rs, '**u**d^{o}rsu mn**ī**ḥ!
6. j**ī**bi‿l-^{c}**u**lbe, ta‿nš**ū**f š**ū** f**ī**^{h} b-q**a**lb-ha / b-q**a**l^{e}b-ha.
7. hu**q**^{c}od h**ō**n j**a**mbi!
8. muš‿^{e}mn**ī**ḥ tuq^{c}od h**ō**n, f**ī**^{h} m**a**jrɑ h**a**wa (See **Book 1, p. 78, footnote 5**).
9. l**a** tit^{e}rki‿l-w**a**lad la-ḥ**ā**lo!

B. Complete the sentences

(Replace the English words with the appropriate expression in Arabic):

10. il-m**ɑ**rɑ btiḥmel il-j**ɑ**rrɑ ^{c}ala r**ɑ̄**s-ha[19]; (she carries it.)
11. ya M**a**ryam, (leave alone) hal-b**i**nt u-(come) la-h**ō**n!
12. h**i**yye 'azġɑr m**i**nnek (leave her [alone])!
13. l**ē**š (did you^{m} remove) il-ġ**ɑ**ṭɑ?
14. baq**ī**m il-ġ**ɑ**ṭɑ. – l**ē**š (are you$^{m\ sing}$ removing it)?
15. b**i**ddak aq**ī**m (the box) min h**ō**n?
16. l-ewl**ā**d b**u**ḍ^{o}rbu (one another).
17. b**i**ddi **a**sboq is-sayy**ɑ̄**rɑ **i**lli (in front of us).
18. f**ī**^{h} (a car) qudd**ā**mi, b**i**ddi (to overtake it).

C. Translate into Arabic:

19. Bring^{pl} the box, I want to see what's inside it.
20. Kamla, write to your mother!

---

19. r**ɑ̄**s-ha = *her head.*

21. What do you[m] want me to write?
22. News (see Book 1, p. 63) from home.
23. Go on your own[m/f].
24. Children, don't go by yourselves!
25. Who's taller (Book 1, pp. 98-99), Kamel or Nabil?
26. They're the same height <they [are] the-size-of (qadd) each other>.
27. Yesterday the box was in the same place.
28. I brought three kilos. Everyone has to bring <must that he bring> the same amount as me.

Solution to the sentence exercise on page 14. The five words in the feminine are: ’**i**dfaᶜi q**a**dd-ma b**i**ddek – bt**i**dfaᶜi – ma tidfa**ᶜī**-š – ma maᶜ**kī**-š

With regard to the final word here, remember what we said in footnote 2 of Book 1, p. 18: -ek + -š (negation) → -k**ī**-š. In the same way:

biz**ū**rek → ma bizūr-k**ī**-š *He doesn't visit you.*
bu**ḍ**ᵒrbek → ma buḍrob-k**ī**-š *He doesn't hit you.*

The verb, of course, takes the same form before -ki as it does before -ni, as explained at the start of this lesson.

id-d**a**rs it̠-t̠**ā**men ᶜ**α**šαr – d**a**rs tamantt**α**ᶜš

18

The Eighteenth Lesson (Lesson Eighteen)

In this lesson we'll learn about verbs of a new type – verbs that conjugate like n**i**zel, which means *to go down*. Instead of the familiar □a□a□ form, the 3rd person singular of these verbs follows the pattern □i□e□ in the past tense. In this type (or, if you like, model) of verb, one of the two vowels *i* or *e* drops in most of the past tense forms. Let's compare k**a**tab and n**i**zel:

he wrote	k**a**tab	n**i**zel	*he went down*
they wrote	k**a**tabu	n**i**zlu	*they went down*
I wrote	kat**a**bt	nz**e**lt	*I went down*

As you can see, in the past tense, n**i**zel changes more than k**a**tab.

Let's take a look at the complete paradigm of the past tense:

I / you[m] *went down*	nz**e**l-t	n**i**zel	*he went down*
you[f] *went down*	nz**e**l-ti	n**i**zlat	*she went down*
we went down	nz**e**l-na	n**i**zlu	*they went down*
you[pl] *went down*	nz**e**l-tu		

And now, a note to reassure you: n**i**zel-type verbs form their present-future tense / subjunctive in **exactly** the same way as k**a**tab [y**i**kteb] or f**a**taḥ [y**i**ftaḥ]. **No** verbs of the model □i□e□ have yu□□o□ as their present-future form.

he understood	f**i**hem	[y**i**fham]
	like	[y**i**ftaḥ]
he held, grasped	m**i**sek	[y**i**msek]
	like	[y**i**kteb]
he went down	n**i**zel	[y**i**nzal / y**i**nzel]

There is nothing new in the future tense, so let's concentrate on the past tense of this type of verb.

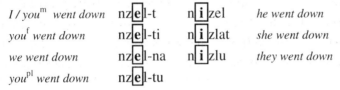

Vocabulary

sime^c [yisma^c]	*to hear*	tilmīz [talāmīz]	*pupil*
nizel [yinzal/-zel]	*to go down*	'āḫer	*last; end*
rije^c [yirja^c]	*to return, to go / come back*		
ti^{c}eb [yit^{c}ab]	*to get tired*	kilme [kalimāt]	*word*
qider [yiqdɑr][1]	*to be able*	kalām[5]	*words; talk*
fiṭen [yifṭɑn]	*to remember*	ḍuh^{o}r	*noon*
fihem [yifham]	*to understand*	maġreb / muġreb[6]	*dusk, early evening*
ḍiḥek [yiḍḥak][2]	*to laugh*	safɑr	*journey*
^{c}iref [yi^{c}rɑf][3]	*to know*	ṭɑrīq [ṭuroq][7]	*way, path*
nām [inām][4]	*to sleep; to go to bed*		
'awwal	*first; beginning*	nukte [nukat]	*joke, funny story*

---

1. In the Galilee region you will usually hear ġider [yiġdɑr], but the form qider is understood and can be used in **all** areas.

2. Before ḍ (and the other emphatic consonants, ṭ, ṣ, ẓ) the vowel *i* is further back in the mouth and less distinct – it sounds almost like *o*. btiḍḥak = btoḍḥak (*you laugh / she laughs*).

3. yi^{c}rɑf (-ref) or ye^{c}rɑf (-ref), because of the influence of the guttural ^{c}.
I know! = ba^{c}ref!

4. nām is a verb of the šūf / jīb type, but the ā- of the past tense doesn't change in the present-future. biddo‿jšūf (*he wants to see*), but biddo‿inām (*he wants to sleep*). *Go to bed / go to sleep!* is rūḥ nām! *I've slept well* = nimt‿^{e}mnīḥ.

5. kalām is a collective noun (one that looks singular but has a plural meaning). It is
■ treated as a masculine singular noun. kalāmak mɑẓbūṭ u-fi maḥallo = *what you say is true* <your talk is true and in its place>, i.e., *appropriate.* kalām fāḍi = *hot air* <empty talk>.

6. Literally: *sunset*. See also Explanations 1.

■ 7. How do we pronounce ṭɑrīq, if the *q* is pronounced like '? Start as if you were going to say ṭɑ-rī-qak / ṭɑ-rī-'ak (*your way*). At the last minute, decide to say a short e instead of -ak, but try to cut it off before you actually say it! ṭɑ-rī-q(e) / ṭɑ-rī-'(e).

Conversation

– ᵉnhɑ̄rak[8] saᶜīd, ya Jamīl.	– Hello <your-day happy>, Jamil.
– ᵉnhɑ̄rak 'asᶜad, ya‿mᶜallem[9].	– Hello <your-day happier>, sir.
– la-wēn? smeᶜna biddak tinzal / tinzel ᶜala ḥēfɑ[10].	– Where are you going? We heard you're going down <want to go down> to Haifa.
– mɑẓbūṭ, mīn qal-lak?	– Yes, I am <true>. Who told you?
– qālū-li... 'ɑbṣɑr[11] mīn, hēk‿ᵉsmeᶜᵉt yaᶜni. hɑ̄, 'issa‿fṭenᵉt: bikūn[12] jɑ̄rna ᶜašān biᶜrɑf wintɑ[13] btinzal.	– They told me … I don't remember who. I mean, that's what I <thus I> heard. Ah, now I remember: it would have been <it will be = it must have been> our neighbor, because he knows when you go.
– 'aywa, banzal ᶜādatan yōm it-talāta u-barjaᶜ fi nafs il-yōm 'aw[14] mɑrrɑ̄t yōm il-'arbᶜa.	– Yes, I usually go down on Tuesday and come back on the same day, or sometimes on Wednesday.
– 'ana‿nzelt‿ᵉmbāreḥ u-immi nizlat maᶜi.	– I went <went down> yesterday, and my mother went <went down> with me.

---

8. **nhɑ̄r** = *day* (the opposite of *night*). When this word appears at the beginning of a sentence, you can, as usual, start the word with a helping ᵉ: **ᵉnhɑ̄r**. But we say **fi-n-nhɑ̄r** (*during the day*), **lēl u-nhɑ̄r** (*night and day*). *A day*, 24 hours, is **yōm**.

9. Literally, *teacher, educator*. This is used not only to address a school teacher, but also other professionals who are experienced enough to teach others.

10. You *go down* from Nazareth to Haifa, and from Zahle to Beirut, of course, but this verb is also used when talking about going from the suburbs to the market, or to the town centre.

11. Lit. *I don't know*. See **Book 1, p.70, footnote 2**.

12. **bikūn**: the future of **kān** signifies a supposition = *he seemingly …/ he must be ….*

13. Note that **winta** is a Galilee word. **'ēmta** is more prevalent in other areas, and even in the Galilee region itself, but you need to know **winta**, too, as you are likely to hear it.

14. **'aw** = *or / or again…* It is used to signify an additional possibility, rather than a choice between two options. In the latter case, the word **willa** is used, especially in questions, or the combination **ya … ya …**: for example, **ya 'ana, ya 'inte!** *[It's] me or you!*

’ana‿rjeᶜᵉt baᶜd iḍ-ḍuhᵒr	I returned in the afternoon <after the noon>,
yaᶜni‿l-maġreb,	that’s to say, in the early evening,
u-hiyye rijᶜat il-yōm iṣ-ṣubᵒḥ.	and she came back this morning <today the morning>.
– šū? ma‿rjeᶜtū-š sawa?	– What, you didn’t come back together?
– la’, ma‿rjeᶜnā-š sawa,	– No, we didn’t come back together,
ᶜala-šān ’immi tiᶜbat min	because my mum gets tired from the
is-safɑr, rɑ̄ḥat la-ᶜind ’aḫūy	journey. She went to my brother’s
u-nāmat ᶜindo.	and stayed there <slept at him>.
– u-inte ma‿tᶜebt-ᵉš?	– And didn’t **you** get tired?
– fiᶜlan, ’ana kamān‿etᶜebᵉt,	– Actually, I got tired, too,
bass muš hal-qadd.	but not that much.
’ana baqdɑr ’arūḥ u-arjaᶜ	I can go and come back
fi nafs il-yōm,	on the same day.
bass hiyye ma btiqdɑr.	But **she** can’t.
– ɑ̄, hāda iši mafhūm.	– No, of course not <yes, that is a thing understood>.

– kull it-talāmīz fihmu‿d-dars?	– Did all the pupils understand the lesson?
– ’is’al-hom!	– Ask them!
– ya ulād, ᵉfhemtu mnīḥ	– Children, did you understand properly
illi qult-o?	<well> what I said <said it>?
– la’, ’Anīs ma fihm-ᵉš[15].	– No, Anis didn’t understand.
– ᵉmbala, fhemt‿ᵉmnīḥ, bass	– Yes I did, I understood fine, but
’uḫti ma fihmat / ma fihmat-š,	my sister didn’t understand.
yaᶜni, fihmat bil-’awwal	I mean, she understood at
u-baᶜdēn tiᶜbat.	first, and then she got tired.
– lāken simᶜat kalāmi?	– But she heard what I said <my words>?
– ’aywa, kullna mnismaᶜ	– Yes, we [can] all hear what you say,
kalāmak la-’āḫer iṣ-ṣɑff,	[even] at the back <to the end> of the class.
smeᶜna kull kilme.	We heard every word.

– lamma smeᶜna han-nukte,	– When we heard that joke,

15. fihem + -š → fihm-ᵉš, or also fihem-š.

’**a**na‿ḍḥ**e**kt / ḍḥ**e**k^{e}t	I laughed and
u-m**a**rati kam**ā**n ḍ**i**ḥkat[16].	my wife laughed, too.
– m**a**ẓb**ū**ṭ, kull in-n**ā**s ḍ**i**ḥku[16].	– That’s right, everyone <true, all the people>
^{e}ḍḥ**e**kna... m**u**tna min iḍ-ḍ**u**ḥ^{o}k!	laughed, we laughed … we died laughing <from the laughter>.

– min k**u**t^{e}r-ma b**i**ḍḥak,	– He’s laughing so much <from the much-what he’s laughing>,
biqd**a**r-š‿iq**ū**l k**i**lme.	he can’t say a word.
– m**ā**-lak?	– What’s up with you <what-to you>?
bt**i**ḍḥak ^{c}al**a**yy?	Are you laughing at me?
– ’a^{c}**ū**ḏu bill**ā**h[17]!	– God forbid!

Explanations

1. Evening – m**a**ġreb / m**u**ġreb

The west in Arabic is il-ġ**a**rb, hence ġ**a**rbi = *western*, so m**a**ġreb / m**u**ġreb, *early evening*, is when the sun is sinking in the west. It’s interesting that the word ġar**ī**b means *strange* (*that’s strange* = h**ā**da ’**i**ši ġar**ī**b), i.e., in the eyes of people from the east, the west is ġar**ī**b!

2. ’**a**wwal and ’**ā**ḫer

The basic meaning of these words is *first* and *last*. We are familiar with ’**a**wwal m**a**rra, which means *the first time* (see **Book 1, page 66**), and, in just the same way, we can also say ’**ā**ḫer m**a**rra, i.e., *the last time*.

These two words are also used in the sense of *beginning* and *end*. There are other words that precisely translate these ideas in a higher register of speech, and you’ll come across them later, but in everyday conversation people usually say:

---

16. See above p.22, footnote 2.

17. This comes from literary Arabic. It means *I seek refuge in God*, i.e., *May God preserve me [from doing what has just been mentioned]*. In literary Arabic, you say not baz**ū**r but ’az**ū**r(u)#. We’ll gradually introduce forms and expressions from the written language, which, because of the influence of education and the media, are becoming increasingly common in colloquial Arabic. As regards ḏ, see Book 1, page [10].

■ fi 'awwal id-d**a**rs	*at the beginning of the lesson*
l**ē**š ma qult-ill**ī**-š min il-'**a**wwal?	*Why didn't you tell me at the outset* <from the first>?
la-'**ā**ḫer is-s**a**ne	*to the end of the year*
fi '**ā**ḫer il-b**ū**ṣ	*at the back of the bus* <end of the bus>

Pronunciation exercises

Before each translation exercise, let's have a bit of a mental work-out. Use the verbs you've just learned and try to move from the 1st person to the 3rd person feminine singular, or to the plural (to get the feel of the difference between, for example, nz**e**lna and n**i**zlu; in the first instance, only the second vowel of n**i**zel is retained, and in the second case, only the first vowel).

This rather boring but essential kind of practice is the only way to become fluent. Read the Arabic below out loud, then cover it up and try to reconstruct it by translating the English column back into Arabic.

■ '**a**na sm**e**^{c}et u-h**i**yye s**i**m^{c}at	*I heard and she heard*
'**i**ḥna sm**e**^{c}na u-h**u**mme s**i**m^{c}u	*We heard and they*$^{m/f}$ *heard*
'**a**na‿qd**e**rt u-h**i**yye q**i**drat	*I could and she could*
'**a**na ma‿qd**e**rt-^{e}š u-h**u**mme ma qidr**ū**-š	*I couldn't and they couldn't*
'**a**na‿rj**e**^{c}et u-h**i**yye r**i**j^{c}at	*I returned and she returned*
'**i**ḥna‿rj**e**^{c}na u-h**u**mme r**i**j^{c}u	*We returned and they returned*
'**i**nti‿fh**e**mti u-h**i**yye f**i**hmat	*You*^{f} *understood and she understood*

Note 1

How do you pronounce a verb that starts with two consonants, for example, qd**e**rt? We've already encountered this problem (see **Book 1, page 22, Explanations 3**.) To remind you:

a. When the verb follows a word ending in a vowel, no helping vowel is needed:

■ '**a**na‿qd**e**r^{e}t	*I could*

b. If the verb follows a word ending in a consonant, or begins a sentence, you can insert the helping vowel ^{e}-:

'**i**nte kam**ā**n‿^{e}qd**e**r^{e}t	*You could, too.*
f**i**^{c}lan‿^{e}t^{c}**e**bna	*We really did get tired* <truly we got tired>.
^{e}ḍḥ**e**kti?	*Did you*^{f} *laugh?*

Note 2

You'll remember the case of b**i**nt / b**i**n^{e}t → b**i**nt‿^{e}kb**ī**re (**Book 1, page 16**). In the exercise above we used the form qd**e**rt in order to emphasize the difference between it and q**i**drat, but just as with kat**a**bt / kat**a**b^{e}t, a helping vowel can be added here, too: qd**er**^{e}t. This happens:

– at the end of a sentence: ’**ē**mta‿nz**e**l^{e}t? (*When did you go down?*)

– or before a consonant followed by a vowel: ^{e}nz**e**l^{e}t m**a**^{c}o (*I went down with him*).

– But before a consonant with no following vowel (remember b**i**nt‿^{e}kb**ī**re) or before the negative particle -š the usual pronunciation is:

■ ’**a**na‿nz**e**lt‿^{e}mb**ā**reh	*I went down yesterday*
t^{c}**e**bt‿^{e}kt**ī**r	*I got very tired*
ma‿fh**e**mt-^{e}š	*I / you didn’t understand*

Once again, **there’s no need to learn all this off by heart**! You just need to pronounce the phrases above out loud and move on. These phenomena will occur again and again and you’ll get used to them without noticing. The whole subject can actually be summed up in the phrases in the box below:

’**i**ḥna‿nz**e**lna	*We went down*
l**ē**š‿^{e}nz**e**ltu?	*Why did you^{pl} go down?*
^{e}fh**e**mna	*We understood*
’**ē**mta‿nz**e**l^{e}t?	*When did you^{m} go down?*
^{e}nz**e**l^{e}t m**a**^{c}o	*I went down with him*
^{e}fh**e**mt‿^{e}mn**ī**h	*I understood well*
ma‿fh**e**mt-^{e}š	*I didn’t understand*

Exercises

A. Translate into English:

1. il-yōm id-dars muš ṣɑᶜeb.
2. ᵉmbala, 'ana‿smeᶜt‿it-tasjīl[18] u-ma‿fhemt-ᵉš.
3. 'iza ma btismaᶜ it-tasjīl kamān u-kamān, muš mumken tifham.
4. btiqdɑr‿ᵉtqul-li 'ēmta fīʰ bɑ̄ṣ?
5. ma baqdɑr-š aqul-lak.
6. ma ḥadā-š hōn bʸiqdɑr‿iqul-lak.
7. il-farše hādi (*this bed*) mnīḥa, nimt‿ᵉmnīḥ.
8. baqdɑr aqūl inno nimt‿ᵉmnīḥ.
9. biddak‿ᵉtnām baᶜd‿iḍ-ḍuhᵒr?
10. la', šukran (*thank you*), ma baqdɑr anām fi-n-nhɑ̄r.

B. Complete the sentences

(Replace the English words with the appropriate expression in Arabic):

11. ma smeᶜt-ᵉš (what you said <your words>).
12. (At the beginning of the lesson) ma‿fhemt-ᵉš
    bass hallaq, (I understand) kull kilme.
13. 'iza bakteb‿ᵉktīr, (I get tired).
14. 'ēmta 'abūk (returns / will return), il-yōm willa bukrɑ?
15. lamma basmaᶜ (jokes), bɑḍḥɑk.
16. simᶜu‿l-quṣṣɑ, bass (they didn't understand) wa-la[19] kilme.

C. Translate into Arabic:

17. The work was easy, we didn't get tired.
18. I go [down] every day but today I couldn't.
19. Couldn't you go down?

---

18. tasjīl (*recording*) is the verbal noun of sajjal (*to record*). We'll learn about the verbal noun in Lesson 27. Incidentally, the Arabic for *CD* is disk [diskāt].

19. Literally *and not a word = not even one word*. So the word wa-la means *not a single [one]*. wa-la mɑrrɑ = *not once, never*; wa-la 'iši = *nothing*; wa-la wāḥad = *nobody*.

20. That's right, I couldn't go down.
21. My neighbor told me that you laughed.
22. True, I laughed, [but] everyone <all the people> laughed, not just me <I>!
23. If you$^{m\ sing}$ want to sleep, you can sleep at our house <at us>.
24. If you$^{f\ sing}$ want to sleep, you can sleep upstairs <above>. There's a bed.
25. When I'm asleep <I sleep> I don't hear anything.
26. When you go (b^{e}tr**ū**ḥ) to Jerusalem, where do you stay <at whom do you sleep>?
27. This time <the time> I stayed with friends <slept at friends'>.
28. We should listen <it's necessary [that] we listen> to the recording again.

id-dars it-tāseᶜ ᶜαšαr – dars tisaᶜtαᶜš

19

The Nineteenth Lesson (Lesson Nineteen)

In this lesson we won't learn any new types of verb, but we'll continue to practice those taught in Lesson 18 and add some new ones of the same type – all of them very useful (*to understand, do, be wrong, go up, go down*, etc. – essential vocabulary).

Let's look back at the beginning of Lesson 18 and the pronunciation exercises in the same Lesson and apply the rules to the new verbs below.

Vocabulary

rikeb [yirkab]	to ride / travel [on]; to get into (a vehicle)		
ziᶜel [yizᶜal]	to be angry; to regret	mustaqbal	future
jumle [jumal]	sentence (grammatical)	ḫiser [yiḫsαr]	to lose
ṭileᶜ [yiṭlαᶜ][1]	to go up; to go out	ġileṭ [yiġlαṭ]	to be wrong
maᶜna [maᶜāni][2]	meaning, significance	ḫileṣ [yiḫlαṣ][4]	to finish / end
natīje [natāʼej] [2]	result[3], consequence	ᶜimel [yiᶜmal][5]	to do
ḥsāb [ḥsābāt] [3]	arithmetic, calculation; bill	mawqaf [mawāqef]	bus stop

Numbers in squares

We've often referred you back to a rule taught in Book 1, or discussed it in more detail. From now on, to save space and make things simpler, you'll be directed instead to a numbered list of rules at the end of the book (page 197). There you'll also find a fuller explanation of this approach.

The number [2] in the Vocabulary above reminds us that the word preceding it begins with a "sun letter" and so *the result* will be in-natīje (and not il-natīje). This method should help remind you of details you may have forgotten.

---

1. See **Lesson 18, footnote 3**. Here, too, you will hear ṭeleᶜ [yeṭlαᶜ] almost ṭoleᶜ [yoṭlαᶜ] .

2. From the same root, we already know yaᶜni = *I mean; that's to say* <[it] means>.

3. natīje [natāʼej] means *result*. natāʼej il-fαḥṣ means *the test results*. When someone is telling a story and gets sidetracked, or has been interrupted and wants to get back to the main story, he/she will say: "in-natīje,..." which means *to get back to the point / to cut a long story short* <the result [is that ...]>.

4-5. See next page.

Conversation

– btifham ᶜαrαbi?	– Do you understand Arabic?
– yaᶜni... baᶜraf‿ᵉšwayy, bass	– Well, I know a little, but
muš‿ᵉktīr, muš kull il-kalimāt.	not much, not every word <all the words>.
mαrrᾱt bafham kull kilme	Sometimes <times> I understand every
fi-l-jumle,	word in a sentence <in the sentence >,
lāken mā bafham il-jumle.	but I don't understand the sentence [itself].
– ma btifham-š il-maᶜna, yaᶜni.	– You mean, you don't understand what it means <the meaning>.
– hāda huwwe.	– That's it!
– šwayy‿ᵉšwayy bᵉtṣīr[6] teᶜrαf.	– Little by little you'll get the hang of it <you'll become you'll know>.
'iza fīʰ ᶜindak ṣαbᵉr	If you've got patience,
u-iza btudros kull yōm,	and if you study every day,
bᵉtšūf in-natīje fi-l-mustaqbal.	you'll see the result in the future.
– 'ēmta yaᶜni? baᶜᵉd ᶜašr‿ᵉsnīn?	– When d'you mean? In ten years?
– la', ᵉnšαllα[7] baᶜᵉd sitt‿ušhor.	– No, hopefully in six months.
ᶜala kull ḥāl, baᶜᵉd sane[8],	In any case, in a year,

4. This is the usual form in Galilee; see **Book 1, Explanations 1, page 94**. But *That's it! It's over! Enough!* is ḫαlαṣ! everywhere.

5. yiᶜmel/-mal, yiᶜref/-rαf: in the subjunctive and present-future in the persons *I*, *you* (m. sing), *he*, *she*, and *we*, where there is no suffix, you will hear both these pronunciations, i.e., with e or a / α. On the other hand, with *you* (f sing), *you* (pl) and *they* (i.e., with the suffixes -i / -u), the vowel a / α is more common. We must mention once again that the vowel before ᶜ sounds more like *e*. To sum up:

you do = bteᶜmel / bteᶜmal – *you* (f) *do* = bteᶜmali – *you* (pl) *do* = bteᶜmalu.

6. We'll have plenty of dealings in future with the verb ṣᾱr and its various nuances. Here, bᵉtṣīr teᶜrαf = *you'll become you'll know*, i.e., *you'll become (with time) one who knows*. Here, too, the second verb (teᶜrαf) is in the subjunctive, i.e., without the prefix b-.

7. See **Book 1, page 32, footnote 7**.

8. We've already noted that if you live in Jerusalem you will usually hear sane (or even sana), rather than sine. Let's remind ourselves, in a single sentence, of some of the differences between Galilee and Jerusalem speech: (see overleaf)

hāda 'iši 'akīd.	that's for sure <that [is] a thing certain>.
– ᵉnšalla.	– Let's hope so!

– šū‿ᶜmeleᵉt?	– What did you do?
– 'ēmta?	– When?
– 'awwal‿ᵉmbēreḥ.	– The day before yesterday.
– ᵉrkebt‿l-bāṣ[9], u-binti	– I caught <went on> the bus and my
rikbat maᶜi,	daughter went with me,
qaᶜdat jambi	sitting <and she sat> beside me,
w-ᵉnzelna ᶜala ḥēfa.	and we went down to Haifa.
– hāy 'awwal marra btinzal[10]?	– Is this the first time you've been / she's been <you're going / she's going down>?
– mīn? hiyye? la', nizlat	– Who? Her <she>? No, she's been
la-ḥāl-ha 'akam min marra.	down on her own a few times.
hiyye btiᶜraf iṭ-ṭarīq	She knows the way
'aḥsan minni.	better than me.
qālat-li matalan: ya-bā[11],	For example, she said to me: "Dad, we've
lāzem ninzal ᶜa-l-mawqaf il-jāy.	got to get off at the next stop <the stop the-coming>."
'ana ma‿ᶜreft-ᵉš wēn 'anzal[12].	I didn't know where to get off.
mnīḥ illi[13] kānat maᶜi.	[It's a] good [job] that she was with me!

---

8. (continued):

■ 'issa bid-hen irūḥu ᶜa-n-nāṣre zayy kull sine.

halqēt (hallaq) bidhom irūḥu ᶜa-l-quds zayy kull sane (sana).

Now they want to go to Nazareth / Jerusalem as [they do] every year.

9. Literally: *I rode the bus.*

10. Here it is unclear if the speaker is asking whether "*you've been*" or "*she's been,*" so clarification is needed, as the question "who?" makes plain. See also **Book 1, p. 43, Explanations 2**.

11. We already know the forms of address (ya) bāba, (ya) māma. You will often also hear yā-ba and yā-mma, especially from older people and in rural areas. bāba, māma apparently sound more modern, and are replacing the older forms of address.

– sme^{c}^{e}t mɑrɑtak zi^{c}lat minnak.	– I heard your wife was angry with you.
– 'ana kamān za^{c}lān minha.	– I'm angry with her, too.
– ^{c}ala 'ēš iz-za^{c}al?	– What [was] the anger about?
lēš‿^{e}z^{c}el^{e}t 'inta?	Why were **you** angry?
– li'anno ġilṭɑt fi l-^{e}ḥsāb.	– Because she got her sums wrong <she made a mistake in the calculation>,
dāyman‿^{e}btiġlɑṭ,	she's always making mistakes,
u-hēk‿^{e}mniḫṣɑr mɑṣɑ̄ri.	and we're losing money because of it <thus we lose money>.
qult-ilha[14]: ġleṭti fi l-^{e}ḥsāb,	I told her: You've made a mistake in the
qālat: la', 'inte‿l-ġɑlṭɑ̄n!	calculation. She said: No, you're the one who's wrong <you are the mistaken-one>!
'inte‿lli‿ġleṭ^{e}t,	It's you who's made a mistake.
ba^{c}dēn‿^{e}fhem^{e}t inno 'ana	Afterwards, I realized <understood> that
^{c}ala ḫɑṭɑ[15].	I was in the wrong,
kān lāzem 'aqul-lha kull hāda	[and] I had to admit it graciously <to tell her
bi-lsān ḥilu[16] u-bi-l-^{e}mnīḥ.	all that in sweet language and in the good>.
bass‿^{e}ṭle^{c}^{e}t la-bɑrrɑ za^{c}lān,	But I went out <outside> angry,
u-ba^{c}d‿^{e}šwayy	and after a while <a little>,
^{e}rje^{c}^{e}t ^{c}a-l-bēt	I came back home and
u-jibt-ilha ḍummet‿^{e}zhūr[17]	brought her a bunch of flowers
u-'issa ḫɑlɑṣ!	and now it's over!
– hā, mnīḥ, 'aḥsan hēk.	Ah, good, that's better <better so>!

The sentences given in Book 1, on page 94 (footnote 4) sound as follows in Galilee:

'ayya sē^{c}a btiḫlɑṣ iṣ-sɑlɑ?	What time do prayers <does the prayer> finish?
^{e}mbēreḥ ḫilṣɑt bakkīr.	Yesterday they <it> finished early.

---

12. 'ana is added here for emphasis: *I myself.* Why is 'anzal in the subjunctive? See **Explanations 6**.

13. See **Book 1, page 55, footnote**

14. This will be explained in Lesson 20.

15. ḫɑṭɑ / ḫɑṭɑ' ['aḫṭɑ̄'] – *mistake, error.*

16. ḥilu means *nice; sweet, sweetened.* ḥilwiyyāt means *sweets, pastries, cakes.*

17. ḍumme means *bunch.* Why ḍummet? This is a construct form, which we'll learn about in Lesson 21.

This is an example of an interesting phenomenon: there are a few verbs that conjugate like k**a**tab in one area but like n**i**zel elsewhere. For example, in one area you'll hear **ђɑ**lɑṣ, ḥ**a**mal, n**a**jaḥ, in another, **ђi**leṣ, ḥ**i**mel, n**i**jeḥ. In Lesson 20, the children will say " nj**e**ḥna!" but the adult speaker will tell you how his brother "n**a**jaḥ." You will be at an advantage if you can identify both forms. You yourself would do best to follow the pronunciation of the area you live in.

Explanations

1. ḥs**ā**b – arithmetic, calculation, bill

This word comes from the root of the verb ḥ**a**sab meaning *calculate*, and also *consider (something / someone) to be (something).*

■ bt**e**ᶜrɑf t**i**ḥseb?	Can you do arithmetic <do you know [how] to calculate>?
ḥ**a**sab‿ᵉḥs**ā**b	He made a calculation
ḥas**a**bt‿ᵉḥs**ā**b	I took [into] account
l**ā**zem t**i**ḥseb‿ᵉḥs**ā**b inno f**ī**ʰ ul**ā**d.	You've got to take into account that there are children.
ma ḥas**a**bteš‿ᵉḥs**ā**b inno ik**ū**nu ᶜišr**ī**n.	I never reckoned on there being twenty of them <I didn't calculate a calculation that they will be twenty>!

2. m**a**talan, f**e**ᶜlan and the suffix -an

In the Conversation above, we learned the word f**e**ᶜlan (*really, actually*), which comes from the root f-ᶜ-l[18] with the added suffix -an. This suffix is used to create adverbs, just like the suffix *-ly* in English (*temporari**ly**, usual**ly***). You already know the word m**a**talan (**Book 1, page 97, footnote 9**). From the root ṭ-b-ᶜ mentioned in the same lesson (footnote 8), which means both *nature* and *stamping* (and hence, *printing*), we derive the word ṭ**ɑ**bᶜan (*naturally / of course*). This is the place to note two more words from the same root: iṭ-ṭɑb**ī**ᶜa (*Nature*) and ṭ**ɑ**beᶜ (*nature, character*) as well as ṭɑb**ī**ᶜi (*natural*). h**ē**k ṭ**ɑ**bᶜo! means *That's what he's like / That's his nature* <thus his-nature>!

18. The root f-ᶜ-l is traditionally used as a model for the Forms of the Arabic verb, which we'll start learning about in Lesson 26. The Arabic word for *verb* is f**i**ᶜel ['afᶜ**ā**l].

A few more examples of words made by adding this suffix:

taqrīban = *approximately, about* (**Book 1, page 86**).

'**a**walan = *A.* or *firstly* (when speaking about a number of points or items)

ṯ**ā**niyan = *B.* or *secondly*

3. zi^{c}el – za^{c}l**ā**n

We can derive adjectives from many of the **n**izel-type verbs we've learned today by adding the suffix -an. You are already familiar with ta^{c}b**ā**n (*tired*), which comes from the verb t**i**^{c}eb [y**i**t^{c}ab] (*to be tired*). Likewise:

■ ġ**i**leṭ	*to be wrong*	ġɑlṭ**ɑ̄**n	*wrong, mistaken* (of a person)
z**i**^{c}el	*to be angry; to be sorry*	za^{c}l**ā**n[19]	*angry, grumpy; sorry*
ħ**i**ser	*to lose*	'**i**nte‿l-ħasr**ɑ̄**n	*You're the loser!*

However, the present-future form of the verb is commonly used in cases where there is a sense of *always, usually, every time that*, and, of course, for the future tense:

b^y**i**z^{c}al	*He's* (always) *angry* (he's an angry person) *He'll be angry* (when he hears about it)
b^y**i**ġlɑṭ	*He's wrong* (every time)*; he'll be wrong*

4. He goes up / out

The verb ṭ**e**le^c means both *to go up* and *to go out*, so, to make the distinction, it's usual to add la-f**ō**q (*up* <to above>). For example:

■ ṭ**e**le^c la-f**ō**q	*He went up* (i.e., above, upstairs)
ṭ**e**le^c la-b**ɑ**rrɑ	*He went out* (i.e., outside)

19. The root denotes anger, and also sorrow. You can be za^{c}l**ā**n when you see a friend sad or ill.

5. The imperative

You'll remember, of course, that the imperative of k**a**tab is '**i**kteb!

In other words, to form the imperative, you take the subjunctive – y**i**kteb – and replace the y**i**- with '**i**-. This rule also applies to verbs of the n**i**zel pattern:

y**i**nzal	*that he go down*
'**i**nzal !	*go down / get off!*
'**i**nzali!	*go^{f} down / get off!*
'**i**nzalu!	*go^{pl} down / get off!*
'**i**ṭlɑᶜi la-f**ō**q!	*go^{f} up(stairs)!*

Let's go straight on to a short exercise on the imperative:

	imperative:	
r**i**keb [y**i**rkab]	....	*get in* (a car)! *ride* (a bicycle)!
ᶜ**i**mel [y**i**ᶜmal]	....	*do$^{m/f\ sing}$!*
r**i**jeᶜ [y**i**rjaᶜ]	....	*come back$^{m/f\ sing}$!*
s**i**meᶜ [y**i**smaᶜ]	....	*listen$^{m/f\ sing}$!*

We won't bother with the other verbs because we don't normally say *be tired! be angry!* or *lose!*

6. More about the subjunctive: where to get off, how to do

We've already pointed out (**Book 1, Lesson 11, footnote 4**) that the subjunctive can be used on its own to suggest intention, prohibition, doubt, etc. The subjunctive in itself implies one of these ideas. In Lesson 11 we had 'aj**ī**b? meaning: *[Do you want] me to bring / [Should] I bring?* In today's Conversation we had w**ē**n '**a**nzel, meaning *Where I [should] get off.*

Let's compare a couple of similar sentences with and without the present-future verb prefix b-, and get the feel of the difference. To remind you, the present-future with the prefix b- denotes a **fact** (that's how it is!).

b**a**ᶜref k**ī**f‿ᵉbt**e**ᶜmal	*I know how you do [it]* (I see a fact)
bt**e**ᶜraf k**ī**f t**e**ᶜmal?	*Do you know how to do [it] / what you should do?* (intention, obligation)
q**a**l-lak '**ē**š b**a**kteb?	*Did he tell you what I'm writing?* (description of fact)
q**a**l-li '**ē**š '**a**kteb	*He told me what to write* (obligation, order)

We'll encounter more examples of this use of the subjunctive later on.

Exercises

A. Translate into English:

1. sm**e**^{c}t‿in-n**u**kte ?
2. l**a**', q**ū**l ta‿nš**ū**f,
3. b**i**dna n**i**ḍḥαk '**i**ḥna kam**ā**n (and he's already laughing).
4. ṭ**α**yyeb, '**i**sma^{c} bi-l-'**a**wwal, ba^{c}d**ē**n‿^{e}bt**i**ḍḥαk.
5. '**i**nzalu h**ō**n, il-m**a**wqaf il-j**ā**y‿^{e}b^{c}**ī**d‿^{e}kt**ī**r.
6. b**a**fham kam k**i**lme fi-l-j**u**mle.
7. k**ī**f l**ā**zem '**a**^{c}mal ('**a**^{c}mel)?
8. š**ū**f k**ī**f b**a**^{c}mel '**a**na w-**i**^{c}mel[20] m**i**tli / z**a**yyi.
9. 'a**ḫū**k z**i**^{c}el m**i**nnak, l**ē**š?
10. li'**a**nno‿ġl**e**ṭ^{e}t u-ḫs**e**rna mαṣ**ā**ri.
11. qadd**ē**š‿^{e}ḫs**e**r^{e}t '**i**nte? - ^{e}ḫs**e**rt‿^{e}kt**ī**r?
12. y**a**^{c}ni, muš haq**a**ll m**i**nno.
13. '**i**rja^{c} la-w**α**rα, '**i**rja^{c}, '**i**rja^{c}, b**a**ss[21]!

B. Complete the sentences

(Replace the English words with the appropriate expression in Arabic):

14. w**ē**n l-ewl**ā**d ? – (They went up) la-f**ō**q.
15. bte^{c}rαf '**i**nte inno '**a**na‿l-ḫ. (the loser).
16. '**ē**mta (does he come back) min iš-š**u**ġ^{o}l ?
17. hal-m**α**rrα ma‿ (we didn't lose) kt**ī**r.
18. mαẓb**ū**ṭ, '**a**na‿ġl**e**ṭ^{e}t, bass h**u**mme kam**ā**n (were wrong).
19. '**i**rja^{c} (backwards), f**ī**^{h} ma**ḥ**all.
20. '**i**za bte**ṭ**lα^{c}i, (take this up).

C. Translate into Arabic:

21. What are you^{f} doing in the morning?
22. I'm going out with my sister, we're going to the market (^{c}a-s-s**ū**q) and coming back home.
23. Do you$^{m\ sing}$ know [how] to ride a bicycle (il-busukl**ē**t / il-baskal**ē**t)?
24. When you$^{m\ sing}$ travel to work, where do you get off?
25. Usually (**Book 1, page 77, Vocabulary**) I get off here.

---

20. w-**i**^{c}mel without hamza (') – see **Book 1, page 110, section 3**.
21. = *Go backwards! Reverse, reverse, stop* <enough>!

26. They didn't come back yesterday and the result[22] [was that] we lost a day.
27. The cat slept outdoors. (See **Book 1, p. 89, Exercise B, 9-10**)
28. What <how>? Yesterday [she] was indoors.
29. True, but the boy opened the door and the cat went out.
30. Every day the cat goes outside and later <afterwards> she comes back to the kitchen

---

Final exercise (if you have the strength – and the head – for it):
Let's do another short exercise to get used to the transition from nz**el**^{e}t to nz**el**t, and from nz**el**t to nz**el**^{e}t. Insert the helping vowel ^{e} where necessary and repeat out loud:

u-**i**nte šu‿^{c}m**el**^{e}t?	And you, what did you do?
31. šu‿^{c}melt mb**ā**reḥ?	What did you do yesterday?
32. '**a**na‿^{c}melt il-b**ā**qi.	I did what was left <the remainder>.
33. $^{e c}$melt kt**ī**r minš**ā**no.	I did a lot for him.
w-^{e}ħs**er**^{e}t f**ī**ha?	Did you lose (business) by it <in it>?
34. '**a**ywa, ħs**e**rt kt**ī**r.	Yes, I lost a lot!
w-^{e}z^{c}**el**^{e}t?	And were you angry?
35. ṭ**ɑ**b^{c}an, ^{e}z^{c}**e**lt kt**ī**r.	Of course, I was very angry!

Maybe you don't yet feel entirely relaxed playing these "games"? That's to be expected, but you do need to go on making an effort now and then. Gradually it will come to seem more natural. It's simply a matter of learning how to cope with "impossible" pronunciation situations like:

j**i**bt d**a**ftɑr (*I brought an exercise book*)
j**i**bt kt**ā**b mb**ē**reḥ (*I brought a book yesterday*)

Did you work out the pronunciation? The answer is in the footnote below[23].

---

22. See footnote 3. Remember that square brackets indicate words that are necessary in English, but not in Arabic.
23. The answer is, of course: j**i**b^{e}t d**a**ftɑr, j**i**bt‿ekt**ā**b‿^{e}mb**ē**reḥ.

dars ᶜišrīn

20

Lesson Twenty[1]

This time we won't make any new forays into verb territory. You need some time to absorb what you've learned so far – time is an important part of the learning process – so we'll turn to other matters.

You're already used to adding the attached suffixes -li, -lak, -lo, etc., to verbs, for example:

katab-lek = *He wrote to you*ᶠ.

In this lesson you'll see that in certain cases (e.g., for emphasis) you can use 'ili, 'ilak, etc., instead. You'll also discover some more uses for il-, as well as other related matters. Let's go over the text first and analyze it afterwards in the Explanations.

Vocabulary

juzdān	purse	jahᵉd/ juhᵒd [5] [juhūd]	effort
'aswaḏ[2]	black	hadiyye [hadāya]	gift, present
imtiḥān	examination	bunni / binni	brown
[imtiḥānāt]	examinations	nijeḥ // najaḥ	to succeed
faḍᵉl [5]	kindness, favor	ᶜaks	opposite, contrary
fišel [yifšal]	to fail	mušwār[3] [mašawīr]	excursion, walk
fašal	failure	liᶜeb [yilᶜab]	to play
najāḥ [2]	success	luᶜbe[4]	game; doll
tabaᶜ	of, belonging to	jāmᶜa [jamiᶜāt]	university

---

1. From now on we'll change to cardinal numbers for the lesson headings, e.g., Lesson 20. Similarly, it's usual to say *page 12* – ṣafḥa tnaᶜš (tnaᶜeš).

2. Fem sōda, pl [sūd], of things. An alternative plural, sūdān, is used in the case of people, hence blād es-sūdān, *Sudan* <the country of the black-people>. A more accurate word for *a black person* is zinj [zunūj] [2].

3. mušwār / mešwār also means *[an] errand*. ᶜalayy mešwār ᶜala ḥēfa means *I've got to go to Haifa (on an errand)*.

4. Not *game* in the sense of *playing*, but a specific game such as *tag* or *hopscotch*; or a round of a particular game. We'll revisit this distinction later.

Conversation

– il-b**ā**bα j**a**b-li hadi**y**ye!	– Dad brought me a present!
– j**ā**b il-hadi**y**ye '**i**li, muš '**i**lek!	– He brought the present for <to> **me**, not for you!
– ya b**ā**bα, la-m**ī**n j**i**bt il-hadi**y**ye?	– Dad, who did you bring the present for?
– had**ī**k il-m**a**rrα, jibt-**i**llek l**u**ᶜbe u-hal-m**a**rrα j**i**bᵉt '**i**ši la-'aħ**ū**ki.	– Last time <that time> I brought you <to you> a doll and this time I brought something for your brother.
bass jibt-**i**lkom kam**ā**n‿ᵉmlabbas.	But I brought you [both] sweets, too.

– katabt-**i**llak makt**ū**b.	– I wrote you a letter.
– il-makt**ū**b h**ā**da, muš '**i**lo?	– This letter's not to him?
– l**a**', kat**a**bt il-makt**ū**b '**i**lak, muš '**i**lo.	– No, I wrote the letter to you, not to him.

– la-m**ī**n hal-juzd**ā**n?	– Whose is this purse <to whom this purse>?
– h**ā**da '**i**li.	– It's mine.
– h**ā**da '**i**lek?	– It's yours?
– l**a**', ᵉġl**e**tᵉt, ḍ**ā**ᶜ[5] m**i**nni juzd**ā**ni,	– No, I was mistaken. I lost my purse <went missing from me my purse>,
bass h**ā**da b**u**nni,	but this [one] is brown and my purse
w-il-juzd**ā**n t**a**baᶜi '**a**swad.	<the purse belonging-to me> is black.
– y**a**ᶜni, 'ak**ī**d muš '**i**lek hal-juzd**ā**n?	– So you're <[it's]> sure this purse isn't yours?
– l**a**', m**i**yye fi-l-m**i**yye!	– No [it isn't], [I'm] a hundred per cent <100 in 100> [certain].
law k**ā**n '**i**li, k**u**nt baq**u**l-lak[6].	If it were mine, I'd tell you.

----

5. ḍ**ā**ᶜ [iḍ**ī**ᶜ] means *to go missing / get lost.* '**i**za biḍ**ī**ᶜ hal-muft**ā**ḥ...! means *If this key gets lost ...!*

6. This is an introductory example of a conditional sentence (*if it is... / if it were...*), a topic we'll deal with later.

– ya ul**ā**d, naj**aḥ**tu fi-l-imtiḥ**ā**n?	– Children, did you pass <succeed in> the exam?
– ᵉnje**ḥ**na[7]!	– We did <we succeeded>!
– š**ā**ṭr**ī**n! dar**a**stu mn**ī**ḥ!	– Well done <clever [ones]>! You studied hard <studied well>!
– mαẓb**ū**ṭ, bass il-f**α**ḍᵉl[8] **'i**lak, ya‿mᶜ**a**llem!	– True, but it's thanks to you <the merit is yours>, Teacher!
– '**a**na b**a**ᶜmel **i**lli ᶜal**a**yy ka-mᶜ**a**llem,	– I'm [only] doing my job <doing what is on me (my obligation)> as a teacher,
bass in-naj**ā**ḥ fi 'id**ē**kom;	but <the> success is in your hands:
'**i**lli b**i**ddo y**i**njaḥ, l**ā**zem y**u**dros.	whoever wants to succeed must study.
'**i**lli b**u**dros‿ᵉmn**ī**ḥ, b**i**njaḥ.	Whoever studies hard will succeed.

– '**i**li '**a**ḫḫ u-**u**ḫt fi-l-j**ā**mᶜa,	– I have a brother and sister at <in the> university.
'aḫ**ū**y ᶜ**i**mel kull j**u**hdo,	My brother put in a lot of effort <made all his effort>
u-n**a**jaḥ, '**a**mma '**u**ḫti f**i**šlat[9]	and succeeded, while my sister failed
u-z**i**ᶜlat‿ᵉkt**ī**r min il-f**a**šal.	and was very angry about her failure <from the failure>.

– '**i**lak n**a**fs[10] t**ā**kol[11] h**a**llaq?	– Do you want to eat now?
– l**a**', ma-l**ī**-š (nefs//) n**a**fs.	– No, I'm not hungry <not to me appetite>.

---

7. The teacher is obviously from Jerusalem, but his pupils are from Galilee.

8. Note also the expression min f**α**ḍlak / -lek meaning *please* <(I ask you,) from your kindness>. The polite invitation *Please (come in / sit down / help yourself,* etc.*)*, is tf**α**ḍḍαl <be so good as to> (to a woman, tf**α**ḍḍαli, and to more than one person, tf**α**ḍḍαlu). This is the imperative of a Verb Form that we haven't learnt yet.

9. To be fair, the reverse is just as likely.

10. n**a**fs means *soul*. This word is also used to denote *desire (to eat) / appetite*. In this sense, it is also pronounced n**e**fs. ḫ**ā**ṭer means *willingness / goodwill; mood; desire (to do)*. See also **Book 1, page 56**, *See you soon / au revoir*.

11. This is the subjunctive of the verb '**a**kal, which we encountered in the past tense in **Book 1, page 71**. We'll learn the complete paradigm soon.

– ṭɑyyeb, taᶜāl‿ᵉnrūḥ mušwɑ̄r fi-l-ḥɑ̄rɑ.	– Fine, let's go out for a walk round <in> the neighborhood / the quarter.
– ma-lī-š ђɑ̄ṭer.	– I don't feel like it <not to me desire>!
– u-inti, ya Lɑṭīfe[12]?	– What about you <and you>, Latifa?
– 'ana kamān ma biddī-š.	– I don't want to, either <I too don't want>.
– 'iza ma-lkī-š ђɑ̄ṭer, balāš il-mušwɑ̄r. lamma 'ili ђɑ̄ṭer 'ɑṭlaᶜ 'inti ma bid-kī-š, u-bil-ᶜaks.	– If you don't feel like it <not to you desire>, there's no need for a <the> walk. When I want to go out, you don't want to, and vice-versa <the opposite>.
– ṭɑyyeb, bukrɑ neṭlɑᶜ mešwɑ̄r 'ēmta-ma biddak, u-wēn-ma biddak!	– OK, tomorrow we'll go out for a walk when[ever] you want and where[ever] you want!

– 'ili ᶜind 'abūk ђamsīn šēkel.	– Your father owes me <I have at your father> 50 shekels.
– bass 'ana kamān 'ili ᶜalēk ђamsīn šēkel.	– But you owe me <I also have on you> 50 shekels too.

---

12. This is a woman's first name. lɑṭīf means *pleasant; delicate; kind.* il-jins il-lɑṭīf means *the fair sex* <the delicate / nice sex>. ya lɑṭīf ! = God! <O kind God!>.

b**u**krɑ b**ɑ**ṭlob min 'ab**ū**y hal-m**a**blaġ u-ḫ**ɑ**lɑṣ!	Tomorrow I'll ask my father for that amount and we'll be quits <and it's over>!
– w**ɑ**llɑ[13] f**i**kra!	– Now that's an idea <by God, an idea>!

Explanations

1. I told you, you told him

There's a construction in the text above that requires explanation: katabt-**ell**ak, meaning *I wrote to you*. We know that in the 1st person and 2nd person masculine (*I, you*) of the past tense the verb ends in -t: kat**a**bt, q**u**lt, etc. What happens when we add -li, -lak, -lek, -lo?

It's possible to say kat**a**bt-lak, q**u**lt-lo (and indeed, you are likely to hear this in rural areas). But it's more usual to add the helping vowel i and to double the l- of -li / -lak / -lek / -lo:

kat**a**bt + lak → katabt-**i**llak	*I wrote to you*
q**u**lt + lek → qult-**i**llek	*I told you*

In the rest of the paradigm, the -l is not doubled:

qult-**i**lha	*I told her; you told her*
qult-**i**lna	*you*^{m} *told us*
katabt-**i**lkom	*I wrote to you*^{pl}
jibt-**i**lhom	*I brought* <*to*> *them*

And in Galilee, as you know, people say -lku, -lhen.

At this point, it's interesting to compare two similar forms and learn to distinguish between them, e.g., q**u**lt + -li (→qult-**i**lli) as opposed to q**u**lt illi... (*that / which / what*):

qult-**i**lli m**a** b**i**ddak	*You told me you didn't* <don't> *want[to].*
q**u**lt illi fi q**a**lbak	*You said what you thought* <what [was] in your heart>.

---

13. A shortened form of the expression w**ɑ**-'ɑll**ɑ̄**h! (*by God!*). It shouldn't be regarded as an oath. The reference to God is obscured, as in the expression y**ɑ**llɑ! (*Come on! / Let's go!*)

Clearly, it's the position of the stress that makes all the difference here. Enough for today! We'll come back to this later with some new verbs.

2. tabaᶜ – of, belonging to

Although people usually say kalbi, *my dog*, and bēt il-jirɑ̄n, *the neighbors' house*, you can also say il-kalb tabaᶜi and il-bēt tabaᶜ il-jirɑ̄n instead. tabaᶜ is normally used:

a. When the noun is qualified by an adjective, e.g.,

    il-bint l-ᵉkbīre tabaᶜ il-jirɑ̄n   *the neighbors' oldest daughter*
    il-bēt l-ᵉjdīd tabaᶜ il-mudīr   *the manager's new house*

In the first case, we could have said bint il-jirɑ̄n l-ᵉkbīre without confusion, but in the second case we have to use tabaᶜ, otherwise bēt il-mudīr l-ᵉjdīd would be understood as *the new manager's house*.

b. After foreign loan-words:

    it-tander tabaᶜi   *my van / my pickup*
    ir-rɑ̄dyo tabaᶜkom   *your radio*

There are other cases, such as constructs like *my driving license,* but we'll leave that for the next lesson.

Note that when the attached pronouns are added, the stress in tabaᶜ moves in accordance with the now-familiar rules (**see Book 1, p.91**).

3. 'ili, 'ilak...

From the Conversation above we can conclude that the particle 'ili - is used:

a. To translate *to me, to you*, etc., when there is a need for emphasis, or when it stands alone in answer to a question:

    katab 'ili   *He wrote to me* (i.e., not to you)
    – la-mīn katab? – 'ili.   – *Whom did he write to? – Me* <to-me>.

b. To say *[That's] mine, yours*, etc. / *That belongs to me, you*, etc., for example:

    hāda 'ili   *That's mine / That belongs to me*
    is-sayyɑ̄ra 'ilo willa la-'aḫūh?   *Is the car his or his brother's?*

c. As an alternative to the word ᶜ**i**nd in the sense of *I've got, he's got*, etc., especially when speaking of abstract things (desire, willingness, inclination, etc.), or of family relationships; for example:

'**i**li ħ**ā**ṭer	*I feel like (doing something)* <to me a desire>
'**i**li '**u**ħt	*I have a sister*

The corresponding negative form is ma-l**ī**-š[14],etc.

'**i**lo n**e**fs / n**a**fs y**ā**kol[15]	*He wants to eat*
ma-l**ō**-š n**e**fs / n**a**fs	*He doesn't feel like [it] / He has no appetite*
'**i**lna ħ**ā**ṭer	*We feel like (going for a walk,* etc.)
ma-ln**ā**-š ħ**ā**ṭer	*We don't feel like [it]*

The Conversation above contains an example of an interesting usage of '**i**li, '**i**lak, etc. *You owe me (money)* is, literally, <I have at / with you>:

'**i**lak ᶜ**i**ndi	*I owe you* <you have at me> <you own money that's with me>

You'll also hear:

'**i**lo ᶜal**ē**k	*You owe him* <he has on you>
b**i**ddak m**i**nni	*I owe you* <you want from me>
l**i**ssa b**i**ddek m**i**nna...	*We still owe you…* <you still want from us …>

To sum up: just memorize and use the first expression, '**i**lak ᶜ**i**ndi; you'll understand the others when you hear them.

----

14. Just as one says b**i**ddek → ma bidk**ī**-š, we say '**i**lek → ma-lk**ī**-š. See **Book 1, page 18, footnote 2**.

15. See footnote 11 above.

Here are two ways to say in Arabic *Life has its ups and downs*:

id-dinya dūlāb:	*The world [is like] a wheel:*
yōm 'ilak, yōm ᶜalēk.	*[one] day for you, [the next] day against you.*
or:	
yōm ᶜasal, yōm bɑṣɑl[16].	*[One] day honey, [the next] day onion.*

4. fi and b-

Strictly speaking, there is a distinction in colloquial Palestinian Arabic between the use of the particles fi and b-.

To say *in / inside*, it's best to use fi	*in the house* = fi-l-bēt
When you mean *by means of / with*, always say b-	*with the knife* = b-is-sikkīne

In everyday speech, however, they get swapped around and you'll hear, for example:

He was in the house	kān bil-bēt
In this box	bil-ᶜulbe hāy
He hit me with a stick	ḍɑrɑb-ni fi-l-ᶜɑṣāy

You should be aware of this phenomenon, but it's best to stick to making the distinction between fi for *in* and b- for *by means of.*

> **Note that** Lebanese and Syrian dialects always use b-, and never fi, except in the case below.

Nonetheless, there is one case where you must always use fi- and not b-: when you add attached pronouns. For example:

ḍɑrɑb-ni bi-s-sikkīne	*He stabbed* <hit> *me with the knife*
but	
misek is-sikkīne u-ḍɑrɑb-ni fī-ha	*He seized the knife and stabbed me with it*
bakteb bil-qalam	*I write with a pen*
but	
jīb il-qalam, biddi akteb fīh	*Bring the pen, I want to write with it!*

16. Don't pronounce bɑṣɑl like ᶜasal. Remember the ṣ of bɑṣɑl is emphatic, and consequently the vowels surrounding it are "dark" and pronounced further back in the mouth.

The paradigm of fi- plus attached pronouns holds no surprises:

f**i**yyi (f**i**yye)	f**ī**k f**ī**ki	f**ī**^{h} (in Galilee also:) f**i**yyo
f**ī**-na	f**ī**-kom	
	f**ī**-hom	

Once again, remember: You don't have to memorize every detail the first time around. All the forms you've encountered in the Explanations will reappear again and again as you progress. For the moment, and when you come to revise the lesson, just concentrate on the summary in the box below.

kat**a**b-lak	katabt-**i**llak
ir-r**ā**dyo t**a**ba^{c}ak	
il-b**ē**t il-ḥ**i**lu t**a**ba^c il-m**a**lek	
j**a**b-lo[17]	j**ā**b h**ā**da '**i**lo
la-m**ī**n k**a**tab?	'**i**li
'**i**li n**a**fs	ma-l**ī**-š n**a**fs
'**i**li ^{c}**i**ndak ḫams**ī**n š**ē**kel	
'**i**li ^{c}al**ē**k ḫams**ī**n š**ē**kel	
l**i**ssa b**i**ddi m**i**nnak ḫams**ī**n š**ē**kel	
k**a**tab bil-q**a**lam	k**a**tab f**ī**^{h}

Exercises

A. Translate into English:

1. '**i**^{c}mal kull j**u**hdak '**i**za b**i**ddak t**i**njaḥ.
2. j**ī**b is-sikk**ī**ne!
3. š**ū** b**i**ddak ti^{c}mal f**ī**ha?
4. min f**a**ḍlak, jib-li[17] it-tasj**ī**l, b**i**ddi **a**sma^{c}o kam**ā**n m**a**rr**a**.

---

17. Remember – when a long vowel is followed by -li, -lak, -lo... it is shortened:
j**ā**b → j**a**b-li, biq**ū**l → biq**u**l-li

5. 'ilo ^{c}indak mītēn (200) šēkel, hēk qal-li.
6. bil-^{c}aks! huwwe ġαlṭᾱn!
7. 'ana biddi minno tlat mīt (300) šēkel.
8. ya mᾱmα, (ma) biddī-š 'anām! biddi al^{c}ab kamān‿^{e}šwayy.
9. ṭαyyeb, hayy il-lu^{c}be taba^{c}ek, 'il^{c}abi fīha!
10. ta^{c}āl, bidna nil^{c}ab lu^{c}be jdīde.

B. Complete the sentences

(Replace the English words with the appropriate expression in Arabic):

11. 'i^{c}mal juhdak 'iza biddak (to succeed).
12. jīb is-sikkīne!
13. šū biddak (to do with it)?
14. (Please,) jib-li‿t-tasjīl, biddi (hear it) kamān mαrrα.
15. (You$^{m\ sing}$ owe him) mītēn šēkel, hēk qal-li.
16. (On the contrary)! huwwe ġαlṭᾱn!
17. 'ana biddi minno (300) šēkel.
18. ya mᾱmα, biddī-š (to sleep), biddi al^{c}ab (a little longer <a little more>).
19. ṭαyyeb, hayy il-lu^{c}be taba^{c}ek, (play with it)!
20. ta^{c}āl, bidna nil^{c}ab (a new game).

Now you can compare what you've written with Exercise A.

C. Translate into Arabic:

21. Do you$^{m\ sing}$ want to eat (tākol) something now?
22. No, I don't feel like it.
23. Do you$^{f\ sing}$ feel like going out (teṭlα^{c}i) with me now?
24. No, I don't feel like going out in the afternoon.
25. In that case <if so>, go$^{f\ sing}$ [and] sleep!
26. Now, that's an idea!
27. – Where's the money? – In my purse.
28. – But the money isn't yours$^{m\ sing}$!
29. – Yes, it is! The money's mine, not yours$^{m\ sing}$!
30. Bring$^{f\ sing}$ the pen and write with it!
31. Where's the lid of (taba^c) this box?
32. The box is here, but where's its lid? (taba^c-ha)?
33. We succeeded! – Yes, but it's thanks to him <the merit [is] his>.

dars wāḥad u-ᶜisrīn

21

Lesson Twenty-One

We have already seen how masculine nouns behave in the construct form (see **Lesson 1, Explanations 8**), e.g., bēt il-mudīr, and with the attached pronouns: bēt-i, bēt-ak...; 'abūy, 'abū-k, etc. But we have not yet learned what happens with feminine nouns that end in -e or -a /-α. Let's compare:

	bēt	bēt Yūsef	bēt il-mudīr
	house	*Yusef's house*	*the manager's house*
		<house-of Yusef>	<house-of the manager>
■	farše	faršet Yūsef	faršet il-walad / faršt‿il-walad
	bed	*Yusef's bed*	*the boy's bed*
		<bed-of Yusef>	<bed-of the boy>

We can see from the example above that the endings -e and -a turn into -et or -t when a feminine noun appears as the first part of the construct form. The same thing happens when we add an attached pronoun or the dual ending -ēn to a feminine noun:

■	faršti / far^{e}šti	*my bed*
	farštēn / far^{e}štēn	*two beds*
	mαrrα	*time, instance*
	mαrrtēn	*twice* <two times>

Here is the complete paradigm of the word farše, with attached pronouns:

■	faršti	faršet-ha
	farštak	faršet-na
	farštek	faršet-ku // -kom
	faršto	faršet-hen // -hom

And here are the paradigms of ḫāle, which means *maternal aunt,* and lahje[1] which means *dialect, vernacular.*

---

1. il-lahje‿l-mαṣriyye (or lahjet mαṣ^{e}r) means *the Egyptian dialect / colloquial Egyptian [Arabic].* We can also say il-lahje‿l-'amrikiyye, which means *the American dialect [of English],* i.e., *American English.*

	ɧ**ā**lti	ɧāl**e**t-ha
	ɧ**ā**ltak	ɧāl**e**t-na
	ɧ**ā**ltek	ɧāl**e**t-kom[2]
	ɧ**ā**lto	ɧāl**e**t-hom[2]
■	l**a**hᵉjti	lahj**e**t-ha
	l**a**hᵉjtak	lahj**e**t-na
	l**a**hᵉjtek	lahj**e**t-kom
	l**a**hᵉjto	lahj**e**t-hom

These paradigms should be read from top to bottom, in both columns, i.e., ɧ**ā**lti, ɧ**ā**ltak, etc. We are already familiar with the attached personal pronouns, and we can see that:
– Before the endings -i, -ak, -ek and -o the final vowel before the -t drops.
– Before the other endings (-ha, -na, -kom and -hom, all of which begin with a consonant), the e is retained, and is even stressed.

There's nothing very new about this, as it reminds us of the stress shift t**a**rak-o → tar**a**k-na and of the difference between

ɧ**ɑ̄**ṭer → ɧ**ɑ̄**ṭrak
ɧɑ̄ṭ**e**r-kom.

Note: the helping ᵉ vowel in the word l**a**hᵉjti is designed to make pronunciation easier. The word f**a**ršti does not require a helping vowel, as it is not difficult to pronounce without it.

Theory apart, how do you deal with this on a practical level? As always, only practice will make perfect. A note of caution, however: once you've got used to saying ɧ**ā**lti, ɧ**ā**ltak, etc., there will be a great temptation to say ɧ**ā**lt-ha, instead of ɧāl**e**t-ha, especially as the incorrect form is not difficult to pronounce.

Nouns ending in -**i**yye behave in much the same way as those ending in -e or -a. The suffix -iyye turns into -**ī**t-[3] before -i, -ak, -ek and -o:

■	šams**i**yye	*umbrella; sunshade*
	šams**ī**ti[3]	*my umbrella*
	šams**ī**to	*his umbrella*

---

2. From now on we'll give only the forms -kom, -hom, and Galileans will remember to replace them with -ku, -hen.

3. Don't forget to make the *i* long: šams**ī**ti. Some people say šams**i**yyᵉti. The main thing is not to say š**a**msito with a short *i*.

Before a consonant however (e.g., before the endings -ha, -na, -kom, -hom), the word assumes a slightly different form:

šamsiyyet-ha *her umbrella*

Take care not to fall into the following common error:

huwwe jāb šamsīto u-hiyye jābat šamsīt-ha (!!)

Another example of how things should be:

niyye = *intention*

■ nīto mnīḥa u-niyyet-ha ᶜα̅ṭle[4] *His intention is good and her intention is bad.*

Before we move on, you should note that a number of words, most of which end in -a or -α, retain the vowel before the -t, even when a possessive pronoun (-i, -ak, etc.) is attached. The most common of these exceptions, which we've already met once (**Book 1, page 49, footnote 7**), is:

mαrα *woman; wife.*

mαrαti, mαrαtak *my wife, your wife*, etc.

According to the rules we've just learned, we would have expected the form mαrti (incidentally, Lebanese and Syrian speakers of Arabic do actually say mαrti). In the construct, however, this α drops, and we say:

■ mαrt‿il-mudīr *the manager's wife*

mαrt 'aḫūy *my brother's wife / my sister-in-law*

Try to work out how you would say *two women*, then read the footnote[5].

Too many explanations? But not too much to remember. As usual, we suggest that you review the summary in the box below:

farše	faršet il-walad
or:	faršt‿il-walad
faršt-o	faršet-ha
ḫālti	ḫālet-na
šamsīto	šamsiyyet-ha
mαrαto	mαrt‿il-mudīr

4. Of course, the opposite can be true, too, in which case we'll say nīto ᶜα̅ṭle u-niyyet-ha mnīḥa. ᶜα̅ṭel [ᶜα̅ṭlīn] means *bad, nasty*. The comparative form is 'αᶜṭαl, which means *worse, nastier.*

5. You are familiar with the word mαrrα, which means *time, instance* (with a double *r*!) and with mαr(r)tēn, which means *twice*. How do you say *two women*? mαrαtēn? No!! In this case we say niswān tintēn <women two>.

Now it's time to listen to the conversation, which will help you to get used to these changing forms. Look out for them and say them out loud.

Vocabulary

ṣeḥḥɑ[6] [2]	health	būlis	police; policeman
ḥɑrārɑ	heat; fever	saḥab [yisḥab]	to pull[9]
salāme [2]	peace; well being	ḥabas [yiḥbes]	to imprison
ḥorr ['aḥrār]	free (i.e. at liberty)	ᶜazam [yiᶜzem]	to invite
sakrān	drunk, intoxicated	ḥorriyye [10]	freedom
qɑṭɑᶜ [yiqṭɑᶜ]	to cut; to cross	kettō // kēks	cake[10]
dahas[7] [yidhas]	to run over / run down	luġa [luġāt]	language
šaqfe [2] [šuqaf]	slice, piece	swāqa [2]	driving
hawiyye [10]	identity; identity card	dawle [2] [duwal]	state, country
ruḫṣɑ [2]	license, permit (e.g., driving license, building permit, etc.)		
ġada[m]	midday meal (lunch, dinner)		
ᶜaša[m]	evening meal (dinner, supper)		
wɑsṭ / wɑsɑṭ[8]	middle; circle, milieu (social)		

Conversation

– ya 'abu Jamīl, kīf ṣeḥḥtak il-yōm?	– Abu Jamil, how are you feeling <how [is] your health> today?
– 'aḥsan, il-ḥamd-illa.	– Better, praise God.
– u-mɑrɑtak, kīf ṣeḥḥet-ha?	– And your wife, how is she feeling <how

---

6. Don't forget that the "emphatic" consonants (ṣ, ḍ, ṭ, ẓ) affect the vowel sounds. The word ṣeḥḥɑ is pronounced almost ṣoḥḥɑ.

7. This word is understood by speakers in all areas, though in Galilee you are more likely to hear dahak used in this sense.

8. The word wɑsɑṭ / wɑsṭ means *middle*; in everyday conversation, however, the word nuṣṣ (*half*) is more often used in this sense: *in the middle of the room* = fi nuṣṣ il-ġurfe; *in the Arab social sphere / in the Arab milieu* = fi-l-wɑsɑṭ il-ᶜɑrɑbi.

9. E.g., *He pulled the rope*. This verb also means *withdraw*, as in withdrawing money from a bank account, etc.

10. This is a "European" rather than a Middle Eastern cake, i.e., one that gets cut into slices. In Galilee people say ketto, from French *gâteau*, while Jerusalemites say kaᶜke or kēk(s) from the English word *cake(s)*; the plural form is more common.

smeᶜᵉt in-ha muš mɑbsūṭɑ.	[is] her health>? I heard she wasn't well.
šū-mā-lhɑ[11]?	What's wrong with her?
– ᶜind-ha šwayyet ḥɑrɑ̄rɑ[12].	– She's got a bit of a fever.
– salāmet-hɑ[13]!	– I hope she feels better soon <her well-being>.
– 'ɑllɑ‿isallmak[14] (isalmak).	– Thank you <[may] God preserve you>!

– yā ḥabībi, ђōd ḥorrītak[15]!	– My friend <my dear>, make yourself at home <take your freedom>!
hōn mitᵉl bētak u-aᶜazz!	Consider this your home – and even more than that <here [is] like your home and more dear>!
hōn 'ōḍtak u-hōn 'ōḍet-na	Here's your room and here's **our** room,
'iḥna – 'ana u-mɑrɑti, yaᶜni,	that's to say, my wife's and mine,
u-hunāk 'ōḍet[16] immi.	and [over] there is my mother's room.

– smeᶜᵉt šū ṣɑ̄r maᶜ 'abu ђalīl?	– Have you heard what happened to Abu Khalil?
haz-zalame bisūq zayy	That man drives as if he were drunk
wāḥad sakrɑ̄n! kān māši	<like one drunk>! He was going

---

11. This will be explained in Lesson 22.

12. You can also use the word ḥamm to mean *fever.* šwayy or šwayye is actually a feminine noun that means *a bit* or *a little* (it is a diminutive form of the word ši [*thing*]). The construct form is šwayyet, in accordance with the rule you learned earlier in this lesson. *A little sugar* = šwayyet sukkɑr.

13. salāmtak is an expression of good wishes used when speaking to a person who is ill, much like the English *Get well soon / I hope you feel better soon.* We are familiar with the word salāme (which means *welfare, safety, well-being*) from the leave-taking formula: – b-ђɑ̄ṭrak! – maᶜ is-salāme!

If you want to say *get well soon* to a woman, you say salāmtek <your well-being> of course. If you're talking about a sick person who is not present (as is the case here), you will say salāmto! or, of a female, salāmet-ha!

14. This will be explained soon.

15. ir-rajol biddo ḥorrīto wil-mɑrɑ bid-ha ḥorriyyet-ha = *Man wants his freedom and woman wants hers.*

16. 'ōḍɑ ['uwɑḍ] = *room.* This Turkish loan word is increasingly being replaced by the Arabic word ġurfe.

b-surᶜα fi wαsṭ‿il-balad.	fast in the center of the town.
'aja[17] wāḥad biddo yiqṭαᶜ iš-šāreᶜ,	Someone came along and wanted to cross <came one, he wants to cross> the road,
lawla šwayy kān dahaso[18].	[and] he almost ran him over <but for a little he would have run him over>.
il-bulīs ṭαlαb minno hawīto...	The policeman asked him for his ID card…
– u-šū ṣār baᶜdēn?	– And what happened afterwards?
– ma baᶜref... in-natīje	– I don't know… The main thing <the result> [is that]
saḥabū-lo‿r-ruɧṣα.	they took away <withdrew> his license.
– 'ayya ruɧṣα?	– What license?
– ruɧṣet l-ᵉswāqa / is-swāqa.	– His driving license.
– ḥabasūʰ?	– Did they put him in prison?
– la', bass 'aɧadu minno ruɧᵒṣto.	– No, they only took his license away.

– mαrαti 'aɧdat is-sayyārα, qult-ilha: ɧōdi	– My wife's taken the car. I told her,
ruɧṣet is-swāqa tabaᶜt-ek[19]	"Take your driving license,"
fa-aɧdat maᶜ-ha ruɧṣet-ha	and she took her license
u-hawiyyet-ha.	and her identity card.

– mudīr il-bank ṣāḥbi,	– The bank manager is a friend of mine <[is] my friend>.
šāf-ni fiš-šāreᶜ,	He saw me in the street [and] said to me
qal-li: tfαḍḍαl !	"Please [accept a lift from me]!"
'ana‿rkebᵉt fi sayyārto...	I got into his car…
– sayyāret mīn?	– Whose car?
– sayyārt‿il-mudīr yaᶜni,	– The manager's car, that is <it means>,
u-aɧad-ni ᶜala bēto	and he took me to his house

17. This will be explained soon.

18. *He would have run him over*. It's too soon to start explaining conditional sentences of the *If such-and-such had happened, so-and-so would have seen it* type. One brief example will suffice to lay the foundations for the future: (*If he had known at the time*) kān katab (*he would have written*) <he was he wrote>.

19. This is another case where it is best to use tabaᶜ, or, if the noun it agrees with is feminine (as is the case here), tabaᶜt- / tabaᶜt-. See the table at the end of the lesson.

u-ᶜazam-ni[20] ᶜa-l-ġada.	and invited me to lunch.
– niyyā-lak[21].	– How nice for you! / Lucky you!

– yā-mmɑ, biddi šaqfet kēks.	– Mummy, I want a slice of cake!
– lā yā-mmɑ[22], bikaffi!	– No dear, that's enough!
'aђadᵉt šaqᵉftak	You'veᵐ had your slice,
u-uђtak 'aђdat šaqfet-ha,	and your sister's had her slice
ђɑlɑs!	and that's it <finish>!

– bʸeᶜref il-luġɑ‿l-ᶜibriyye w-il-luġɑ‿l-ᶜɑrɑbiyye, yaᶜni il-luġtēn / il-luġatēn[23].	– He knows Hebrew and Arabic, that's to say, both languages <the two languages>.
– bidhom dawle fɑlɑsṭīniyye[24] jamb dawlet 'isrɑ̄'īl – yaᶜni dawltēn / dawlatēn[23].	– They want a Palestinian state alongside the State of Israel – in other words, two states.

---

20. *I invite; I invite you*ᵐ = baᶜzem, baᶜᵉzmak. *I invite them* = baᶜzem-hom.

21. The word hana (hanā'#) means *enjoyment*: haniyyan! (hanī'an!#) is an expression of good wishes (we'll come back to this later). haniyyan lak <enjoyment to you> has shortened to become niyyā-lak, which means *how lucky / pleasant for you!* The Arabic word for *luck* or *fate* is ḥɑẓẓ (ma-lōš ḥɑẓẓ = *He's unlucky* <he has no luck>), but the word šɑns (from the French *chance*) is also often used in this sense. You will hear people say šɑns-na! (*That's our good luck!*) and 'inte u-šɑnsak! (*Try your luck* <you and your luck>)!

22. We are familiar with the terms bɑ̄bɑ and mɑ̄mɑ, but in rural areas (especially villages in Galilee), you will hear yā-bɑ and yā-mmɑ. Note that each parent addresses both sons and daughters by the term used to address himself or herself: a father will say yā-bɑ to both his son **and his daughter**! The accepted explanation for this is that this is how each parent teaches his / her sons and daughters to address him or her. However, parents continue to use these expressions long after their children have passed the toddler stage.

23. In educated speech the word luġɑ behaves like mɑrɑ: *his language* can be either luġto or luġato#, and, in the dual, luġtēn or luġatēn#. The same is true of *two countries*, which you will hear pronounced as either dawltēn or dawlatēn#.

24. The word for *Palestine* is fɑlɑsṭīn (filɑsṭīn#); the -s is pronounced ṣ because of the ṭ → fɑlɑṣṭīn). *Palestinian* is fɑlɑṣṭīni, fɑlɑṣṭīniyyeᶠ [fɑlɑṣṭīniyyīn].

The rules we've learned today enable us to go back and take another quick look at some familiar words that end in -e or -a / -α. Let's see how they behave when an attached pronoun is added to them, or when they appear in the construct form:

■ *a box*	^{c}**i**lbe // ^{c}**u**lbe
a box of matches	^{c}**i**lbet kibr**ī**t
two boxes	^{c}il^{e}bt**ē**n
a minute	daq**ī**qa
a minute's silence	daq**ī**qet ṣ**α**mt#
two minutes	daqīqt**ē**n
a word	k**i**lme
two words	kil^{e}mt**ē**n
the school	il-m**a**drase
Yusef's school	m**a**draset Y**ū**sef
his school	madr**a**sto [8*]
our school	madras**e**t-na
two schools	madrast**ē**n
a story / tale	q**u**ṣṣα
the story of the king's daughter / the king's daughter's tale	q**u**ṣṣet b**i**nt il-m**a**lek
our story	quṣṣ**e**t-na
two stories	quṣṣt**ē**n (quṣt**ē**n)
a worker^{m} / laborer^{m}	^{c}**ā**mel
a worker^{f} / laborer^{f}	^{c}**ā**mle / ^{c}**ā**mile
checkout clerk / assistant <cash-register worker>	^{c}**ā**mlet sand**ū**q
Yusef 's family; the Yusef family	^{c}**ē**let Y**ū**sef
his family; our family	^{c}**ē**lto; ^{c}ēl**e**t-nα[25]
What will be the outcome / the result?	š**ū** b^{e}tk**ū**n in-nat**ī**je?
What's that the result of <this [is] result-of what>?	h**ā**da nat**ī**jet '**ē**š?
It happened [as] a result of a technical hitch.	h**ā**da ṣ**ᾱ**r nat**ī**jet ḫ**a**lal f**a**nni.

25. Remember the rule that says that an unstressed long syllable (i.e., one not in bold type) shortens: we say ^{c}**ē**le (with a long **ē-**), but ^{c}ēl**e**t-na = ^{c}el**e**t-na.

Where's your daughter's doll?	**wēn luᶜbet bintak?**
Here's your[f] doll / her doll.	**hayy luᶜobtek / luᶜbet-ha.**

Read all the sentences above out loud, then cover the right-hand column with a piece of paper, read the English, and try to reconstruct the Arabic.

Explanations

1. 'inno (inno), 'innak...

Let's go over a few details concerning inno, which means *that* in phrases like *He said that... She heard that... We know that...*

- **qāl inno biddo‿irūḥ** *He said that he wanted* <he wants> *to go.*

Often the inno is dropped, as *that* is in English:

- **smeᶜet biddo‿irūḥ** *I heard he wanted to go.*
  qāl ziheq[26] *He said he was fed up.*

The word for *that* is actually inn-, to which we add an attached pronoun. This is usually the third person masculine singular pronoun -o, even when the subject of the phrase that follows is *I* or *you*. However, we've already seen that it is also possible to add a pronoun in the appropriate person:

- **smeᶜet inno 'inte marīḍ** *I heard that you [were] ill* or, quite simply:
  smeᶜet innak marīḍ *I heard that you [were] ill.*

---

26. **ziheq [yizhaq]** means *he was fed up / he'd had it up to here.* **zheqᵉt min hal-ᶜīše** *I'm fed up living like this* <I'm fed up with this life>. How do you pronounce **zheqᵉt**? In three syllables: **ᵉz-he-qᵉt**. It's not so hard, but let's hope you never need to use the word...

Let's take this opportunity to distinguish once again between *that* (inno) and *that / which / who / whom* (illi):

■ sm**e**ᶜet inno q**u**lt '**i**ši — *I heard that you had said something.*
sm**e**ᶜet il-kal**ā**m illi q**u**lto — *I heard what you said*
<I heard the talk that you said>.

b**a**ᶜref iz-z**a**lame‿lli q**ā**l inno muš m**u**mken — *I know the man who said that it was <is> impossible.*

2. Dear = expensive; beloved

Something that costs a lot of money is ġ**ā**li, while a beloved person is ᶜaz**ī**z – but he or she can also be described as ġ**ā**li.

ᶜaz**ī**z fem ᶜaz**ī**ze [ᶜazīz**ī**n]; cp: 'aᶜ**a**zz
ġ**ā**li fem ġ**ā**lye [ġāly**ī**n]; cp: '**a**ġla

■ hal-w**a**lad ᶜaz**ī**z ᶜal**ē**na — *This boy's dear to us.*
il-bɑnḍ**ō**rɑ‿l-y**ō**m ġ**ā**lye — *Tomatoes are dear now.*
ġ**ā**li u-ṭ**ɑ**lɑb‿ᵉrħ**ī**ṣ — *His wish is my command*
<a dear [man] and he asked for a cheap [thing]>.

You may also hear a slightly different version of this proverb:

ġ**ā**li wiṭ-ṭ**ɑ**lɑb‿ᵉrħ**ī**s — *Your wish is my command*
<[you are] dear and the request is cheap>.

In other words: *You are so precious to us that we will do anything for you.*

3. My strength, our brothers, etc.

Before we finish dealing with the business of f**a**ršto, let's take a look at a couple of special cases, i.e., words like

q**u**wwe[27] — *strength, power*
'**i**ħwe — *brothers*

The second word above, which is the plural form of '**a**ħħ or'**a**ħu (*brother*) looks like a feminine singular noun, and, indeed, behaves rather as if it were one, as we shall see.

---

27. The double -w of q**u**wwe should be pronounced as in the English *bo<u>w w</u>indow* or *bo<u>w-w</u>ow*.

Let's look at the paradigm of both words with the attached pronouns:

q**u**wwti	*my strength*	'**i**ḫ^{e}wti	*my brothers*
q**u**wwtak	*your^{m} strength*	'**i**ḫ^{e}wtak	*your^{m} brothers*
q**u**wwtek	*your^{f} strength*	'**i**ḫ^{e}wtek	*your^{f} brothers*
q**u**wwto	*his strength*	'**i**ḫ^{e}wto	*his brothers*
quww**e**t-ha	*her strength*	'iḫw**e**t-ha	*her brothers*
quww**e**t-na	*our strength*	'iḫw**e**t-na	*our brothers*
quww**e**t-kom	*your strength*	'iḫw**e**t-kom	*your brothers*
quww**e**t-hom	*their strength*	'iḫw**e**t-hom	*your brothers*

To pronounce the word q**u**wwti (listen to the recording), you have to start slowly: q**u**-we-ti (no need to double the -w), then repeat it faster and faster, dropping the -e as you do so. This may sound obvious, but it really does help.

The combination ḫ^{e}w in the word '**i**ḫ^{e}wti should be pronounced (more or less) ḫ + *eh-u*. Listen carefully to the recording for the exact pronunciation.

This has been another jam-packed lesson, but, as always, its contents can be summarized in a table. All you have to do is repeat the following forms out loud:

f**a**rše	f**a**ršti	f**a**ršet Y**ū**sef	faršt**ē**n
š**a**qfe	š**a**q^{e}fti	šaqf**e**t-na	šaq^{e}ft**ē**n
haw**i**yye	haw**ī**ti	hawiyy**e**t-ha	hawīt**ē**n
m**ɑ**rɑ	m**ɑ**rɑti	m**ɑ**rt 'aḫ**ū**y	m**ɑ**rt‿il-mud**ī**r
'**i**ḫwe	'**i**ḫ^{e}wti	'iḫw**e**t-na	

ġ**u**rfet in-n**ō**m taba**ᶜ**-na / taba**ᶜ**et-na[28]

ru**ḫ**ṣet is-sw**ā**qa tabaᶜak / tab^{aᶜ}tek (taba**ᶜ**tek)[29]

28. *Our bedroom* <the sleeping-room belonging-to-us>. n**ō**m = sleep (noun).

29. *Your$^{m/f}$ driving license.*

Exercises

A. Translate into English:

1. k**ī**f lahj**e**t-kom? zayy l**a**hjet m**ɑ**ṣᵉr?
2. l**a**', lahj**e**t-na h**ī**‿l-l**a**hje‿l-fɑlɑṣṭ**ī**n**i**yye.
3. h**ā**di sayy**ɑ̄**ret m**ī**n? la-m**ī**n is-sayy**ɑ̄**rɑ h**ā**y?
4. h**ā**y sayy**ɑ̄**ret 'aḫ**ū**y.
5. is-sayy**ɑ̄**rɑ '**i**lo w**i**lla lal-mud**ī**r?
6. l**a**', h**ā**di sayy**ɑ̄**rto. 7. bass ᶜ**i**ndo sayy**ɑ̄**rɑ t**ā**nye.
8. n**a**ᶜam, ᶜ**i**ndo sayyɑ̄rt**ē**n. – niyy**ā**-lo!
9. h**ā**t ir-r**u**ḫṣɑ t**a**baᶜak!
10. ᶜ**i**ndo t**a**lat '**i**ḫwe u-s**ā**ken maᶜ '**i**ḫᵉwto.
11. l**ē**š ma j**i**bt-ᵉš haw**ī**tak?

B. Complete the sentences

(Replace the English words with the appropriate expression in Arabic):

12. hal-m**ɑ**rrɑ m**a** '**a**ḫad (his license) m**a**ᶜo.
13. (Did you^{pl} invite) Y**ū**sef ᶜala‿l-ᶜ**a**ša?
14. n**a**ᶜam, (we invited him).
15. il-f**a**rše (was) fi-l-q**u**rne.
16. is-sayy**ɑ̄**rɑ (ran over) il-w**a**lad.
17. (I crossed) iš-š**ā**reᶜ h**ō**n.
18. (I cut) š**a**qfet ḫ**u**bᵉz.
19. j**ī**b (your^{m} identity card) u-([the] identity-card-of) m**ɑ**rɑtak kam**ā**n..

C. Translate into Arabic:

20. We meant well <our intention was good>.
21. The children can sleep in this room. This is their room.
22. Your bed is longer than hers <than her bed>.
23. We want to invite Yusef to lunch.
24. I want to invite him.
25. Sit$^{m\ sing}$ there in the corner.
26. Our brothers are in their room.
27. Cut^{f} two slices, a slice for yourself <to you> and a slice for me <to me>!
28. I'm in good health, thank God <my health is good, praise to God>.
29. Today the patient doesn't have a fever <the patient, he doesn't have….>.
30. I've understood everything. – Good for you!

By the way, how do the Egyptians say "the Egyptian dialect"?
il-l**a**hga‿l-mɑṣr**e**yya, with g instead of j and -**e**yya instead of -**i**yye.

dars tᵉnēn u-ᶜišrīn

22

Lesson Twenty-Two

We've come across the verb ṣ**ɑ̄**r [iṣ**ī**r], which conjugates like j**ā**b (**see Book 1, pages 26 and 62**) several times already. Apart from indicating a new situation, or a transition from one state to another (something new has happened / a new process has got underway), ṣ**ɑ̄**r also means *he / it became* or *he / it started to*. You may recall the expression ṣ**ɑ̄**r 'a**ḥ**san from Book 1, p. 71. and there have been other examples, too. Let's look at some of the contexts in which ṣ**ɑ̄**r appears, and learn how to use it. We'll start by looking at the following examples:

š**ū** ṣ**ɑ̄**r?	*What happened / What's happened?*
il-w**a**lad ṣ**ɑ̄**r y**u**rkoḍ	*The boy began to run / The boy started running*
k**ā**n faq**ī**r u-ṣ**ɑ̄**r ġ**a**ni	*He was poor and he became rich / and he got rich*
šw**a**yy‿ᵉšw**a**yy	*Gradually* <a little a little = slowly slowly>
biṣ**ī**r yif**h**am	*he begins / he'll begin to understand*

Note that ṣ**ɑ̄**r can mean *got* in the sense of *became*, indicating a transition between one state and another. We can feel the difference between the following pairs of sentences:

ᶜ**i**ndi sayy**ɑ̄**rɑ	*I have a car* (i.e., *I am already in possession of a car*)
ṣ**ɑ̄**r ᶜ**i**ndi sayy**ɑ̄**rɑ	*I've got a car [now] / I got a car*

(i.e., I didn't have a car before, but now I do – the situation has changed).

f**ī**ʰ bɑnḍ**ō**rɑ	*There are tomatoes [at the greengrocer's]*
ṣ**ɑ̄**r f**ī**ʰ bɑnḍ**ō**rɑ	*There are tomatoes now / Tomatoes have come in*

(i.e., they didn't have any before, but now they've got them).

bt**i**fham ᶜ**ɑ**rɑbi	*She understands Arabic*
ṣ**ɑ̄**rat t**i**fham ᶜ**ɑ**rɑbi	*She's started to understand Arabic / She understands Arabic now* (though she didn't before).
buḍr**o**b-ha	*He hits her.*
ṣ**ɑ̄**r yuḍr**o**b-ha	*He started to hit her.*

From the sentences above we can see that ṣ**ɑ̄**r can also mean *he / it started to*, indicating the gradual or sudden onset of a new situation. The second verb is in the subjunctive, i.e., without initial b-. However, ṣ**ɑ̄**r is not used to indicate a deliberately planned beginning, and so would not be appropriate in a sentence like *He began to study at university* or *When did be begin to build the house?*

To indicate the start of deliberate actions such as these we use a different verb, which we shall learn in due course (in Lesson 29).

As ṣ**ɑ̄**r is used in so many different contexts it is a very commonly heard verb, as you will see from the Conversation below:

Vocabulary

w**a**ja^{c} ['awj**ā**^{c}]	pain	š**i**ta [2]	winter; rain[3]
f**ɑ**ḥɑṣ [yifḥɑṣ]	to examine	f**ɑ**ḥṣ	examination
d**a**raje [2] [daraj**ā**t]	step, stair; degrees[1]	b**a**rd	cold (n)
d**a**raj (d**ɑ**rɑj)[2]	steps, stairs; degree	ya-r**ē**t!	if only!
ṭɑb**ī**b ['ɑṭibb**ā**']	doctor / physician	ḥ**a**rb^{f} [ḥur**ū**b]	war
m^{c}**a**llem [3]	teacher^{m}	h**a**zze [8] [-zz**ā**t]	shock, jolt
m^{c}**a**llme [3] [8] [-m**ā**t]	teacher^{f}	m^{c}allm**ī**n	teachers
m**u**dde [8]	period of time, while (n)		
k**i**ber [y**i**kbɑr]	to grow / get bigger; to grow up; to grow older		

Conversation

– š**ū** ṣ**ɑ̄**r?	– What's happened?
– ma ṣ**ɑ̄**r-š (→ ṣ**ɑ**r-š) '**i**ši.	– Nothing's happened!
– ^{e}mb**a**la, il-jir**ɑ̄**n qāl**ū**-li inno ṣ**ɑ̄**r m**a**^{c}o ḥ**ā**des.	– Yes it has. The neighbors told me he'd had an accident.
– ma biṣ**ī**r-š (biṣ**i**r-š)! ma ṭ**e**le^{c}-š min il-b**ē**t.	– Impossible <[it] doesn't happen>! He hasn't left the house.

---

1. *Temperatures* = daraj**ā**t il-ḥɑr**ɑ̄**rɑ. The word ḥɑr**ɑ̄**rɑ means both *temperature* (of the atmosphere, or of a person's body) and *rash* (on the skin). Nouns ending in -a or -e are usually feminine, and most of them have a "regular" plural form, i.e., they add -**ā**t to form the plural. Where this is the case, we shall not indicate the plural form in full, but use a shortened version instead: [-□**ā**t]. Here, for example, we have d**a**raje [-j**ā**t], i.e., [daraj**ā**t] and m^{c}**a**llme [-m**ā**t], i.e., [m^{c}allm**ā**t].

2. This is a collective noun in the masculine singular: id-d**a**raj h**ā**da = *these steps.*

3. In the Middle East, winter is the rainy season.
fi-š-š**i**ta b**a**rd‿^{e}kt**ī**r fi r**ū**sya = In winter it's very cold in Russia.

– wiqeᶜ [4] ᶜa-d-daraj.	– He fell on the stairs.
ruḥt 'azūro qal-li:	I went to see him [and] he told me,
'ana‿wqeᶜᵉt ᶜala rās̄i	"I fell on my head and
u-ṣār ᶜindi wajaᶜ rās [5].	now I've got a headache."
'aẖadūʰ ᶜa-l-mustašfa	They took him to hospital
u-ṣār-lo jumᶜa hunāk.	and he's been in there for a week <and [there] became to him a week there>.
– faḥaṣūʰ?	– Did they examine him?
šu-mā-lo?	What's wrong with him?
– ṣār-lo hazzet moẖẖ [6].	– He's got concussion <brain jolt>.
– salāmto!	– I hope he's better soon <his well-being>!
– 'alla‿isalmak!	– Good health to you too <may God keep you well> !

– il-yōm, 'ana mašġūl‿ᵉktīr,	– Today I'm very busy.
bukra‿nšalla	Tomorrow I hope to have time
biṣīr fīʰ ᶜindi waqt / waqᵉt.	<[there] will become there-is at me time>.

– baᶜd‿il-ḥarb ṣār fīʰ	– After the war new problems cropped up,
mašākel‿ᵉjdīde [7] wil-waḍeᶜ ṣār	and the situation got worse.
'aᶜṭal, maẓbūṭ willa la'?	Am I right or not <accurate or not>?
– ᵉnšalla hallaq biṣīr ẖēr!	– Let's hope things will get better now!
– 'ā, ṣār il-waqt!	– Yes, it's about time <[it's] become the time>.

– halqēt šita, baᶜᵉd šahᵉr	– It's winter now. In a month's time

---

4. wiqeᶜ belongs to the same group of verbs as nizel, and is conjugated in the same way: huwwe wiqeᶜ, hiyye wiqᶜat, 'ana‿wqeᶜᵉt (like nzelᵉt), which you should pronounce 'a–naw–qe–ᶜet. This verb has an irregular form in the present-future tense, which we'll talk about later on.

5. wajaᶜ rās means *[a] headache*, in both the literal and figurative sense.
ma biddī-š wajaᶜ rās = *I don't want [any] headaches / [any] hassle.*

6. . moẖẖ (muẖẖ) means *brain. He's brainless* = ma ᶜindō-š moẖẖ.

7. muškile [mašākel] = *problem, difficulty*. Why do we say jdīde in the feminine singular, even though the noun is plural? We'll explain this soon (in Lesson 25).

betṣīr id-dinya[8] rαbīc.	<after a month> it'll be spring <the world will become spring>.
– il-yōm iṣ-ṣuboḥ kānat id-dinya ṣαḥu[9] bass bacd_iḍ-ḍuhor ṣār fīh šita.	– It was fine this morning <today the morning the world was clarity> but in the afternoon it came on to rain <[it] became there-is rain>.

– 'aђūy rāḥ cala 'amērka[10].	– My brother's gone to America.
– qaddēš ṣαr-lo[11] hunāk?	– How long has he been there?
– sane u-nuṣṣ.	– A year and a half.
– yacni ṣαr-lak[11] sane u-nuṣṣ ma šuft-eš 'aђūk?	– In other words, it's been a year and a half <[it] means it's become to you...> since you saw your brother <you haven't seen your brother>?
– la', ruḥt 'azūro qabel šahrēn.	– No, I went to visit him two months ago.
– kīf huwwe? ṣār yicrαf 'inglīzi?	– How is he? Has he learned English <has he become he knows English>?
– 'ā, ṭαbcan! bil-'awwal ma kān yifham[12] wa-la kilme, bass il-yōm ṣār yifham kull 'iši.	– Yes, of course! At first he didn't understand a word but now <today> he can understand everything.
– niyyā-lo! ya-rēt 'aqdαr (hadqαr)	– Good for him! I wish I could go there too

---

8. Natural phenomena such as the seasons of the year and changes in the weather are attributed to "the world" = id-dinya (id-dunya#). This feminine noun means *the world around us / the natural environment*, while il-cālam is used to refer to *the world* as a geographical or political entity. We say <the world [is] rain; the world [is] winter; the world's got warm / clear; the world [is] rain[ing]; the world [is] thunder[ing]; the world [is] morning; the world [is] noon>, etc.

9. ṣαḥu / ṣαḥew means *clear / fine weather* (no rain, no strong winds, clear skies, etc.)

10. The Arabic pronunciation of *America, American* is 'amērka, 'amērkāni, or 'amrīka, 'amrīki. The feminine is -niyye, -kiyye and *the Americans* are il-'amērkān.

11. Why a short vowel? See **Book 1, pages 28 and 35**.

12. This composite verb (kān + subjunctive) denotes a habitual action in the past <didn't use to understand>. See **Explanations** below.

'arūḥ 'ana kamān la-muddet	for a year or two <if only I can go I too
sine sintēn,	for a period of a year, two years>.
hēk baṣīr 'a^{c}raf il-luġa mnīḥ.	Then <thus> I'd get to know the language well.

– biddi aṣīr doktōr,	– I want to be a doctor <to become a doctor>.
šu biddi a^{c}mel?	What should I do?
– lēš ma sa'alt-^{e}š l-^{e}m^{c}allem?	– Why didn't you^m ask the teacher?
– mà sa'alto! qult-illo:	– But I did ask him! I said to him,
ya 'ustāz, 'iza wāḥad biddo iṣīr	"Sir, if you want to be <if one wants to become> a doctor,
doktōr, šū b^{y}i^{c}mal?	what do you do <what does he do>?"
ṣār yiḍḥak, lēš / lēh[13]?	He started to laugh. Why?
– ^{c}ašān ba^{c}dak // lissāk‿^{e}zġīr,	– Because you're still young, [and] when you
lamma tikbar, btirja^c‿^{e}btis'alo.[14]	grow up you'll ask him again <you'll go back you'll ask him>.

---

13. lē is a less commonly used form of lēš. In Egypt, however, lē is the standard word for *why*?

14. This sentence has a couple of interesting features, which we'll deal with in the **Explanations** below.

– kān faqīr u-ṣār ġani[15], u-ṣār ᶜindo maṣāri u-kull ’iši.	– He was poor and he got <became> rich. Now he’s got money and everything…
– ya-rēt ṣar-li nafs‿iš-šī.	– If only the same thing would happen to me <if only [there] became to me the same thing>!

Explanations

1. The various meanings of ṣār

a) First of all, we’ve learned another meaning of the verb ṣār: *to be possible* (if it happens, it must be possible!)

biṣīr	*It’s possible / It’s reasonable / It could happen*
’iza bajib-lak[11] bukra, biṣīr?	*If I bring [it] to you tomorrow, is it OK?*
ma biṣīr-ᵉš (biṣir-š)!	*It’s not OK / That’s impossible!*

b) When used with l- + an attached pronoun (ṣār-li, -lak, -lo, etc.), ṣār can also mean *I’ve been / I haven’t been* (somewhere, for such-and-such a period of time). For example:

■ ṣar-lak[11] zamān sāken hōn?	*Have you lived here long* <[it] became to you [a long] time living here>?
ṣar-lo jumᶜa ma rāḥᵉ-š la-hunāk	*He hasn’t gone there for a week.*

In sentences like *I’ve been... for a long time / I haven’t... for a long time,* we have the option of using ’ili, ’ilak, ’ilo, etc., instead of ṣar-li:

’ilo šahrēn ma dafaᶜᵉ-š	*He hasn’t paid in two months / It’s been two months since he paid* <[it] became to him two months…>

2. On various words in the Conversation:

The Conversation contains a number of interesting words:

a) ṭabīb# [’aṭibbā’] means *doctor*. The word ṭebb [2] means *[the science of] medicine*, and daras iṭ-ṭebb fi-l-jāmiᶜa‿l-ᶜibriyye = *He studied medicine at the Hebrew University.*

---

15. faqīr [fuqara] means *poor*. The comparative form is ’afqar. The Arabic for *rich* is ġani (f ġaniyye) [ġunaya / ġanāya / ’aġniyā’#]; cp ’aġna.

Some speakers use the word ḥakīm <wise man> for *doctor*, and the related noun is used in the expression il-ḥikme‿l-ᶜαrαbiyye, which means *folk medicine* <Arab medicine>. The most commonly used word for *doctor* is, however, the one we learned in the early lessons of Book 1: doktōr [dakα̅trα]. Of parents who have searched far and wide for a cure for their ailing child we say in Arabic:

■ 'aђadūʰ la-ᶜind kull id-dakα̅trα — *They took him to all the doctors!*

b) fαḥαṣ [yifḥαṣ] means *to examine / to test*, and fαḥṣ [fuḥūṣα̅t / fuḥūṣ#] means *examination.*

■ ṭαlαb min id-doktōr inno yifḥαṣo — *He asked the doctor to examine him.*

3. lamma = when

A verb that follows lamma will usually be
- in the subjunctive, with a future meaning
- in the present future (i.e., with the prefix b-), with a present-habitual meaning (i.e., describing a repeated customary action):

■ lamma‿trūḥ, ђodo maᶜak — *When you go, take him with you* (in the future)
lamma bᵉtrūḥ ᶜa-l-madrase — *When you go to school...* (every day)

We'll come back to this use of the subjunctive. For now, this brief introduction will suffice.

4. To repeat / do again / say once more, etc.

There are a number of ways to say this in Arabic. One of these is to use the verb rijeᶜ (*return; repeat*): *I do again* = barjaᶜ baᶜmel <I return I do>. The appropriate tense is used in both verbs: past, present (with b-), subjunctive or imperative:

■ tāni yōm rijeᶜ sa'al-ni — *The next day he asked me again* <second day he returned he asked me>.
lāzem tirjaᶜ tis'alo — *You'll have to ask him again* <[it] must you return you ask him>.
'irjaᶜ 'is'alo — *Ask him again* < return ask him>!

5. ya-rēt = if only...! / I only hope that...!

The word yarēt precedes the expression of a wish – *if only...!*, etc.

– It is used with the **past tense** to express regret for something that has already happened: *If only things had happened otherwise... / If only such-and-such had never happened...* Usually the appropriate attached pronoun (-ni, -ak, etc.) is added: ya-rēt-ni, ya-rēt-ak, etc.

– It is used with the **subjunctive** to express a wish for the future: *If only it could happen / If only it could never happen...!* etc.
Examples:

■ yar**ē**t-ni‿^{c}**re**f^{e}t h**ā**da min q**ab**^{e}l[16]	*If only I'd known that before!*
yar**ē**t-ni k**u**nt maḥ**a**llak!	*If only I were in your place!*
yar**ē**to ma‿ir**ū**ḥ-^{e}š!	*I only hope that he doesn't go!*
yar**ē**t 'aš**ū**fo!	*I only hope I see him!*
yar**ē**t ik**ū**n ^{c}indi maṣ**ā**ri q**a**ddo!	*I only hope I'll have as much money as him!*

Note the difference in usage between yar**ē**t, which is followed by a verb in the **subjunctive** (= the expression of a wish), and 'inš**a**lla / (^{e}nš**a**lla), which is followed by the **present-future** (if God wills it, it will happen, i.e., the expression of a fact in the future), despite the fact that we translate 'inš**a**lla as *I hope / you hope / he hopes,* etc., which sounds in English like the expression of a wish.

■ yar**ē**t y**i**rja^{c}!	*I only hope he comes back!*
^{e}nš**a**lla b^{y}**i**rja^{c}!	*I hope he'll come back!*

6. A summary of the various meanings of ma

The little word ma has a variety of meanings and uses, some of which you learned quite a long time ago:

a) As a negative particle it is used alone or with the suffix -š in phrases like ma bidd**ī**-š / m**a** b**i**ddi[17] (*I don't want [to]*).

b) It is used when a preposition precedes a verb. Compare:

■ q**ab**^{e}l	*before*
q**ab**^{e}l s**ē**^{c}a	*an hour ago* <before an hour>
q**ab**^{e}l-ma ir**ū**ḥ[18]	*before he goes*
m**i**t^{e}l	*like*
m**i**tlak	*like you*^{m}
m**i**t^{e}l-ma q**u**lti	*as you*^{f} *said* <like you^{f} said >

---

16. How do you pronouce yar**ē**t-ni‿^{c}**re**f^{e}t? As always, start by saying slowly ya-r**ē**t–ni^{c} –**re**–fet, then repeat it, gradually speeding up to the rate of normal speech.

17. m**a** b**i**ddi is the form used in Syria, where the final -š is never added..

18. q**ab**^{e}l-ma is always followed by the subjunctive, even if the verb refers to an action in the past: q**ab**^{e}l-ma y**i**rja^{c} = (I managed to finish) *before he came back.*

c) In literary Arabic ma means *what*, and it is sometimes borrowed and used in this sense[19] in the colloquial language, too, e.g.,

■ mā-lak / šu-mā-lak? = *What's wrong* <with you>*?*

In this context we should mention the expression mah-ma, which means *whatever*.

Note that although the verb is in the past tense, it can also refer to the present:

■ mah-ma qult	*Whatever you say...*
mah-ma ṣār	*Whatever may have happened...; Whatever happens ...*

d) *But I / you / it did!* (to remind yourself, go back and take a look at **Book 1, p. 64, footnote 5**), in conversational exchanges such as:

■ – kān lāzem‿irūḥ...	*– He should have gone...*
– mà rāḥ!	*– But he did go!*

In other words: this ma is used to deny what has just been said. Take care to distinguish between the two following sentences, which are identical except for the placing of the stress, as indicated by the position of the words below:

mā rāḥ ↘	ma rāḥ! ↗
He didn't go.	*But he did go!*

7. Composite past tense: kān + subjunctive

You'll remember the composite phrase kān biddo (*he wanted*), and in the Conversation above you'll have noticed the expression ma kān yifham (*he didn't understand*) with reference to a lack of understanding that continued for a long period of time, not a one-time occurrence: *at first he didn't understand English...* Here are some more examples:

■ kunt 'akteb...	(When I was little) *I used to write...*
kān yismaᶜ ir-rādyo.	(Every day) *he used to listen to the radio.*
kān yiḍḥak.	(Every time I suggested it) *he would laugh.*
kānat tiġsel...	(Before she bought a washing machine) *she used to do the laundry...*
'abūy kān‿iqūl...	*My father used to say...*

---

19. We came across this word in the expression mā šā' allāh, which means *how beautiful!* <[it is] what God wanted>. As you already know, *what* in colloquial speech is normally šū or 'ēš.

Note that the verb **kān** in these composite verbs often translates into English as *I / you / he* ***used to*** or *I / you / he* ***would***. We'll discuss this at greater length in another lesson. In the meantime we'll make do with the examples above and concentrate on one important point: the verb after **kān / kunt**..., etc. is in the subjunctive.

Exercises

A. Translate into English:

1. bil-'awwal kān hayyen, baᶜdēn ṣar 'ɑṣᶜɑb.
2. bard‿il-yōm!
3. mɑẓbūṭ, bard bɑrrɑ, miš fi-l-ġurfe.
4. 'iza btiftaḥ iš-šubbāk, biṣīr bard fi-l-ġurfe kamān.
5. lamma kān walad ma-kan-š yeᶜrɑf yikteb,
6. 'amma‿l-yōm[20] ṣɑ̄r yikteb‿ᵉmnīḥ.
7. qabᵉl sane kunt 'afham qalīl‿ᵉktīr,
8. 'amma‿l-yōm, ṣert 'afham 'aktɑr.
9. qabᵉl ᶜašr‿ᵉsnīn, kān ᶜindo bass bintēn.
10. il-yōm ṣɑ̄r ᶜindo ḫams‿ᵉwlād.
11. ᵉmbāreḥ qult-illo: ma ᶜindī-š. il-yōm rijeᶜ ṭɑlɑb nafs‿iš-šī.
12. qabl‿il-ḥarb kānu mitēn, il-yōm ṣɑ̄ru ḫamᵉs miyye.
13. qabᵉl yōmēn ṭeleᶜ min il-bēt u-mā rijeᶜ. 'ɑbṣɑr šū ṣɑ̄r maᶜo.
14. 'immi wiqᶜat ᶜa-d-daraj, kasrat 'īd-ha[21]. – salāmet-ha!

B. Complete the sentences

(Replace the English words with the appropriate expression in Arabic):

15. (At first) kān hayyen, baᶜdēn ṣɑ̄r (harder).
16. ([It's] cold) il-yōm!
17. (If you^{m} open)‿š-šubbāk biṣīr bard (inside the room) kamān.
18. lamma kān walad, (he didn't know [how] to) yikteb,

---

20. This phrase means *nowadays* <today>, *on the other hand....* **'amma** means *but / on the other hand.*

21. This word can mean either *hand* or *arm*, depending on the context. What's the plural? We'll learn it in Book 3.

19. (but now <today>) ṣ**ɑ̄**r y**i**kteb‿^{e}mn**ī**ḥ.
20. l**i**ssa m**a** r**i**je^{c}, '**ɑ**bṣɑr (what's happened to him).
21. '**i**mmi (fell) ^{c}a-d-d**a**raj, k**a**srat (her arm).
22. l-ewl**ā**d (began) y**u**r^{o}kḍu.

C. Translate into Arabic:

23. At first [it] was difficult, now it's got <become> easier.
24. Yesterday there were[22] no tomatoes.
25. I heard that tomatoes had come in <that [it] became there are tomatoes>.
26. Did the doctor examine you^{m}?
27. Yes, he examined me[23].
28. I'd like to <I want to> examine you$^{m \& f}$.
29. The doctor said that he wanted to examine him.
30. He wanted to be <to become> a doctor.
31. But his father told him, "No, you're going to be <you'll become> a lawyer."[24]
32. This exercise[25] is difficult. That's enough, go$^{m \& f}$ to bed!
33. Yes, it's high time <[it's] become the time>!

This has been another very full lesson. Do you feel that you're in over your head? Don't panic, you're bound to have remembered some of it – the general meaning of the verb ṣ**ɑ̄**r, at least, and perhaps also a few new words. The **Explanations** are there to help you to understand, and, by explaining things, to prepare you for the lessons that follow. Don't worry if you don't remember everything the first time you come across it.

---

22. Remember that *there was / there were* = k**ā**n fīh.

23. Don't forget the change in the position of the stress (see **Book 1, p. 91**).

24. The word for *lawyer* is muḥ**ā**mi.

25. *Exercise* = tamr**ī**n [2] [tamār**ī**n].

d**a**rs tal**ā**te u-ᶜišr**ī**n

23

Lesson Twenty-Three

In this lesson we'll make the acquaintance of the active participle (active part.), also referred to as the present participle, and the passive participle (passive part.), also known as the past participle. As you'll see, we've already come across both these forms, and in this lesson we'll focus mainly on the **various meanings** of each.

The active participle of k**a**tab is:

k**ā**teb	*writer, he-who-writes / has-written; registrar, scribe*$^{\text{m sing}}$
k**ā**tbe	*writer, she-who-writes / has-written; registrar, scribe*$^{\text{f sing}}$
kātb**ī**n	*writers, those-who-write / have-written; registrars, scribes*$^{\text{m pl}}$
kātb**ā**t / kātib**ā**t	*writers, those-who-write / have-written; registrars, scribes*$^{\text{f pl}}$

The passive participle of katab is:

makt**ū**b[1]	*written*$^{\text{m sing}}$
makt**ū**be	*written*$^{\text{f sing}}$
maktūb**ī**n	*written*$^{\text{m/f pl}}$

We have already come across a number of these participles (e.g., s**ā**ken; mašġ**ū**l, etc.) and now it's time to see how they are used; additional points will be clarified in the **Explanations** below. In this lesson we won't learn many new words; instead, we'll "slot" verbs familiar to us from earlier lessons into the new word patterns we've learned today, i.e., we'll use their active and passive participles.

Vocabulary

r**a**faᶜ [y**i**rfaᶜ]	to lift, raise; to turn up, make louder		
š**i**reb [y**i**šrɑb]	to drink	'**ā**le [-l**ā**t][2]	machine, apparatus
d**a**wa [2] ['**a**dwiye]	medicine	m**u**lk [aml**ā**k]	property, possessions
ṣ**ō**t [2] ['aṣw**ā**t]	voice; sound	fa-	then; so; hence, thus
balad**i**yye [-iyy**ā**t]	municipality, town hall		

1. This word, as we have already seen, also means *letter* <[that which is] written>. However, when it means *letter* it has a different plural: [makāt**ī**b], which means *letters*.

2. See **Lesson 22, page 63, footnote 1**.

Sentences and Conversation

Signs used in the sentences that follow: an action in the present can be either habitual — (*I do... every day*) or taking place only at this particular moment • (*I am doing .... now*). Verbs designating the future are not marked.

—	b**a**nzal kull y**ō**m ^{c}ala ḥ**ē**fa.	I go <go down> to Haifa every day.
	b**u**krɑ b**a**nzal ^{c}al ḥ**ē**fa.	Tomorrow I'm going to Haifa.
•	'**i**ssa '**a**na n**ā**zel min ^{c}**i**ndo.	I'm coming down from his place <from at-him> right now.
•	š**u**fto n**ā**zel min il-b**ɑ̄**ṣ.	I saw him getting off the bus <coming down from the bus>.
•	š**u**ft-ha n**ā**zle ^{c}a-d-d**a**raj.	I saw her coming down the stairs.
•	šufn**ā**-kom nāzl**ī**n min f**ō**q.	We saw you^{pl} coming down from upstairs.
—	^{c}**ā**datan b**i**rja^{c} bil-b**ɑ̄**ṣ.	Usually he comes back by bus / on the bus.
	q**ā**l b**i**rja^{c} b**a**^{ce}d yōm**ē**n.	He said he'd <he'll> come back in two days <after two days>.
•	h**a**llaq '**a**na r**ā**j^{c}a min il-m**a**ktab.	Now I'm$^{f\ sing}$ coming home from the office.
•	f**ā**t ^{c}**i**ndo u-h**ū** r**ā**je^{c} [3] min iš-š**u**ġ^{o}l.	He dropped in on him on his way home from work <he went in at-him and he coming back from the work>.
•	u-**a**na r**ā**je^{c} [3], bajib-lak il-jar**ī**de.	On my way back <and I coming back> I'll bring you the newspaper.
	ṣ**ɑ̄**r[4] r**ā**je^{c} min zam**ā**n.	He's been back for a long time <he became having-come-back since a [long] time>.
—	d**ā**yman b^{y}**e**ṭlɑ^{c} min il-b**ē**t is-s**ē**^{c}a s**i**tte u-n**u**ṣṣ.	He always leaves <goes out from> the house at six thirty.
•	'**a**na r**ɑ̄**yeḥ la-^{c}**i**ndo, ba^{c}d**ē**n b**ɑ**ṭlɑ^{c} la-^{c}**i**ndak.	I'm going to [see] him, then I'll come up to [see] you.
•	š**u**f^{e}t 'aḫ**ū**k ṭ**ɑ̄**le^{c} min id-dukk**ā**n.	I saw your^{m} brother coming out of the shop.
—	kull y**ō**m baš**ū**f 'aḫ**ū**ki fi ḥ**ē**fa.	Every day I see your^{f} brother in Haifa.

---

3. This expression (u- + a personal pronoun [*I, you, he,* etc.] + a present participle) means *when / while...* See **Explanations 3.**

4. On ṣ**ɑ̄**r + the active participle, see **Explanations 2.**

bukrα 'akīd[5] bašūfo.	Tomorrow I'll definitely see him / I'll see him for sure.
• 'ana šāyef [6] 'aḫūk min hōn.	I can see <I am seeing> your^{m} brother from here.
• 'ana šāyfak ḥāmel baṭṭαniyye – 'ēš biddak teᶜmal fīha?	I can see you^{m} carrying a blanket – what are you going to do with it <what do you want to do….>?
— kull yōm bamroq min hōn.	I pass by here every day.
• šufto māreq fi-š-šāreᶜ.	I saw him passing by in the street.
• šufᵉt nās mārqīn jamb il-baladiyye.	I saw people passing by next to the town hall.
— ᶜādatan basmaᶜ‿ᵉmnīḥ, bass	Usually I can hear <I hear> well, but this
• hal-mαrrα 'ana muš sāmeᶜ.	time I can't hear!
'iza basmaᶜ 'iši baqul-lak.	If I hear anything I'll tell you.
• halo! miš sāmeᶜ / miš sāmᶜa[7].	Hello! I can't hear <I'm not hearing>$^{m/f}$.
'irfaᶜ ṣōtak!	Speak up <raise your voice>!
'irfaᶜ ir-rādyo!	Turn up the radio!
• muš sāmᶜīn!	[We] can't hear!
• il-walad ᶜemel ḥālo muš sāmeᶜ.	The boy pretended he couldn't hear <the boy made himself not hearing>.
• 'iᶜmel ḥālak nāyem[6]!	Pretend you're asleep <make yourself sleeping>!

■ 5. 'akīd = *[for] sure / [for] certain,* when stating a fact: hāda 'iši 'akīd! means *It's certain / That's for sure!* However, *I'm sure that / I'm certain that* = 'ana mit'akked inno...

6. The verbs šāf, jāb, nām, etc. add a -y after the **-ā**. For the grammar freaks among you, the explanation is as follows: it would be more accurate to say that the roots of these verbs are considered to be š-y-f, j-y-b and n-y-m respectively. In the active participle the **-ā** is added as it is in any other verb (šāyef is modeled on the same pattern as kāteb). However the first sentence of this footnote sums up the situation more briefly and practically, and so it is the formulation we shall use. The present participle nāyem (which means *asleep* or just *lying down*) behaves in just the same way. What do we do if we want to say that someone has actually fallen asleep? We'll learn that later.

7. We say kāteb^{m} → kātbe^{f}, nāyem^{m} → nāyme^{f}, but sāmeᶜ ^{m} → sāmᶜa^{f} because of the ᶜ. Likewise, we say ṭāleᶜ → ṭālᶜa (ṭālᶜα), rāyeḥ → rāyḥa (rāyḥα) as explained in **Book 1, page 59** in the section on the **feminine ending**.

– btifham ᶜɑrɑbi?	Do you understand Arabic?
• fāhem ᶜalayy?	Do you / Can you understand me? (just now).
• ’ana muš fāhme wala kilme.	I don’t understand a word <and not a word>.

– biddi as’alak su’āl.	– I’d like to ask youᵐ a question <I want to ask you….>
– tfɑḍḍɑl!	– Go aheadᵐ <please>!
– bteᶜref tiḥseb?	– Can you do arithmetic <do you know [how] to calculate>?
– ṭɑbᶜan!	– Of course!
– qaddēš talāte fi ḫamse?	– How much is three times five <three in five>?
– hāda ṣɑᶜeb, mā ᶜindi ’āle ḥāsbe.[8]	– That’s difficult, I haven’t got a calculator / adding machine <a calculating machine>.
’is’al ’aḫūy l-ᵉzġīr.	Askᵐ my little brother.
– yā šɑ̄ṭer, taᶜ la-hōn!	– Come here, sonny <oh clever one, come to here>.
qul-li: qaddēš talāte fi ḫamse?	Tell me: how much is three times five?
– ḫamᵉstɑᶜeš.	– Fifteen.
– brāvo ᶜalēk!	– Well done <bravo on you>!
’inte ’aštɑr min ’aḫūk.	You’re smarter than your brother.
– ṭɑyyeb, b-ḫɑ̄ṭer-kom...	– Well, I’ll be seeing you…
– la’, bidna nišrɑb finjān qahwe.	– No, we were just going to have <we want to drink> a cup of coffee.
– yā (a)bu Samīr, qahwet-kom mašrūbe!	– No thanks, Abu Samir, I don’t want coffee just now <oh Abu Samir, your coffee’s [been] drunk – i.e., consider me to have accepted your offer and to have had coffee>.
lāzem ’arūḥ.	I’ve got to go.
– ma biṣir-š hēk!	– You can’t do that <[it] isn’t possible thus>.
hāda muš maḥsūb,	This doesn’t count <this is not counted> [as a visit].
taᶜāl zūr-na kamān mɑrrɑ!	Come and visit us again <another time>.
– tikrɑm!	– Thanks, I will <you will be honored>!

---

8. Or mākinet‿ᵉḥsāb.

il-b**i**ss ṣ**ɑ̄**r š**ā**reb il-ḥal**ī**b	The cat[m] has drunk the milk <has become having-drunk the milk>.
il-b**i**sse ṣ**ɑ̄**rɑt š**ā**rbe‿l-ḥal**ī**b	The cat[f] has drunk the milk.
id-dokt**ō**r q**a**l-li: mamn**ū**ᶜ 'i**m**mak t**i**šrɑb had-d**a**wa.	The doctor told me: your mother mustn't take this medicine <[it is] forbidden [that] your mother drink…>!
fa-'**a**na‿rj**e**ᶜet ᶜa-l-b**ē**t qaw**ɑ̄**m, laq**ē**t[9] 'i**m**mi š**ā**rbe‿d-d**a**wa.	Then I went home straight away and found that my mother had taken the medicine <I found my mother having-drunk the medicine>!

Now if we review some of the verbs you already know we can easily form their passive participles:

il-b**ā**b maks**ū**r	The door's broken.
'**ē**š mɑṭl**ū**b m**i**nni?	What's required <asked> of me?
'inte mas'**ū**l[10] ᶜan haš-š**a**ġle.	You're responsible for this matter.
ᶜala‿l-m**u**stawa‿l-mɑṭl**ū**b[11]	at the required level / to the required standard <on the asked-for level>
iṭ-ṭ**ɑ̄**wle madh**ū**ne	The table's painted.
w**a**lad matr**ū**k	an abandoned child / boy
m**u**lk matr**ū**k	abandoned property
'amw**ā**l matr**ū**ke[12]	abandoned assets
lᵉ-ḥṣ**ɑ̄**n mɑrb**ū**ṭ‿ᵉb-ḥ**a**bᵉl	The horse is tethered <tied> by a rope.

---

9. laq**ē**t = *I found / I discovered…* We haven't learned this verb yet, but we need it here to demonstrate the use of the active participle in the sense of *having already done / having already finished doing…*

10. mas'**ū**l means *responsible* – literally *he who is asked*, just like the English *responsible*, i.e., the person who's got to supply the answers. *Responsibility* = mas'ūl**i**yye, and f**ī**ʰ ᶜal**ē**k mas'ūl**i**yye kb**ī**re means *You've got* <there is on you> *a big responsibility.*

11. m**u**stawa [mustaw**ā**y**ā**t] means *level, standard.* The root s-w-a (s-w-y) indicates *equality*, and you are already familiar with the word s**a**wa, which means *together*: cooperation and togetherness are based on equality, on being on the same level.

12. Why is the adjective in the feminine singular here? We've already come across other examples of this curious phenomenon, which will be explained in Lesson 25.

'**a**na ma^{c}z**ū**m ^{c}ind‿^{e}ṣḥ**ā**b	I'm invited to friends' <at friends>.
maṭb**ū**^{c} – maft**ū**h	printed – open
mamn**ū**^{c} – masm**ū**ḥ	forbidden – permitted / allowed
h**ā**da '**i**ši ma^{c}r**ū**f	Everyone knows that <this [is] a known thing>.
h**ā**da mafh**ū**m	That's obvious / That goes without saying <this [is] understood>.
il-^{c}**i**lbe ma^{c}m**ū**le min ḫ**a**šab	The box is made of wood.

What are the feminine forms of the passive participles above (maks**ū**r, maṭl**ū**b, etc.)? Try to work them out for yourselves and compare the result with the solution at the end of the lesson *.

Explanations

1. The active participle

The active participle serves a number of different purposes:

a) In certain verbs only: it indicates the **immediate present** (i.e., what's happening right now). Let's compare the following sentences:

'**a**na š**ā**yef (š**ā**yfe^f)	*I can see / I see* (at this very moment)
('**a**na) baš**ū**f	*I see* (in general, every day); *I'll see*

This applies especially to -

– Verbs that describe the action of the **senses:**
I [can] see, hear, feel (also: *I [can] understand*) *right now*
– Verbs that indicate **movement** or **position:**
I'm sitting, I'm standing, I'm lying down; I'm going, I'm coming, I'm coming / going back, I'm passing, I'm going up, I'm coming down, etc.

Note: The active participle is negated with muš / miš, not with ma… (± -š), as the past and present-future tenses are. We saw examples of this in the Conversation: muš s**ā**me^c (*[I] can't hear*); likewise '**a**na muš š**ā**yef '**i**ši, which means *I can't see anything.*

b) In all other verbs (i.e., the vast majority of verbs in Arabic) the present participle indicates an **action that has already taken place**, e.g., *having written; [he who] has written.*

■ kāteb il-maktūb	*the person^{m} who wrote the letter / the writer of the letter*
huwwe fāteḥ dukkān[13]	*He's opened a shop / He's got a shop* <he's having-opened a shop>.
laqēto šāreb kull il-qannīne	*I found he'd drunk the whole bottle* <I found him having-drunk all the bottle>.

We see, therefore, that kāteb does not mean quite the same thing as the English active participle *writing* in sentences like *I'm writing*; it is perhaps closer to the word *writer*, as in *the writer of the article,* or to words like *signatory* or *initiator*, which indicate a completed action: the writer has already written the article, the signatory has signed the letter and the initiator has initiated the action.

c) Because of this, the active participle in Arabic also provides the **title** of persons or things that perform specific actions on a regular basis – like the English *writer, laborer, worker*, etc.

ṭαlαb	*he asked*	ṭᾱleb[14]	*student* (one who seeks / asks for knowledge)
katab	*he wrote*	kāteb	*writer; scribe, registrar*
^{c}emel	*he did*	^{c}āmel	*workman, laborer*

And we can add:

sāken	*living* (part.); *resident, inhabitant*
māne^{c} [15]	*preventing* (part.); *impediment; objection*

These nouns that designate a profession or role usually take the plural form □u□□ā□.

ṭullᾱb (ṭullāb) (*students*); kuttāb (*writers*); ^{c}ummāl (*laborers*); sukkān[16] (*residents*).

---

13. People will say to the proprietor of a shop: ṣαr-lak zamān fāteḥ had-dukkān? which means *Is it a long time since you opened this shop / Have you had this shop long?* Similar sentences can be constructed with the verb tarak (*he left*): ṣαr-lak zamān tārek haš-šuġ^{o}l? = *Has it been long since you left this job?*

14. The feminine is ṭᾱlbe [ṭᾱlibāt] = *[a] female student.*

15. The expression 'iza ma-fī-šš māne^{c}... means *if there's no reason why not... / if there's no objection...* Although māne^{c} is not a title and does not designate a profession, the idea is the same, as, in essence, it means *preventer / that which prevents.*

16. ^{c}adad is-sukkān means *the number of residents* or *the population.* However, when sāken means *live / living* (rather than *[a] resident*) it takes the plural form sāknīn. – wēn sāknīn? = *Where do you / they live?*

d) The active participle can also serve as an adjective:

s**a**baq	*he preceded / arrived before...*	s**ā**beq	*previous*
n**i**šef	*it dried out* (intrans)	n**ā**šef	*dry*

(remember Book 1, p. 71)

Very often the active participle translates into English as a word ending in -er or -ing (*He's a writer; I saw him writing*). The important thing to remember is that, except in the case of the verbs mentioned in section **a)** above, the active participle in Arabic (unlike the English version) indicates an action that has **already taken place**, e.g. *having written.*

Now it's time to go back to the conversation and re-read it, paying special attention to the points mentioned above. Note that the present-future tense, when used to indicate an action in the future, has not been marked. The two markers ▬ and ● are used to distinguish between an action in the habitual present (*I go*) and one in the immediate present (*I am going [now]*).

2. ṣ**ā**r with the active participle

You can see from some of the examples in the Conversation that, when used with the auxiliary verb ṣ**ā**r, the active participle **always** designates a completed action. This is true even of verbs of the kind discussed in section **a)** above.

We say:

■ ṣert k**ā**teb il-makt**ū**b min zam**ā**n! *I wrote^{m} the letter ages ago!*

And there is nothing odd about this, as the word k**ā**teb indicates a past action in any case, and the verb ṣ**ā**r serves only to emphasize the notion that "this has already been done." Now compare the following sentences:

h**ū** n**ā**zel	*He's coming / going down* (right now)
ṣ**ā**r n**ā**zel	*He's come / gone down* <he has become having-gone-down>.

In this case the verb ṣ**ā**r changes the meaning of the participle – from present to past.

You don't have to be able to do more than recognize this structure when you come across it. Frequent encounters with it in the Conversations will familiarize you with it, and eventually you'll begin to use it yourself quite naturally.

3. while..., as he was...

In the Conversation earlier in the lesson we encountered the phrases *I saw him as he was....* (u-h**u**) and *on my way back* (u-**a**na r**ā**je^{c}...<and I coming back>).

By placing u- or w- before a noun or personal pronoun we can create phrases like those that begin in English with *while..., as I was..., on their way...* etc. Let's take a look at the following sentences:

■ u-inte rājeᶜ, fūt ᶜa-l-bōṣṭɑ.	*On your way back, pop into the post office...*
ṭeleᶜ min il-bēt u-hū ḥāmel šanta.	*He came out of the house carrying a suitcase* <and he carrying...>.
hādi ṣūrto[17] u-huwwe zġīr.	*This is a picture of him when he was young* <and he young>.
hāy ṣūret-ha u-hiyye zġīre.	*This is a picture of her when she was young.*
'ajɑ[18] jɑ̄rna w-il-walad nāyem.	*Our neighbor came while the boy was sleeping* <and the boy sleeping>.
šuft-ha mārqa u-walad ᶜala 'īd-hɑ[19].	*I saw her pass by with a boy in her arms.*
fāt ᶜindna u-sakkīne fi 'īdo / ufi 'īdo sakkīne.	*He came into our house with a knife in his hand.*
bʸiḥki[20] u-mlabbase fi tummo.	*He talks with a sweet / candy in his mouth.*

Exercises

A. Translate into English:

1. ya Maḥmūd, (± la-)wēn rɑ̄yeḥ? – ᶜa-l-maktab.
2. w-inti wēn rɑ̄yḥɑ? – 'ana kamān rɑ̄yḥɑ ᶜa-l-maktab.
3. 'ana šuft-hom rɑ̄yḥīn maᶜ bɑᶜeḍ.
4. wēn il-bineṭ? – šuft-ha ṭɑ̄lᶜɑ la-fōq.
5. mɑẓbūṭ, 'ana‿ṭleᶜet la-fōq, laqēt-ha[9] nāyme.
6. ṣɑbɑ̄ḥ il-ḫēr, ya ulād! šū? lissā-kom nāymīn? qūmu qawɑ̄m!
7. lamma šāfat-ni fihmat inno lāzem tinzal.
8. lissāt-ha fōq, 'ana sāmeᶜ ṣōt-ha.
9. la', ṣɑ̄rat nāzle min zamān!

---

17. The word ṣūrɑ [2] [8] [ṣuwɑr] means *picture, photograph.*

18. A special lesson will be devoted to this verb.

19. See **Lesson 22, footnote 21**.

20. We've already come across baḥki (*I speak*), on page 5. We'll be getting to know this verb better soon, in Lesson 28.

10. id-dukkān[21] maftūḥa min iṣ-ṣub^{o}ḥ lαḍ-ḍuh^{o}r.
11. 'aywa, šufto qāᶜed (sitting) fi dukkānto.
12. ruḥ^{e}t la-ᶜind il-jirān, laqēt-hom qāᶜdīn fi-l-ḥakūrα.
13. ma tuqᶜod-š ᶜa-l-kursi, hū[J] maksūr / hiyye[G] maksūrα.

B. Complete the sentences

(Replace the English words with the appropriate expression in Arabic):

14. šufto (sitting) bαrrα.
15. kānat (sitting) fi (her room).
16. is-sandūq hāda ([is] broken), jīb (another one).
17. (I've written <I've become having-written>) hal-maktūb.
18. ma‿ᶜreft^{e}-š inno (that was <is> forbidden)
19. kān (carrying) šanta zġīre.
20. hāy ṣūrti (when I was) walad.
21. ṭelᶜat min il-bēt (carrying) walad‿^{e}zġīr ᶜala 'īd-ha.

C. Translate into Arabic:

22. I found the door open. – I found the key broken.
23. I told John: Come out! He didn't seem to understand. That's strange, I don't understand^{m} what happened.
24. They told me he understood <understands> Arabic. Why didn't he come out?
25. He seemed to think <he understood> that he had to <has to> go up, because you told him ''eṭlαᶜ!'
26. Next time tell him: ''eṭlαᶜ la-bαrrα!'
27. That's right, he's up [there]. Hey, John, come down at once!
28. I can see <I see> your^{m} sister coming out of the house.
29. I saw the *mukhtar* coming out of his house.
30. I saw laborers passing by in the street.
31. The pupils came out of the headmaster's / principal's [office] <from at the headmaster>.
32. The former headmaster / principal invited me to lunch . – I'm invited <to at him> as well!
33. How much is two times three? – I can't tell you, the calculator's at the office.

---

21. The word dukkān is feminine. You may also hear the form dukkāne, which is regularly used with the attached pronouns (as in the next sentence), in the construct form (dukkānet 'alᶜāb means *toyshop*) and in the dual: dukkāntēn = *two shops*.

Getting to the root of things

And finally, a couple more interesting points – which, as usual, you can skip if you're tired – regarding two words with which we are already familiar: mɑẓbūṭ (*right / correct*) and maᶜlūm (*naturally / of course!* <known>), from the roots ẓ-b-ṭ and ᶜ-l-m respectively.

■ ẓɑbɑṭ [yuẓboṭ] means *to control / regulate; to fit*
il-muftāḥ bʸuẓboṭ = *The key fits.*
muftāḥ ẓābeṭ = *a suitable key / [the] right key*
(active participle used as an adjective).
ẓābet [2] [ẓubbāṭ] = *officer*
(i.e., *he who controls / regulates;* active participle used as a noun and job title).
ẓɑbṭ = *control; precision* – hence biẓ-ẓɑbṭ, which means *precisely / exactly.*
ma baqdɑr 'aqul-lak biẓ-ẓɑbṭ = *I can't tell you exactly.*

ᶜilem (ᶜelem) [yiᶜlam]# means *to know*
ᶜilᵉm = *science; knowledge*
ᶜala ᶜilmi = *as far as I know* <on [the basis of] my knowledge>
ᶜilm‿in-nafs = *psychology* <the science of the mind>
ᶜālem [ᶜulamā'] = *scholar, scientist, knowledgeable person* <one-who-knows>
'ɑllāhu# 'aᶜlam = *God alone knows / God only knows* <God knows-better>!
maᶜlūm = *known, obvious.* maᶜlūmāt means *information* <known [things]> .
bʸijmaᶜ maᶜlūmāt = *He gathers information.*

The above gives you a brief glance into word "families," without obliging you to go into things too deeply. Remember what you like, and whatever has aroused your interest.

And we'll finish up (yes, really, this time…) with an excellent proverb:

■ il-mɑyy – 'arḫɑṣ il-mawjūdāt u-atman il-maf q̈ūdāt[22].
Water – cheap when you've got it, dear when you haven't
<…the cheapest of things-that are-there, the most valuable of things-that-are-lost>!

---

* The feminine forms of the passive participles (see the end of the Conversation) are:
maksūrɑ, mɑṭlūbe, mɑrbūṭɑ, maᶜzūme, mɑṭbūᶜɑ, maftūḥa, mamnūᶜa, masmūḥa, maᶜrūfe, mafhūme.

---

22. wajad# = to find; hence mawjūd = *present / there / in existence* <found>.
fɑq̈ɑd (faqad) = to lose; hence maf q̈ūd (mafqūd) = *lost / missing.*
taman (t̲aman#) = *price, value;* tamīn (t̲amīn#) means *valuable / dear.*

Lesson Twenty-Four

In this lesson we'll focus on two very useful verbs that have an unusual conjugation: '**a**kal (*he ate*) and '**a**ђad (*he took*). You've already encountered both of them in the past tense, where there's no difficulty as they behave exactly like k**a**tab.

In the present-future tense / subjunctive, however, their conjugation is not only irregular, but varies from one region to another.

Form A (the prevalent colloquial form)		**Form B**	
Present-future	Subjunctive	Present-future	Subjunctive
b**ō**kol	'**ō**kol	b**ā**kol	'**ā**kol
bt**ō**kol	t**ō**kol	bt**ā**kol	t**ā**kol
bt**ō**kli	t**ō**kli	bt**ā**kli	t**ā**kli
b^{y}**ō**kol	y**ō**kol	by**ā**kol	y**ā**kol
bt**ō**kol	t**ō**kol	bt**ā**kol	t**ā**kol
bn**ō**kol (mn**ō**-)	n**ō**kol	bn**ā**kol (mn**ā**-)	n**ā**kol
bt**ō**klu	t**ō**klu	bt**ā**klu	t**ā**klu
b^{y}**ō**klu	y**ō**klu	by**ā**klu	y**ā**klu

Conclusion: There's actually very little here that you need to remember. The two forms are almost identical, except that Form B has -**ā** instead of -**ō** (b-t**ō**kol / b-t**ā**kol) and, as usual, the y- of the third person may be dropped after the b- prefix: by**ō**kol is commonly pronounced b**ō**kol:

- hal-w**a**lad b**ō**kel‿ᵉkt**ī**r. *This boy eats a lot.*

However, in the subjunctive the y- is clearly heard:

- muš l**ā**zem y**ō**kol‿ᵉkt**ī**r! *He shouldn't eat a lot!*

Form B, which is current in Syria and Lebanon, is also used by speakers of Palestinian Arabic, especially when adopting the more "educated" form of speech – i.e., a higher register, in television interviews, for instance – because it's closer to the t**a**'kol, y**a**'kol, etc., of literary Arabic. If you prefer, you can use Form B, but you need to be familiar with Form A because that's how most people speak.

Incidentally, you'll also hear the second syllable pronounced -kel instead of -kol. One of the speakers on the recording, reading an example from Explanations 1, says: bt**ō**kel q**a**tle. You'll soon get used to all these variations.

Imperative: kol! (kōl!!) koli, kolu = *eat*^{m}! (*eat!!*) *eat*^{f}, *eat*^{pl}!

The **active participle** is a little different from those you have met so far. The ' of the root is replaced by m-: m**ā**kel, m**ā**kle^{f} [mākl**ī**n] = *having eaten*[1]

– '**a**ђad is conjugated exactly like '**a**kal.

laq**ē**t il-k**a**lb m**ā**kel il-l**a**ḥme	*I found [that] the dog had eaten the meat* <I found the dog having-eaten …>
'aђ**ū**y m**ā**ђed b**i**nto	*My brother is married to his daughter* <my brother [is] having-taken his daughter>

Here's an initial exercise: try to conjugate the verb '**a**ђad (out loud) using '**a**kal as your model.

And now let's move on to the Conversation and practice these two verbs.

Vocabulary

'**a**ђad ᶜala ђ**ɑ̄**ṭro	to take offense; to take to heart		
'**a**ђad‿eb-ђ**ɑ̄**ṭro	to offer condolences		
takl**ī**f [2]	manners, etiquette, formality		
ᶜal**ā**me [8] [-m**ā**t]	mark[s] / grade[s] (at school); sign		
ṭ**ɑ**rɑf ['ɑṭr**ɑ̄**f]	end (extremity); side (in a dispute)		
š**i**beᶜ [y**i**šbaᶜ]	to be satisfied / sated / replete		
ṣy**ɑ̄**ḥ$^{m\ sing}$ [2]	shouting, shouts	ġ**ɑ̄**r [iġ**ɑ̄**r][2]	to be jealous of
ḥ**a**ble	(length of) rope	ṣuᶜ**ū**be [2] [8]	difficulty
k**a**maš [y**i**kmeš]	to take a handful	f**ɑ̄**r [fir**ɑ̄**n]	mouse
m**i**sek [y**i**msek]	to take, catch, seize	ml**a**bbase [3]	sweet, candy
q**a**tle	beating, thrashing <killing>	r**ɑ̄**s [r**ū**s]	head
tall**ā**je [2] [8]	fridge	bɑrr**ɑ̄**de^{G}	fridge
f**u**stoq / f**u**sdoq	peanuts $^{m\ sing}$	l**a**ḥme	meat
ḥ**a**bbe [8]	grain; pill; single unit	hw**ā**y [3]	blow, hit

---

1. '**a**kal means *he ate* (something specific). To talk about eating a meal, there are special verbs relating to each of the three main meals of the day. You'll have to wait a little longer to learn to say: "Do you want to eat (e.g., lunch) with us?"

2. How is ġ**ɑ̄**r [iġ**ɑ̄**r] conjugated? Like j**ā**b [ij**ī**b], except that the -**ɑ̄**- is retained in the present-future tense, as in n**ā**m [in**ā**m] – *to sleep*. These two verbs have one more "brother": ђ**ɑ̄**f [iђ**ɑ̄**f] = *he feared*. ђ**e**ft = *I was afraid. Are you afraid of him?* (habitually) is bᵉtђ**ɑ̄**f m**i**nno? But *I'm afraid* (just now), is '**a**na ђ**ā**yef (active participle indicating the immediate present), like š**ā**yef and n**ā**zel; see Lesson 23.

[3]

Conversation

– biddak tōkol 'iši?	– Would you like something to eat <do you want to eat something>?
tfaḍḍal!	Please [help yourself].
– la', šukran[4], 'akalt‿ektīr, 'issa‿šbeᶜet[5].	– No, thanks, I've eaten plenty [and] I'm not hungry any more <I'm replete now>.
– kol, ya zalame, hōn ma fi-šš taklīf!	– Eat, man! We don't stand on ceremony here <here is no formality>.
– ᶜam-baqul-lak[6], 'ana šabᶜān u-muš qāder 'ākol / 'ōkol luqme.	– I'm telling you, I'm full <I'm replete> and I couldn't eat [another] bite.
– ṭayyeb, hallaq bnišrab qahwe.	– OK, let's have coffee now <now we'll drink coffee>.
(After they've drunk their coffee:)	
– ᶜamār / dāyme[7]!	– Thank you! <Prosperity / May it always be like this for you>!
– ṣaḥḥtēn!	– Your health <double health >!

---

3. See p. 80.

■ 4. šukran comes from the root š-k-r. šakar [yuškor] means *to thank, to say thank-you*. You could also say 'aškor-ak / -ek (*I thank you*). This is literary Arabic, which doesn't use the suffix b-. šukr means *thanks, gratitude*. The proper response to šukran is ᶜafwan (*Don't mention it* <excuse [me]>), or the more formal la šukr ᶜala wājeb! <no thanks [are due] for [fulfilling] an obligation>.

5. *We have eaten enough* <we have been sated> is ešbeᶜna. *They have eaten enough* is šibᶜu. *Replete* (adjective or immediate present) is šabᶜān, šabᶜāne [šabᶜānīn].

6. See **Explanations 5.**

7. See **Explanations 3**.

– w**ē**n il-l**a**ḥme? fi-t-tall**ā**je[8]? (fi-l-bɑrr**ɑ̄**d^{G}?)	– Where's the meat? In the fridge?
– l**a**', ᶜala-ṭ-ṭ**ɑ̄**wle.	– No, [it's] on the table.
– '**i**za‿l-k**a**lb bišūf il-l**a**ḥme, 'akīd rɑḥ-yāk**o**l-ha[9].	– If the dog sees the meat, he's sure to eat it <certain he's going to eat it>.

– il-b**i**sse bt**ō**kol il-fir**ɑ̄**n, '**i**za bᵉtš**ū**f f**ɑ̄**r, bt**i**hjem ᶜal**ē**ʰ, bt**ō**klo.	– The cat^{f} eats <the> mice; if she sees a mouse she jumps on it [and] eats it.
– f**ī**ʰ h**ō**n f**ɑ̄**r ᶜam-bʸ**i**lᶜab taḥt‿iṭ-ṭ**ɑ̄**wle.	– There's a mouse playing here under the table.
– j**ī**b il-b**i**sse, 'ak**ī**d rɑḥ-t**ō**klo u-ђ**ɑ**lɑṣ!	– Bring the cat, she's sure to eat it and we'll be done with it <[it's] finished>.

– š**u** ᶜam-t**ō**kol[6]?	– What are you eating?
– ᶜam-b**ā**kol f**u**stoq[10]...	– I'm eating peanuts …
– h**ā**t, '**a**na kam**ā**n b**i**ddi **ā**kol m**i**nno.	– Give [me them], I want some, too <I also want to eat from them>.
– tf**ɑ**ḍḍɑl, ђ**ō**d q**a**dd-ma b**i**ddak!	– Please, take as much as you like!
š**ū**!? bass ḥabbt**ē**n[11]? '**i**kmeš k**a**mše!	– What! Just a couple? Take a handful!

– š**ū** haṣ-ṣy**ɑ̄**ḥ (hal-ᵉṣy**ɑ̄**ḥ)? [3] š**u** m**ā**-lha?	– What's [all] this shouting? What's [wrong] with her?
– Mun**ī**rɑ '**a**klat‿ᵉhw**ā**y[12] ᶜala r**ɑ̄**s-ha.	–Munira got hit on the head <ate a blow on her head>.

---

8. tall**ā**je means *refrigerator* <ice-maker>. t**a**lᵉj [2] means *snow,* but also *ice* in colloquial Arabic.

9. **Explanations 6**.

10. f**u**stoq$^{m\ sing}$ is a collective noun. f**u**stoq ḥ**a**labi are *pistachios* (from the Syrian town of ḥ**a**lab, i.e., Aleppo).

11. ḥ**a**bbe – see **Explanations 7**.

12. '**a**kal = *to eat*, means also *to receive* (something unpleasant). See **Explanations 1.**

– m**ī**n illi ḍɑr**ɑ**b-ha? Sam**ī**r?	– Who hit her? Samir?
– l**a**', muš '**a**na!	– No, not me <not I>!
– '**u**skot, w**i**lla btōkel q**a**tle[12].	– Be quiet, or you'll catch it <eat a beating>!
ya Mun**ī**rɑ, taᶜ**ā**li,	Munira, come [and] take a sweet /
ђod**ī**-lek‿ᵉmlabbase u-ђ**ɑ**lɑṣ!	candy for yourself, and that's the end
'**u**sᵒkti '**i**nti kam**ā**n!	of it! You, be quiet, too!

– muš b**i**ddak[13] t**ō**ђod il-w**a**lad	– Don't you want to take the boy
ᶜa-s-s**ī**nama?	to the cinema?
– '**i**za b**ō**ђed ᶜal**ā**me mn**ī**ḥa	– If he gets good marks <a good mark>
fi-l-m**a**drase,	at school,
'**a**na b**u**krɑ b**ā**ђdo m**a**ᶜi ᶜala ḥ**ē**fa.	I'll take him with me to Haifa tomorrow.
– w-il-b**i**nt‿ᵉbtōђ**o**d-ha kam**ā**n?	– Will you take the girl, too <and the girl, will you take her also>?
– '**ɑ̄**, maᶜl**ū**m bāђ**o**d-ha,	– Yes, of course I'll take her;
'iza ma bāђod-h**ā**-š, bᵉtġ**ɑ̄**r[14]!	if I don't take her, she'll be jealous!

– j**ɑ̄**rna m**ā**t, '**ɑ**llɑ yirḥamo,	– Our neighbor has died, God rest his soul <God have mercy on him>.
l**ā**zem‿ᵉnr**ū**ḥ ᶜ**i**nd m**ɑ**rɑto	We must go and offer [our] condolences
w-ewl**ā**do n**ō**ђed‿ᵉb- ђ**ɑ̄**ṭer-hen //-hom.	to his wife and children.

'aђ**a**dna‿b-ђ**ɑ̄**ṭro	We offered him [our] condolences.
'aђ**a**dna‿b-ђ**ɑ̄**ṭer-ha	We offered her [our] condolences.

– il-w**a**lad ᶜ**i**ndo ṣuᶜūb**ā**t (-b**ɑ̄**t)	– The boy has difficulties at school.
fi-l-m**a**drase,	
l-ewl**ā**d it-tāny**ī**n bi**ḍ**ḥaku ᶜal**ē**ʰ,	The other children laugh at him and call him
biqūl**ū**-lo: ya kasl**ā**n!	lazybones <they said to him: lazybones>!
kt**ī**r by**ā**ђod ᶜala ђ**ɑ̄**ṭro.	He's taking it very much to heart.

13. muš (miš) b**i**ddak... can be used to ask a negative question when expecting a positive reply: *Don't you want to....? (I think you do.)* ma b**i**dd**a**k-š ... is sometimes used in the same way.

14. This sounds more or less like bᵉdġ**ɑ̄**r. The ġ affects the t, turning it into d. Don't slip into pronouncing it bᵉtђ**ɑ̄**r.

Explanations

1. [He] took – 'a**ḫ**ad / m**i**sek

The verb '**a**ḫad means *he took (for himself), he took (something somewhere),* as in the Conversation and in the following sentence:

- m**ī**n '**a**ḫad il-jar**ī**de? — *Who's taken the newspaper?*

When the meaning is *he caught, grasped, seized, took hold of,* a different verb is used, m**i**sek [y**i**msek]:

- m**i**sek is-sikk**ī**ne u-ḍɑr**ɑ**b-ha f**ī**hɑ — *He seized the knife and stabbed* <hit> *her with it.*
  m**i**skat '**ī**di — *She grasped my hand.*
  ᵉms**e**kto min d**ā**no — *I grabbed him by* <from> *the ear.*
  b**i**msek il-ḥ**a**ble min iṭ-ṭɑrɑf**ē**n — *He takes hold of both ends of the rope* <takes hold of the rope from the two-ends>.

Another meaning of '**a**ḫad is *he received* (e.g., good marks, a letter, a prize):

'aḫ**a**dᵉt makt**ū**b m**i**nno — *I got a letter from him.*
il-ᶜal**ā**me‿(i)lli 'aḫ**a**d-ha — *the mark he received* <received-it>

But when we receive something unpleasant, we *eat* it:

- bt**ō**kol q**a**tle[15] — *You'll get a thrashing!*

---

15. The real meaning of q**a**tal [y**u**qtol] is *to kill*, but q**a**tle is used here colloquially to mean *a beating*, in the same way that everyday English uses exaggeration for effect: *He'll murder you when he finds out!*

'akal muђālafe[16]	*He got a "ticket"* (for a speeding or parking offence).
'akalna hawa	*We're left empty-handed / We've been had* <we've eaten air / wind>.

2. 'aђad ᶜala / b- + ђɑ̄ṭer

In the Conversation there were two more examples of the verb **'aђad**:

a. 'aђad ᶜala ђɑ̄ṭro, literally, *He took (offense, sorrow) upon his mood*, meaning *he took offense / he got upset / he took [something] to heart.* In other words, something came over his mood and affected him badly.

b. 'aђad‿eb-ђɑ̄ṭer‿eflān[17] is literally *He took (part) in someone's (bad) mood*, in other words, *He commiserated with someone*, or *He offered his condolences to someone.*

The literal translations should help you not to confuse the two expressions.

3. ᶜɑmɑ̄r! dāyme!

The word ᶜɑmɑ̄r belongs a family that also includes ᶜɑmɑ̄rɑ (*building*). The basic meaning of the root from which both are derived is *to fill; to build; to prosper*. The benediction maḥall ᶜāmer, shortened to ᶜāmer! means *[May the] place [be] prosperous!* and refers to the home and family being visited. In Galilee you say ᶜɑmɑ̄r! to your host after drinking coffee, or at the end of a meal. In other areas, it is more usual to say dāyme! <perpetual[f]>, meaning: *May your hospitality (and the prosperity that makes it possible) be permanent* <perpetual>! The root of dāyme is d-w-m, which is already familiar from dāyman, meaning *always*. (For the suffix -an, see **Lesson 19, Explanations 2**.)

4. btākol → btāklo

You will have noticed that before a suffix beginning with a vowel, i.e., -i, -o, -u, -ak, -ek, the *o* following the second root letter -k- drops (we'll include forms beginning with bā-, btā-, byā-, etc., in the examples, for a change):

btākol	*You eat*	btākli	*You[f] eat*
bāђod	*I take*	bāђdek	*I take you[f]*
byākol	*He eats*	byāklo	*He eats it*
lāzem yōkol	*He must eat*	lāzem yōklu	*They must eat*

---

16. muђālafe is the verbal noun (see Lesson 27) of a verb we have yet to learn, and means literally *law-breaking*. Here it's short for *a "ticket" for an offence against the law*. Similarly, hawiyye, meaning *identity*, is short for *identity papers / identity card.*

17. flān / fulān# means *so-and-so* (noun). flāni, flāniyye[f] (adjective) means *such-and-such.* fi-l-yōm l-eflāni means *on such-and-such a day.*

You've seen that this also happens to the vowel *e* in the same circumstances:

ħ**ā**ṭer	*mood*	b-ḥ**ā**ṭrak	*goodbye*
m**i**sek	*He caught*	m**i**skak	*He caught you*

However, when a suffix starts with a consonant (-ni, -ha, -na, -kom, -hen, etc.) the *o* and the *e* don't drop; on the contrary, they attract the stress, in accordance with the now familiar rule [5] (see also **Book 1, page 91**):

ħāṭ**e**r-ha, bōk**o**l-ha, mis**e**k-na (*he caught us*).

There's nothing really new here, but it's been useful to practice with new verbs.

Worth noting

The rules governing stress shift within words don't apply to the helping vowels (*e* / *o*) that are inserted to "oil the wheels": b**i**nt → b**i**nᵉt; š**u**ġl → š**u**ġᵒl, and so forth. Strictly speaking, the words are b**i**nt and š**u**ġl. Compare the following:

m**i**sek + -na = mis**e**k-na	b**ō**kol + -ha = bōk**o**l-ha	*
'**i**bᵉn + -na = '**i**bᵉn-na	š**u**ġᵒl + -ha = š**u**ġᵒl-ha	**

* The stress shifts to the second syllable, next to the attached pronoun.

** The stress is unchanged. The helping vowels are like stowaways that have no rights, so cannot attract the stress.

Now it will be clear to you why we don't write b**i**nᵉt like m**i**sek, nor š**u**ġᵒl like b**ō**kol, even though the pronunciation is similar. The transcription will tell you whether or not the stress moves.

5. The immediate present prefix ᶜam-

As you saw in the Conversation, the prefix ᶜam- indicates the immediate present: *I'm cooking (just now).*

In Lesson 23 you learned that in verbs of movement or position and verbs describing the action of the senses (*go, go up, go down; see, hear*, etc.) the active participle, e.g., n**ā**zel, s**ā**meᶜ, is used to denote the immediate present. But what about the other kinds of verb? To give them the sense of *just now*, the prefix ᶜam- is attached to the present-future:

b**a**kteb	*I habitually write*	ᶜam-b**a**kteb	*I'm writing now*
bt**e**ᶜmal	*You do*	ᶜam-bt**e**ᶜmal	*You're doing now*
bt**i**ġsel	*She does the laundry*	ᶜam-bt**i**ġsel[18]	*She's doing the laundry now*

18. Or *You're*[m] *doing the laundry now*, if that happens to be the case. There's no need to make an effort to pronounce the b- in ᶜam-bt, as people simply say ᶜam-t**i**ġsel, ᶜam-t**e**ᶜmal, etc.

6. The future prefix rɑḥ-

The prefix rɑḥ- / raḥ- before a subjunctive verb is used to denote the future tense. You have seen that the present-future tense is used to talk about both the present and the future (just as we ask in English about a future journey: *When are you going?*), so the meaning is not always clear. The prefix rɑḥ- eliminates confusion.

| 'ēš rɑḥ-iṣīr? | *What will happen?* |
| šū rɑḥ-teᶜmal? | *What will you do?* |

It's worth noting that bidd- (biddi, biddak, etc.), in addition to meaning *I, you want...*, can also be used to denote the future tense, as well as to mean *should, needs to, requires (time, etc.)*, for example:

1. biddo_imūt	*He's dying / He will die*
2. 'ēmta biddak tirjaᶜ?	*When will you return?*
3. hāda biddo waqᵉt	*It takes time.*
4. biddek ᶜamaliyye	*You*ᶠ *need an operation*

The only unambiguous way to indicate the future is to use the prefix rɑḥ-. The first sentence above could, in the appropriate context, be understood as *He wants to die*, and the second as *When do you want to return?* Using rɑḥ- eliminates the doubt: rɑḥ-imūt = *He will die*; rɑḥ-tirjaᶜ = *You will return*.

Note that the prefixes, ᶜam- and rɑḥ- are shortened forms of rāyeḥ (*[is] going [to] ...*) and ᶜammāl (*[is] doing / [is] busy [with]...*), which can themselves be used for the same purpose – but we'll stick to using the short forms for now.

7. Something small and round ...

The word ḥabbe ⟨8⟩ means *a grain, a pill, a pimple*, or an individual item of fruit, vegetables, sweets. etc. The plural ḥabbāt signifies a number of units, while (ᵉ)ḥbūb ⟨3⟩ denotes an unspecified quantity.

ḫod ḥabbet 'asbirīn!	*Take an aspirin tablet!*
jibt-illo kīlo banḍōrɑ, 'aḫad talat ḥabbāt	*I brought him a kilo [of] tomatoes [and] he took three (tomatoes).*
ḥabbtēn baṭāṭɑ	*a couple of potatoes* (or a few more, not precisely two)
ᵉḥbūb	*tablets* (medicine); *grains* (of cereal crops)

However, the kind of seeds used for roasted sunflower and pumpkin seed snacks are known as **biz**^{e}r <seeds>, a collective noun (m sing).

bɑnḍ**ō**rɑ, too, is a collective noun, meaning not *a tomato*, but *tomatoes*. In Arabic, when we want to speak about a single tomato, we use the word ḥ**a**bbe, i.e., ḥ**a**bbet bɑnḍ**ō**rɑ. This is also the case with other fruits and vegetables that are denoted by a collective noun in Arabic.

Has there been too much new material this time? Too many lengthy explanations? As usual, remember you don't have to commit it all to memory first time around. At the end of this lesson, just memorize the sentences in the box below, which summarize the main points.

'**a**ḫad il-jar**ī**de
m**i**sek is-sikk**ī**ne
šū bte^{c}mal (^{c}**ā**datan)?
šū bte^{c}mal b**u**krɑ?
šū ^{c}am-bt**e**^{c}mal?
šū r**ɑ**ḥ-t**e**^{c}mal?

All the words in the box are familiar to you, but to make the differences crystal clear, here are the translations:

He took the newspaper.
He grabbed the knife.
What do you do (usually)?
What are you doing tomorrow?
What are you doing just now?
What are you going to do?

Exercises

A. Translate into English:

1. kunt biddi ākol il-laḥme, laqēt il-kalb mākel-ha.
2. il-bint dāyman‿ᵉbtōђod ᶜalāme mnīḥa.
3. ’aђadti‿d-dawa‿l-yōm?
4. lāzem tōђdi ḥabbtēn iṣ-ṣubᵒḥ u-ḥabbe baᶜd‿ilᶜaša.
5. yā ’imm Ṣɑ̄leḥ, šu ᶜam-bteᶜmali? – ᶜam-baġsel.
6. u-baᶜdēn, šu rɑḥ-teᶜmali?
7. rɑḥ-anšor il-ġasīl ᶜala‿l-ḥabᵉl.
8. ya ’abu Māzen, šu ᶜam-bteᶜmal? – ᶜam-bakteb mɑq̈ɑ̄le[19].

19. mɑq̈ɑ̄le [mɑq̈ɑ̄lāt] means *article* (in a newspaper). When speaking about the written word, people switch into “educated” Arabic usage and so pronounce the q here as in literary Arabic (see **Book 1, page [11]**). mɑq̈ɑ̄le is derived from the root q-w-l (*say*) with the added prefix m- and the feminine suffix -e.

9. il-jarīde rɑḥ-tunšor[20] il-mɑq̈ɑ̄le tabaᶜi (tabaᶜti).
10. lāzem‿ᵉtrūḥu ᶜind‿il-jirɑ̄n tōђdu‿b-ђɑ̄ṭer-hom.

B. Complete the sentences

(Replace the English words with the appropriate expression in Arabic):

11. ziᶜlat minno, ktīr 'aђad (...) ђɑ̄ṭro.
12. biddi arūḥ (to offer condolences to them).
13. wēn l-ewlād? šū (are-they-doing-just-now)?
14. laqēt-ha (having-eaten[f]) kull il-fustoq.
15. ṣɑr-lak zamān (you left) il-bēt?
16. 'immi bid-ha (an operation).
17. ᶜādatan mā-fīʰ (difficulties).

C. Translate into Arabic:

18. Where's the meat that was on the table? – The cat[f] ate it.
19. Where's the meat that I brought yesterday? – No-one (ma-ḥadā-š) has eaten it.
20. My daughter got a good mark / grade at school.
21. She told me: Dad, I got a good mark! Do you[m] know what mark she got?
22. Take[m] the book to school.
23. I've no room in the bag (šanta), I'll take it another time.
24. You[m] need to take that medicine before lunch.
25. How long did it take you[m] <take with you>? (See **Book 1, page 71, footnote 3**.)
26. The children are-playing-just-now in the street.
27. I was angry with my daughter, I told her: Be quiet!
28. She was very hurt (→ very much took [it] upon her ђɑ̄ṭer).
29. How many times do I have to take the medicine, and when?
30. Only two tablets after lunch.
31. Tell[m] him to take as many peanuts as he wants.
32. He's always wrong. He's sure to be <[for] sure he will be> wrong again.

---

20. The verb našɑr [yunšor] has two meanings: *to hang out (laundry)* and *to publish*. See **Book 1, p. 85.**

dars ђamse u-ᶜišrīn

25

Lesson Twenty-Five

To complete your knowledge of the k**a**tab / n**i**zel type of verbs, you need to learn a few irregular verbs. These all begin with *w*, i.e., their first root letter is w-:

■	w**a**ᶜad	*he promised* (past tense conjugated like k**a**tab)
	waᶜ**a**dna	*we promised*
	w**i**ṣel	*he arrived* (past tense conjugated like n**i**zel)
	w**i**ṣlat	*she arrived*

The present-future tense can also be conjugated like katab / nizel. For example:

■	bt**i**kteb	*you^{m} write*	bt**i**wᶜed (bt**e**wᶜed)	*you promise*
	bt**i**nzal	*you^{m} go down*	bt**i**wṣal (bt**e**wṣal)	*you arrive*

The combination -ew- should be pronouced not like English *ew*, but like the *e* of b<u>e</u>tter followed by a short *oo*.
However, native speakers tend to shorten the syllable to **tu**- instead of **ti**-w / **te**-w, and **yu**- instead of **yi**-w / **ye**-w, etc. and you can adopt this pronunciation:

I arrive / shall arrive	b**ɑ**wṣal		
you^{m} arrive / will arrive	bt**e**wṣɑl	bt**ū**ṣɑl	
you^{f} arrive / will arrive	bt**e**wṣɑli	bt**ū**ṣɑli	
he arrives / will arrive	b^{y}**e**wṣɑl	b^{y}**ū**ṣɑl	
she arrives / will arrive	bt**e**wṣɑl	bt**ū**ṣɑl	
we arrive / shall arrive	bn**e**wṣɑl	bn**ū**ṣɑl	(mn**e**w-/mn**ū**-)
you^{pl} arrive / will arrive	bt**e**wṣɑlu	bt**ū**ṣɑlu	
they arrive / will arrive	b^{y}**e**wṣɑlu	b^{y}**ū**ṣɑlu	

We can now use this model to conjugate w**i**jeᶜ [y**ū**jaᶜ][1] meaning *to hurt / to be painful* and w**i**qeᶜ [y**ū**qaᶜ] meaning *to fall*, as well as a small number of other verbs of the same type.

---

1. š**ū** b**ū**jaᶜak = *Where does it hurt* <what hurts you>? The verb w**i**jeᶜ is never used in the simple past tense since it describes an ongoing situation (pain). Past pain is expressed by the composite past tense, i.e. k**ā**n + subjunctive. See **Explanations 1**. *I had a stomach-ache / my stomach ached* k**ā**n b**ɑ**ṭni yūj**a**ᶜni. b**ɑ**ṭen means *belly / abdomen.*

Notes on pronunciation:

As usual, in the 3rd person singular (*he*), we can drop the *y* of the present-future tense, and say:

- bʸ**ū**qaᶜ → b**ū**qaᶜ = *he falls*
  bʸ**ū**ṣɑl → b**ū**ṣɑl = *he arrives*
  bʸ**ū**jaᶜ → b**ū**jaᶜ = *it hurts*

Of course, this happens only after the b- prefix of the present-future tense. In the subjunctive, the y- is clearly heard:

- 'a**ḥ**san-ma y**ū**qaᶜ — *so that he won't fall* <better than that he fall>
  q**a**bᵉl-ma y**ū**ṣɑl — *before he arrives*
  r**ɑ**ḥ-y**ū**jaᶜak — *it'll hurt you*

Vocabulary

d**ɑ̄**r [id**ī**r]	to turn; to direct (towards)	q̈**ɑ**rye [3] [q̈**u**rɑ]	village
b**ā**l	mind	s**ū**q [2]	market
d**ɑ̄**r b**ā**lo	to pay attention, notice	ḫ**u**ḍrɑ	vegetables $^{f\ sing}$
ḫ**ā**l [2] [ḫw**ā**l]	uncle (mother's brother)	b**ā**ᶜ [ib**ī**ᶜ]	to sell
ᶜam**ū**d [ᶜumd**ā**n]	pillar, pole, column	ḥad**ī**d	iron
r**a**kan [y**i**rken]	to rely (on someone)	f**i**ᶜlan / f**e**ᶜlan	actually, really
tr**ē**n [trēn**ā**t] [2]	train	'aḫ**ī**r [4]	last
r**ɑ**'san	straight away; directly	ši ['**a**šya / '**e**šya]	thing
m**u**dde [8]	period of time, [a] while	š**ay**'# ['ašy**ā**']	thing

Conversation

– š**u**ft il-w**a**lad ᶜam-bʸ**u**rkoḍ	– I saw the boy running
fi-š-š**ā**reᶜ, qult-**i**llo:	in the street, I said to him:
ya w**a**lad, d**ī**r b**ā**lak!	"Boy, be careful <pay attention>!
b**i**ddak t**ū**qaᶜ! u-f**e**ᶜlan w**i**qeᶜ,	You'll fall!" And he actually did fall.
u-**a**kal‿ehw**ā**y ᶜala r**ɑ̄**so	He hit his head <he ate a blow on his-head>

---

2. Pay special attention to the different pronunciations of ḥ**ā**l (= *condition*) and ḫ**ā**l (= *uncle*). If you ask a native Arabic speaker k**ī**f ḫ**ā**lak? he'll wonder how you came to know his mother's brother. You'll remember from Book 1 that the word for *uncle* on the father's side of the family is ᶜamm.

3. The q in q̈**ɑ**rye is always pronounced as in literary Arabic. See **Book 1, page [11]**.

4. See **Explanations 4**.

u ṣ**ɑ̄**r r**ɑ̄**so y**ū**jaᶜo.	and his head started to hurt <hurt-him>.
– '**a**na kam**ā**n rɑk**ɑ**ḍᵉt	– I ran, too, and I almost fell
u-kunt r**ɑ̄**yeḥ '**a**wqaᶜ,	<was going to fall>, [but]
k**ā**n hun**ā**k ᶜam**ū**d min ḥad**ī**d,	there was an iron pillar <a pillar from
ᵉms**e**kt‿il-ᶜam**ū**d	iron> there and I grabbed hold of the
u-m**a**‿wq**e**ᶜt-ᵉš.	pillar and didn't fall.

(The speakers are waiting for a friend at the railway station.)

– '**a**yya s**ē**ᶜa b**ū**ṣɑl it-tr**ē**n?	– What time does the train arrive?
– ᶜ**ā**datan b**ū**ṣɑl is-s**ē**ᶜa	– It usually arrives at half past two
tint**ē**n[5] u-nuṣṣ,	<the hour two and half>;
h**a**llaq ṣ**ɑ̄**r tal**ā**te '**i**lla ᶜ**a**šɑrɑ	it's now ten to three <three less ten>
u-ma w**i**ṣl-ᵉš.	and it hasn't arrived [yet].
ᵉmb**a**yyen ṣ**ɑ̄**r m**a**ᶜo '**i**ši.	Something must have happened to it <it seems happened with it a thing>.
– fi-l-m**u**dde‿l-'aḫ**ī**re,	– Lately <in the last period of time>
b**ū**ṣɑl is-s**ē**ᶜa tal**ā**te '**i**lla t**u**lt...	it's [been] arriving at twenty to three <three less a third>...
– bass[6] y**ū**ṣɑl it-tr**ē**n,	– The minute the train arrives,
r**ɑ**ḥ-n**u**ḍrob telef**ō**n la-ḫ**ā**li	we'll phone <we'll hit a telephone to> my uncle
b**a**ᶜᵉd ḫ**a**mᵉs daq**ā**yeq bik**ū**n	[and] in five minutes he'll be here
h**ō**n, u-b**ō**ḫ**o**d-na ᶜala b**ē**to.	and he'll take us to his house.

– '**i**msek '**ī**d il-w**a**lad '**a**ḥsan-ma	– Take the boy's hand so that he won't fall.
y**ū**qaᶜ.– u-**i**nti kam**ā**n d**ī**ri b**ā**lek	– And you[f], too, take care <pay attention>
'**a**ḥsan-ma t**ū**qaᶜi!	not to fall!

– šu-m**ā**-lak? b**ū**jaᶜak b**ɑ**ṭnak?	– What's wrong with you? Does your stomach hurt <hurt you>?
– 'ak**a**lt‿ᵉkt**ī**r u-ṣ**ɑ̄**r b**ɑ**ṭni yūj**a**ᶜni,	– I ate a lot, and my stomach started aching.

---

5. We've seen that w**ā**ḥed / w**ā**ḥad has a feminine form: w**a**ḥade. The word tᵉn**ē**n also has a feminine form: tint**ē**n. *It's one / two o'clock* = is-s**ē**ᶜa w**a**ḥade / tint**ē**n.

6. bass + a verb can mean *just as....* bass r**i**jeᶜ... means *just as he came back / the minute he came back* <he'd **only** [just] come back (and already...)>. To express this idea in the future, bass is used with the subjunctive, e.g., bass y**i**rjaᶜ = *as soon as he gets back / the minute he gets back.*

u-rɑ̄si kamān būja^{c}ni.	And my head's aching, too.
– 'iza būja^{c}ak rɑ̄sak, ђod ḥabbet 'asbirīn[7] u-birūḥ il-waja^{c}.	– If your head aches, take an aspirin and the ache will go [away].

– 'ēš biddak?! wa^{c}adtak...	– What do you want [from me]? I promised you …
– 'aywa, btew^{c}ed ^{e}btew^{c}ed!	– Yes, you keep promising <you promise you promise>!
balāš il-kalām! bidna‿nšūf 'iši.	No more talk! Let's <we want to> see a result <see something>!
– 'iza bawe^{c}dak[8], btiqdɑr tirken ^{c}alayy(e)...	– If I make a promise [to] you, you can rely on me…
– ya zalame, btew^{c}ed-ni u-mā bte^{c}mal 'iši.	– Man, you promise me but <and> you don't do a thing!
kīf biddi arken ^{c}alēk?!	Why should I <how do I want to> rely on you?

– 'awwal kān ijib-li ђuḍrɑ min il-q̈ɑrye u-kunt abī^{c}-ha[9] fi-s-sūq, bass il-yōm bijīb-ha rɑ'san ^{c}ala‿s-sūq u-bibī^{c}-ha la-ḥālo.	– He used to bring me <first he was bringing me> vegetables from the village and I would sell them in the market, but now <today> he takes <brings> them straight to the market and sells them himself.

– il-yōm ṣɑ̄r ye^{c}ref yiḥseb‿^{e}mnīḥ.	– He's good at arithmetic now <today he knows arithmetic well>.
zamān kān yiġlɑṭ (yeġlɑṭ) fi-l-^{e}ḥsāb u-kunna niђsɑr (neђsɑr) u-kunt 'az^{c}al minno.[10]	[At one] time he used to make mistakes in arithmetic and we'd lose [money] and I'd get angry with him.
– 'ana kamān, lamma kunt‿^{e}zġīr, l-^{e}m^{c}allem kān iqul-li:	– Me too. When I was young the teacher used to say to me:

---

7. There is no *p* in Arabic, so when it occurs in words derived from other languages it is usually pronounced b. For example, *Paris* = barīz.

8. bawe^{c}dak, btew^{c}ed-ni: compare with bat^{e}rko, batrek-ha in Lesson 17.

9. See **Explanations 3.**

10. Compare with the **Conversation, p. 33**.

"dīr bālak, ya šāṭer,	"Watch out, sonny,
fīʰ 'aġlāṭ‿ᵉktīre[11] fi ḥsābak.	there are a lot of mistakes in your arithmetic;
'iḥseb kamān marra."	do the calculation[s] again."
bass bala fāyde li'anno kunt	But [it was] no use <but with no benefit>, because I used fool around
'alᶜab u-aḍḥak waqt‿id-dars.	<to play> and laugh during lessons [the lesson]!

The cat mews / meows is
il-biss bimawwi,
which reminds us of
bikaffi,
a verb form you'll
learn in Book 3.

But what about
cats in Lebanon? See the end of the
lesson.

Explanations

1. More about the composite past tenses – the auxiliary verb kān

The examples in this lesson and in Lesson 22 demonstrate that adding the auxiliary verb **kān** (**kunt**, **kānat**…) to any other verb puts that verb into the past tense:

Munīr[12] nāzel	*Munir is going down* (now)
Munīr kān nāzel	*Munir was going down*
Yūsef ᶜam-bʸikteb darso	*Yusef is writing his lesson* (now)
Yūsef kān ᶜam-(b)yikteb darso	*Yusef was writing his lesson*

---

11. See **Explanations 3**. ġalaṭ ['aġlāṭ] means *mistake, error*. (*They think so-and-so …*) *but they're wrong* <but this is a mistake>! = … bass hāda ġalaṭ!

12. Munīr is a male first name meaning *shining*. nūr = *light* in literary Arabic; remember: ṣabāḥ in-nūr!

'Aḥmad biddo yiṭla^{c} (yeṭla^{c})...	*Ahmed wants to / is going to go out*
'Aḥmad kān biddo yiṭla^{c}	*Ahmed wanted to / was going to go out*
Jamīla rāyḥa tiṭla^{c} min il-mustašfa	*Jamila is going to get out of hospital*
Jamīla kānat rāyḥa tiṭla^{c} ...	*Jamila was about to go out* (when I arrived)

As you can see, the **immediate present** and **future** tenses can be turned into the **continuous past tense** simply by inserting kaan before the verb, without changing anything else.

To form the **habitual past tense** (*used to / would*), we drop the b- prefix of the habitual present, and insert the auxiliary verb kān. In other words, **the habitual past** = kān + subjunctive. For example:

■ b^{y}ikteb darso kull yōm	*He writes his lesson every day.*
kān yikteb darso kull yōm	*He used to write his lesson every day.*
	(Usually at 10 o'clock...)
bijīb il-jarīde	*he brings the newspaper.*
kān ijīb il-jarīde	*he would bring the newspaper.*
hiyye b^{e}tzūr-na	*She visits us.*
kānat‿^{e}tzūr-na	*She used to visit us.*

> lamma jīt...
> kān nāzel
> kān ^{c}am-b^{y}ikteb
>
> ^{c}ādatan...
> kān yinzal
> kān yikteb

A boring (but highly beneficial) exercise ...

To help you commit the habitual past to memory, it's a good idea to write down the following and read them out loud:

kunt 'ajīb	*I used to bring*	kunt 'a^{c}mal (-mel)	*I used to do*
kunt‿^{e}tjīb	*you^{m} used to bring*	kunt te^{c}mal	*you^{m} used to do*
kunti‿tjībi	*you^{f} used to bring*	kunti te^{c}mali	*you^{f} used to do*
kān‿ijīb	*he used to bring*	kān ye^{c}mal	*he used to do*

Repeat the exercise with 'azūr, 'abī^{c}, 'adros, 'adfa^{c} (or any other verb you know). And most importantly: say them out loud!

2. It's easier to fall than to say "I fell"!

How do you pronounce wq**e**ᶜna and wq**e**ᶜt? We've already run into this question with nz**e**lt and seen that it all depends on the surrounding words.

a. w- at the beginning of the word:
- we can either add the helping vowel e- and say ᵉw--q**e**ᶜ--na
- or "borrow" a vowel from the previous word, e.g., m**a**‿wq**e**ᶜna (pronounce maw- like *mouth)*, meaning *we didn't fall.*

b. What about wq**e**ᶜt? Let's recall some similar cases:
At the end of a sentence

■ šu š**u**fᵉt — '**a**na‿wq**e**ᶜᵉt

Before a consonant followed by a vowel

š**u**fᵉt z**a**lame — '**a**na‿wq**e**ᶜᵉt fi-š-š**ā**reᶜ

Before the negative particle -š

ma š**u**ft-ᵉš — m**a**‿wq**e**ᶜt-ᵉš

Before two consonants

š**u**ft‿ᵉkt**ī**r — '**a**na‿wq**e**ᶜt‿ᵉmb**ā**reḥ

There's nothing new here. We just wanted to take you through it step by step to save confusion. Listen to the recording again, memorize the four Arabic phrases above (*I fell; I fell in the street; I didn't fall; I fell yesterday*) and you'll know how to fall (or not) in Arabic.

3. by**ū**t‿ᵉkb**ī**re – big houses

Plural nouns denoting inanimate objects, whether concrete or abstract, masculine or feminine, are qualified by a feminine singular adjective, as in the heading above (*big*^f sing *houses*^m pl).
In the Conversation, we had 'ɑġl**ɑ̄**ṭ ‿ᵉkb**ī**re <(*big*^f sing *mistakes*^m pl), and in Lesson 22, maš**ā**kel‿ᵉjd**ī**de (*new*^f sing *problems*^f pl). A few more examples:

■ 'amw**ā**l matr**ū**ke — *abandoned property*
kalim**ā**t ᶜɑrɑb**i**yye — *Arabic words*
mɑrr**ɑ̄**t‿ᵉkt**ī**re[13] — *many times*

Likewise, verbs and attached pronouns relating to plural inanimate objects also take a feminine singular form, for example:

---

13. You will also hear: kt**ī**r mɑrr**ɑ̄**t, like English *many times.*

Lesson 25

■ kull il-jarāyed našrat il-ḫabar   *All the newspapers published* [f sing] *the news item.*

btuṭlob 'ašya ('ešya) ktīre   *You're asking a lot <many[f] things>.*

il-'ašya illi btuṭlob-ha   *the things you're asking for <it[f]>*

As you encounter further examples of this phenomenon, this rule will become second nature.

4. 'āḫer, 'aḫīr, 'āḫαr & Co.

a. Last

You'll remember the expression **'āḫer mαrrα** (**Lesson 18, Explanations 2**). The feminine form of **'āḫer** (in the sense of *last*) is not normally used, but if you want to employ the usual formula of noun + adjective, you can use a word derived from the same root: **'aḫīr, 'aḫīre**[f]. **fi-l-mudde l-'aḫīre** means *lately* <in the last period of time>. There is a third word, also from this root: **'aḫrāni 'aḫrāniyye ['āḫrāniyyīn]**.

■ il-bēt il-'aḫrāni fi-š-šāre[c]   *the last house in the street*

l-ewlād il-'āḫrāniyyīn   *the last children* (in the queue, etc.)

Which should you use? Preferably, **'āḫer before** a masculine or feminine singular noun and **il-'āḫrāniyyīn after** a plural noun. We'll make do with this practical solution for now.

b. Other, another

Other, too, presents options. You'll be accustomed to using **tāni**, the usual colloquial word for *other*. However, we're gradually getting familiar with more formal "educated" speech, and now it's time to look at the "official" form:

■ **'āḫαr, 'uḫrα**[f] **['āḫαrīn]** #   *other*

At this level of speech, the correct form is **mαrrα 'uḫrα** = *another time*, and in accordance with the rule we learned in **Explanations 3** above, **'ašyā' 'uḫrα** = *other things* (#).

To finish, we'll review what you've learned about these words with a short list to help you to avoid confusing them:

■ 'āḫer 'iši   *last thing*

šay' āḫαr#   *another thing* (educated speech)

hāy 'āḫer mαrrα!   *That's the last time!*

ṭαyyeb, mαrrα 'uḫrα   *OK, another time...*

Exercises

A. Translate into English:

1. ’**a**yya s**ē**^{c}a‿wṣ**e**ltu?
2. ’**i**ḥna‿wselna bakk**ī**r (early).
3. ’ab**ū**y u-**i**mmi wi**ṣ**lu b**a**^{c}d‿iḍ-ḍ**u**h^{o}r.
4. ’**i**s’al ’**i**mmak š**u** būj**a**^{c}-ha.
5. ḍ**ɑ**r**ɑ**bna t**a**lifōn / t**e**lefōn lad-dokt**ō**r.
6. bass t**ū**ṣɑl ’uḍ**r**ob-li t**a**lifōn!
7. id-doktōr q**ā**l: muš‿^{e}mn**ī**ḥ t**ō**ḫod‿^{e}kt**ī**r min had-d**a**wa!
8. ^{c}aš**ā**n h**ē**k k**ā**n b**ɑ**ṭni yūj**a**^{c}ni!
9. kunt ’**ā**ḫod t**a**lat ḥabb**ā**t kull y**ō**m.
10. ’ab**ū**y b^{y}**e**^{c}raf q**u**ṣɑṣ ḥ**i**lwe.

B. Complete the sentences

(Replace the English words with the appropriate expression in Arabic):

11. ’ab**ū**y (used to know) q**u**ṣɑṣ ḥ**i**lwe.
12. ’aḫ**ū**y (used to phone me) mɑrrt**ē**n fi-š-š**a**h^{e}r.
13. (As soon as) r**i**je^{c}, ’**a**na tar**a**kt il-b**ē**t.
14. sme^{c}na (he wants to sell) sayy**ɑ̄**rto.
15. k**a**tab (other) kalim**ā**t, bass ’**a**na ma (didn’t notice <didn’t pay attention>).
16. il-kalim**ā**t illi (he wrote <them (it)>).
17. l**a**mma f**u**t^{e}t ^{c}ala‿l-ġ**u**rfe, il-w**a**lad (was playing).
18. l**a**mma k**u**nna zġ**ɑ̄**r, (we used to play) fi-š-š**ā**re^{c}.
19. h**ō**n f**ī**^{h} (many problems).
20. f**ī**^{h} hun**ā**k sanad**ī**q (broken).

C. Translate into Arabic:

21. What time did you^{pl} arrive? – We arrived at six o’clock.
22. Does your^{f} head ache <hurt-you>? Take an aspirin.
23. Once I used to sell tomatoes. Now I sell cars.
24. Now I know a lot of words.
25. He knows foreign languages (Lessons 16 and 21).
26. Which [are] the languages that you^{m} know <know-it>?
27. The words I understand <it>.

28. My son collects stamps. – I too, when I was young, used to collect stamps.
29. She takes a tablet every day; yesterday she made a mistake [and] she took two <two tablets>.
30. Before, she used to take four tablets.

Falling sounds different in the country …

For those of you who come into contact with people from rural areas, we are bound to reveal that their pronunciation of the verbs we've learned in this lesson is a little different. In the present-future tense, instead of t**i**w- / t**ū**- people simply say t**i**- (dropping the w), and the paradigm is:

b**a**wqa^c / b**a**qa^c, bt**i**qa^c, bt**i**qa^{c}i, b**i**qa^c, mn**i**qa^c, bt**i**qa^{c}u, b**i**qa^{c}u

You'll fall! = b**i**ddak t**i**qa^c!
When will he arrive? = '**ē**mta b**i**ṣɑl?

It's good to be able to understand these forms when you hear them, but you yourself should use those given at the beginning of the lesson, as they are understood everywhere.

There have been plenty of pitfalls in this lesson! Hopefully your bruises will fade and you'll be left feeling you've taken another big step forward!

Now to our Lebanese cats! If you ask the inhabitants of, say, Beirut, what their cats say, they will answer: "n**ā**w nāw" (like *now* in English). So in Lebanon il-b**i**ss bin**a**wwi! Why? A project for a dialect researcher, perhaps.

d**a**rs s**i**tte u-ᶜišr**ī**n

26

Lesson Twenty-Six

So far we've dealt only with verbs belonging to the pattern known as Form 1, or f**a**ᶜal: k**a**tab, n**i**zel, š**ā**f,etc. In this lesson we are going to broaden our horizons: we're going to discover all the **Forms** of the Arabic verb, and begin to make their acquaintance.

Arabic roots can slot into a wide variety of verb patterns, which most English-language Arabic-grammar books refer to as Forms – a practice we'll adopt; we'll also capitalize the word "Forms" when we use it to refer to the various verbal patterns. Arabic verbs can assume any one of ten of these Forms, which are enumerated below. When the same root appears in more than one Form, there will often – though not always – be some similarity of meaning. The special pattern of each Form will be indicated by additions to the boxes in the second column. Note that the Arabic names of the Forms are all derived from the root f-ᶜ-l.

Form	**Pattern**	**Root**	**Verb**	**Translation**	**Name**
f-1	□**a**□a□	s-k-t	s**a**kat	to be silent*	f**a**ᶜal
f-2	□**a**□□a□	s-k-t	s**a**kkat	to hush; to silence	f**a**ᶜᶜal
f-3	□**ā**□a□	s-f-r	s**ā**far	to travel, go, set out	f**ā**ᶜal
f-4	'**a**□□a□	z-ᶜ-l	'**a**z ᶜal	to annoy, upset	'**a**fᶜal
f-5	t□**a**□□a□	q-d-m	tq**a**ddam	to advance, move forward	tf**a**ᶜᶜal
f-6	t□**ā**□a□	q-r-b	tq**ā**rab	to approach each other	tf**ā**ᶜal
f-7	in□**a**□a□	f-t-ḥ	(i)nf**a**taḥ	to open (intrans), be opened	inf**a**ᶜal
f-8	i□t**a**□a□	š-ġ-l	(i)št**a**ġal	to work	ift**a**ᶜal
f-9	i□□**a**□□	ḥ-m-r	(i)ḥm**a**rr	to turn red, to blush	ifᶜ**a**ll
f-10	ist**a**□□a□	ᶜ-m-l	(i)st**a**ᶜmal	to use	ist**a**fᶜal

* Note: s**a**kat means literally *he was silent*. However, as the 3rd person masculine singular is the basic form of the Arabic verb, we have translated it here as an infinitive, which is the basic form of the verb in English.

When you're introduced to a group of people in a social situation, you'll almost certainly not remember all their names at first, nor will you make instant friends of all of them. We'll learn each of these verb Forms in detail in **Books 3** and **4**.

At this point we'll limit ourselves to one encouraging observation:

– All these verbs behave like ka**tab in the past tense, i.e.,**

1. They all take the same suffixes.
2. In all of them the stress shifts in the same way it does in k**a**tab: in the 3rd person, the first syllable is stressed, while in the other persons (*I, you*^{sing}*, we, you*^{pl}) the stress is on the second syllable (if you want to remind yourself, take another look at **Book 1**, **p. 46**).

The only slight difference is to be found in the 3rd person feminine singular (*she*), which generally contains 3 vowels, unlike Form 1 verbs (f**a**ᶜal), which have only two. Compare:

■ s**a**kat	*he kept silent*	s**a**kt-at	*she kept silent*
s**a**kkat	*he silenced*	s**a**kkat-at	*she silenced*

Let's look at a few examples of the verbs above and see how closely they resemble k**a**tab, as far as stress and endings are concerned:

■**Form 2**[1]	n**a**zzal	*he brought down; he let down*
	n**a**zzalat	*she brought down*
	nazz**a**lna	*we brought down*
Form 3	s**ā**fαr	*he traveled*
	s**ā**fαrαt	*she traveled*
	sāf**α**rna	*we traveled*
Form 4	'**az**ᶜal	*he annoyed / he upset*
	'**az**ᶜalat	~~*they*~~ *annoyed*
	'azᶜ**al**t	*I annoyed; you*^{m} *annoyed*
Form 8	išt**a**ġal	*he worked*
	išt**a**ġalat	*she worked*
	ištaġ**a**lna	*we worked*
Form 10	ist**a**ᶜmal	*he used*
	ist**a**ᶜmalat	~~*they*~~ *used*
	istaᶜm**al**tu	*you*^{pl} *used*

---

1. Yes, verbs voweled □**i**□e□ in Form 1 have "a" vowels in the other verbal Forms, e.g., z**i**ᶜel (*he was angry*) becomes '**az**ᶜal in Form 4. In future we shall refer to the various Forms as f-1, f-2, f-3, f-4, etc.

This brief survey of the different Forms of the verb is like a map that will help you to find your way through new territory, even if you don't know all the details of it yet. Now, for example, you can identify the verb tf**ɑ**ḍḍɑl as belonging to Form 5 (f-5), and from now on our conversations and explanations will contain verbs belonging to a variety of Forms, in the past tense, at least. This means we can use a more varied vocabulary and make use of excerpts from "real life" conversations.

It's important to emphasize once again that the first part of this chapter doesn't contain material that you have to start memorizing straight away. And now let's move on to the real business of the lesson:

Form 2 (f-2) – f**a**^{cc}al

For the moment we're going to do no more than take a look at Form 2 of the verb, which has the pattern f**a**^{cc}al, and which is distinguished by the doubling of the second root letter. It's very important to ensure that the doubled consonant is clearly heard and that you pronounce it more strongly and linger over it longer. If you don't do this people will not be able to hear whether you are saying s**a**kkat or s**a**kat.

Let's look at the full paradigm of f-2:

Past		**Present-future**	
nazz**a**lt[2]	*I brought down*	ba-n**a**zzel	*I bring down*
nazz**a**lt		b^{e}t-n**a**zzel	
nazz**a**lti		b^{e}t-n**a**zzli	
n**a**zzal		bi n**a**zzel	
n**a**zzalat		b^{e}t-n**a**zzel	
nazz**a**lna		b^{e}n-n**a**zzel	(m^{e}n-n**a**zzel[G])
nazz**a**ltu		b^{e}t-n**a**zzlu	
n**a**zzalu		bi n**a**zzlu	

The **active participle** is mn**a**zzel[3], its feminine form is mn**a**zzle and the plural is [mnazzlīn].

---

2. Or nazz**a**l^{e}t, of course.

3. In literary Arabic these forms are pronounced mun**a**zzel#, muk**a**mmel#, etc. In colloquial Arabic this pronunciation is used only by highly educated speakers, or in phrases borrowed from the "official" language. In ordinary conversation people say ■ l-^{e}m^{c}allmīn (*the teachers*), but they will talk about dɑ̄r il-mu^{c}allimīn (*the teachers' training college*).

Like the examples we saw earlier (see **Lesson 23, Explanations 1b**) this active participle, too, indicates an action that has already been completed in the past, i.e., *having-brought-down.* The active participle of the verb k**a**mmal, for example (*to continue / to keep going until the end* – i.e., *to finish*), is (e)mk**a**mmel, which means *having-finished.*

laq**ē**to mk**a**mmel iš-š**u**ġol — *I found he'd finished the job* <I found him having-finished…>

The passive participle is (e)mk**a**mmal[3], mk**a**mmle[f], [mkamml**ī**n].

■ laq**ē**t il-b**ā**b‿emsakkɑr — *I found the door closed.*

Before we move on to the **Conversation**, you should declaim the paradigm of the verb k**a**mmal out loud, in both the past and present-future tenses (kamm**a**lt… bak**a**mmel…) so as to put your theoretical knowledge into practice – in other words, to get your tongue used to pronouncing it and your ears accustomed to hearing it!

Vocabulary

b**a**llaš[4]	to begin	w**a**qqaf	to stop (i.e., *to pull up*)
k**ā**mel	complete; perfect	b**ɑ**ṭṭɑl	to stop (i.e., *to leave off*)
k**a**mmal	to complete / continue	ḫ**ɑ**llɑṣ	to finish
ᶜam**ɑ̄**rɑ [-r**ɑ̄**t]	building	ḥ**a**mmal[6]	to load
ᶜ**a**mmɑr	to build	s**a**kkɑr	to close (trans)
l**i**ḥeq [y**i**lḥaq]	to catch up [with]; to manage [to]		
bl**o**kk[5]	block, brick (for building)		
'**a**ššɑr	to signal / sign	r**a**wwɑḥ	to go home
'**u**ġniye ['aġ**ā**ni]	song	tr**a**kk[7]	lorry, truck
m**u**ṭreb [muṭrib**ī**n]	singer	bid**ā**ye [8]	beginning, start

4. This verb is used mainly in the Galilee region (and also in Syria and Lebanon). Jerusalemites prefer to use a different verb, which you'll learn later.

5. From the English *block.* The Arabic word, which you will hear more often in and around Jerusalem, is ṭ**ū**b, a masculine singular collective noun that means *bricks.*

6. You will remember the verb ḥ**a**mal or ḥ**i**mel, which means *to carry.* The Form 2 verb ḥ**a**mmal means *to cause someone / something else to carry*, i.e., *to load, burden with.* This verb sometimes assumes a broader sense and can mean *to transport / to haul.*

7. From the English *truck.* Most foreign words in Arabic form the plural by adding -**ā**t, e.g., tr**a**kk [trakk**ā**t], sh**e**kk (*check*) [shekk**ā**t]; you will also hear tr**ē**n**ā**t, taksiyy**ā**t.

Conversation

– ballašna bi-š-šuġ^{e}l min‿iṣ-ṣub^{e}ḥ u-kammal-na‿š-šuġ^{e}l ḥatta‿l-maġreb.	– We started work in the early morning <from the morning> and went on working until the evening.
– ḫallaṣtu, ya^{c}ni? –	– You mean you've finished?
– ḫallaṣna. sakkarna l-^{e}bwāb u-rawwaḥna. kull yōm, bass‿^{e}nḫalleṣ iš-šuġ^{o}l[8], m^{e}nsakker l-^{e}bwāb u-m^{e}nrawweḥ ^{c}a-l-bēt.	– We've finished. We closed the doors and went home. Every day, as soon as we finish work, we close the doors and go home.
– u-bāqi‿l-^{c}ummāl ḫallaṣu kamān?	– Did the rest of the workers finish too?
– ba^{c}d-hen / lissa ma ḫallaṣū-š. nšalla biḫallṣu[9] bukra...	– They haven't finished yet. Hopefully they'll finish tomorrow...
– u-bisak^{k}ru l-^{e}bwāb u-biraw^{w}ḥu ^{c}a-l-bēt.	– And they'll close the doors and go home!
– maẓbūṭ, ṣert te^{c}ref it-tartīb ^{c}indna fi-l-warše[10].	– Exactly! You've learned how things are done at our building site <you've become you know the arrangement by us at the building site>.
– u-iḫ^{e}wtak, šu bi^{ce}mlu / bi^{c}malu?	– And your brothers, what do they do?
– hinne ^{c}ind-hen‿^{e}trakk, sayyāret šaḥ^{e}n ya^{c}ni, biḥammlu blokkāt ^{c}ala‿t-trakk min il-ma^{c}mal, u-bijībū-hen ^{c}a-l-warše. binazzlu l-^{e}blokkāt min is-sayyāra w-il-bannāy(e)[11] b^{y}ibnu‿l-ḥiṭān[12].	– They've got a truck, a lorry <haulage car>, that's to say, they load bricks onto the truck from the factory and bring them to the building site. They take the bricks off the truck, and the builders build the walls

---

8. See **Lesson 25, footnote 6**.

9. Remember what we said about **biddak / bidna** (**Book 1, Explanations 1, p. 35**): when the doubled consonant is not followed by a vowel, the doubling is weakened, or barely audible. This is why **biḫallṣu** is pronounced **biḫal(l)ṣu**, and why, in the next sentence, we find **bisak^{k}ru** and **biraw^{w}ḥu**.

10. **warše** [**waršāt / wiraš**] = *workshop; building site.*

11. This is the plural from of **banna**, which means *builder.* We'll learn the verb from this root very soon.

12. See next page.

– il-yōm iṣ-ṣubᵒḥ ma‿lḥeqt-ᵉš il-bᾱṣ.	– This morning I didn't catch the bus.
ᶜādatan biwaqqef ta‿inazzel	Usually it stops to let passengers off
rukkāb[13] bass il-yōm ma waqqaf-ᵉš.	but today it didn't stop.
– kān lāzem‿ᵉt'aššer-lo!	– You should have signaled to it!
– mà 'aššart-illo! ᵉmbayyen ma	– But I did signal to it! But he can't have
šāf-nī-š.	seen me <it seems he [i.e., the driver] didn't see me>.
baᶜdēn maraqu	Then three buses passed
talat bᾱṣᾱt wαrα bαᶜᵉḍ,	one after another.
ma waqqafū-š.	[but] they didn't stop.
baᶜdēn 'aššart la-taksi, waqqaf.	Then I signaled to a taxi [and]
ᵉrkebᵉt fiyyo // fīʰ.	it stopped. I got into it
lamma‿wṣelna ᶜa-l-bōṣṭα fi ḥēfa,	[and] when we got to the post office in
qult-illo: waqqef-li hōn.	Haifa I told him: "Stop here for me."
waqqaf fi mawqaf[14] il-bᾱṣ	He pulled up at the bus stop
wᵉ-nzelᵉt.	and I got out.

---

simeᶜ	*he heard*
sammaᶜ	*he caused (someone else) to hear*
– ṣᾱḥbi Kāmel sammaᶜ-ni 'uġniye	– My friend Kamel played me <caused me to hear / let me hear>
ᶜajbat-ni ktīr.	a song I liked very much.
dāyman bijib-li 'isṭiwᾱnᾱt	He's always bringing me Arabic
ᶜαrαbiyye. biddi asammeᶜ-kom	records. I want to play you
'isṭiwᾱne[15] jdīde.	a new record.
Kāmel jab-li‿yyāha‿mbāreḥ.	Kamel brought me it yesterday.

---

12. ḥēṭ [ḥiṭᾱn] means *wall*. Don't get this word mixed up with ђēṭ [ђiṭᾱn] which means *string, thread.*

13. The word rākeb means *passenger* (i.e., someone who rikeb a means of transport). On its plural form, see **Lesson 23, Explanations 1c**.

14. In literary Arabic mawq̈ef# means both *position / attitude* (towards a particular subject) and *bus stop*. In colloquial speech people usually distinguish between mawqaf (*bus stop*) and mawq̈ef (*position / attitude*): šu mawq̈efak min hal-mαwḍūᶜ? # = *What's your position on* <from> *this issue?*

15. Records are what we used to listen to before CDs, MP3 players, etc. were invented.

fīha 'aġāni ḥilwe ktīr la-Fayrūz. — It's got a lot of beautiful songs of Fairuz's on it.

hiyye 'afḍal[16] muṭribe ᶜindi. — She's my favorite singer <she's the preferable singer at me>.

ṣōt-ha ktīr ḥilu. — Her voice is very beautiful.

biddi asammeᶜkom iyyā-ha. — I want you to hear her <I want to cause you to hear her>.

– tfaḍḍal! — – Go ahead!

ṭeleᶜ – ṭallaᶜ — *he went out – he brought out / took out*

– ṣar-li talat‿ᵉsnīn ᶜam-badros. — – I've been studying for three years now <it's become to me 3 years I'm studying>

'abūy biddo iṭalleᶜ-ni min il-madrase ḥatta‿išaġġel-ni maᶜo fi-l-karāj. — [and] my father wants to take me out of school so that I can go to work <so that he can make me work> with him at the garage / auto repair shop.

bass 'ana biddi akammel ᶜilmi. — But I want to complete my education <my knowledge>.

– 'ana bil-ᶜaks: 'abūy buṣrof[17] — – I'm [just] the opposite: my father spends

---

16. 'afḍal is a comparative adjective meaning *preferable* – see **Book 1, pp. 98, 102**. You will also hear people say il-muṭribe‿l-mufaḍḍale ᶜindi <the preferred singer at me>, using the passive participle of the verb faḍḍal (f-2), which comes from the same root and means *to prefer.* bafaḍḍel arūḥ la-ḥāli = *I prefer to go alone.*

17. The verb ṣaraf [yuṣrof] means *to spend money; to change / exchange money*: biddi aṣrof had-dolarāt = *I'd like to change these dollars* (into another currency). The noun ṣarrāf means *moneychanger.*

mαṣ**ᾱ**ri ktīr ḥ**a**tta‿iᶜall**e**m-ni,	a lot of money educating me <in order to teach me>
ᶜaš**ā**n ak**a**mmel dir**ᾱ**sti[18].	so that I can finish my studies.

---

l-ᵉmᶜ**a**llem biᶜ**a**llem iṭ-ṭull**ᾱ**b.	The teacher teaches the students.
biᶜall**e**m-hom d**a**rs‿ᵉjd**ī**d,	He teaches them a new lesson.
biᶜall**e**m-hom‿iyy**ā**ʰ.	He teaches them it.

– ya m**ᾱ**mα, l-ᵉmᶜ**a**llme	– Mummy, the teacher[f]
ᶜallam**a**t-na ’**u**ġniye.	taught us a song.
– ’**ē**š il-’**u**ġniye illi	– What song did she teach you
ᶜallam**a**t-kom‿iyy**ā**ha?	<what the song that she taught you it>?
– b**i**ddek tismaᶜ**ī**-ha?	– Do you want to hear it?
– ṭ**α**bᶜan b**i**dna nism**a**ᶜ-ha!	– Of course we want to hear it!
sammᶜ**ī**-na‿yy**ā**ha!	Sing it for us <make us hear it> !

---

f**i**hem – f**a**hham	*he understood – he explained* <he caused (someone else) to understand>
– ’**a**na muš f**ā**hme hal-j**u**mle,	– I don’t understand this sentence,
b**i**ddi tfahh**e**m-ni‿yy**ā**ha.	I want you to explain it to me.
– ṭ**α**yyeb, ’**i**smaᶜi!	– OK, listen!
bid**ā**yet il-j**u**mle...	The beginning of the sentence…
– u-kam**ā**n h**ō**n...	– And here, too…
–’ismaḥ**ī**-li bass ak**a**mmel!	– Just let me finish <allow me just to finish>!
– ṭ**α**yyeb, k**a**mmel, k**a**mmel!	– Fine, go ahead, finish <finish, finish>!

18. The noun dir**ᾱ**se [2] [8] means *study / studies.*

Explanations

1. Subjunctive, imperative or – Off with its head!

You will already have noticed that the prefixes for the present-future tense of f-2 (i.e., Form 2, which we learned earlier in this lesson) are identical to those we used with šāf and other verbs: beṭkammel, bikammel, just like beṭšūf, bišūf.

Here, too, we form the subjunctive by dropping the prefix b- / be-: tkammel, ikammel.

The imperative is formed by dropping initial t- of the 2nd person:
tkammel → kammel!

To sum up:

bet-kammel	*you*m *continue / complete; she continues / completes*
ḥatta‿t-kammel	*so that you*m */ she continue / complete…*
kammel!	*complete! / continue! / go on!*

A pronunciation exercise, just to remind you:

ḥatta‿tkammel	*so that you*m */ she continue…*
lāzem‿etkammel	*you*m */ she must continue*
ḥatta‿ikammel	*so that he continue…*
lāzem‿ikammel	*he must continue*

There's nothing new here, as you are already accustomed to phrases like lāzem‿etšūf, ḥatta‿išūf, etc.

2. The meaning of Form 2 (faccal) verbs

What is the meaning of Form 2 (f-2) verbs?

a. From the examples above you will already have realized that their principal meaning is **causative**, i.e., *to cause (something to happen), to make (someone do something)*, etc. Here are some more examples:

zakar *he remembered*	zakkar *he reminded* (i.e., *caused someone else to remember*)
simec *he heard*	sammac *he played* (a recording, a song, etc – i.e., *he caused someone else to hear*)
nḍīf *clean* (adj)	naḍḍaf *he cleaned*
kāmel *complete, perfect* (adj)	kammal *he completed*

b. With certain verbs, Form 2 (**fa**^{cc}al) has an **intensive** function, i.e., it indicates a particularly powerful action, or an action that is repeated several times:

k**a**sɑr	*he broke*	k**a**ssɑr	*he smashed*
m**a**za^{c}	*he tore*	m**a**zza^{c}	*he tore up / he tore to pieces*
q**a**daḥ[19]	*he drilled a hole*	q**a**ddaḥ	*he drilled several holes*
ђ**a**zaq	*he drilled a hole*	ђ**a**zzaq	*he drilled several holes*

3. (He brought me) it = iyy**ā**- + attached pronoun

As we've already seen, in sentences such as *He saw me* and *I saw him*, Arabic does not use a separate word for *me* or *him*, but tacks an attached pronoun (-ni, -ak, etc.) on to the end of the verb (and that, of course, is why they're called "attached pronouns").

There is, however, an exception to this:

■ il-jar**ī**de — *the newspaper,*
j**ā**b-ha la-'ab**ū**y — *he brought it to my father.*
j**a**b-lo‿yy**ā**-ha — *he brought him it* <he brought-to-him it>.

Why do we use the little word iyy**ā**-[20] here? Because the verb already has one attachment (-lo), and so there's no room for another one (we can't say j**a**b-lo-ha). So we use the particle iyy**ā**-, which, with the addition of the appropriate ending, indicates a direct object (*him, her, them*, etc.)

■ '**ē**mta b^{e}tj**i**b-li l-^{e}kt**ā**b? — *When will you bring me the book* <...bring to-me the book>?
b**u**krɑ baj**i**b-lek‿iyy**ā**^{h} — *I'll bring you it tomorrow* <... I'll bring to-you it>.
jibt-**i**lli‿l-^{c}**u**lbe? — *Did you bring me the box* <you brought to-me the box>?
'**a**ywa, jibt-**i**llak‿iyy**ā**-ha. — *Yes, I brought you it / I brought it to you.*

Note: The word iyy**ā**- can also serve as the direct object of b**i**ddi, b**i**ddak, etc., for precisely the same reason: the expressions b**i**ddi, b**i**dd-ak, b**i**d(d)-ha, etc. already include an attached pronoun, and so there's no room left to add another one.

---

19. The verb q**a**daḥ is used in rural speech, while townies prefer to say ђ**a**zaq. For the noun *hole* they say q**u**d^{e}ḥ and ђ**u**z^{o}q respectively [qd**ū**ḥ / ђz**ū**q] [3].

20. You'll have noticed that we say ‿iyy**ā**- after a consonant and ‿yy**ā**- after a vowel: j**a**b-lo‿yy**ā**-ha = j**a**b - loyy**ā** - ha

We can't say b**i**d-ha-ha (*she wants her / it*) or b**i**d-na-hom (*we want them*). We have to say b**i**d-ha‿yy**ā**-ha (*she wants her / it*) and b**i**d-na‿yy**ā**-hom (*we want them*). Here are some more examples:

■ ħ**o**d iṣ-ṣ**u**wɑr illi b**i**ddak‿iyy**ā**-ha[21]. — *Take the pictures that you want.*
r**ū**ḥ la-ᶜ**i**nd 'ab**ū**k, b**i**ddo‿yy**ā**k. — *Go to your father, he wants you*[m].
h**ē**k b**i**ddi‿yy**ā**k! — *That's how I want you* (to be / to behave)!

(A woman on the radio said sadly, speaking of her disappointment in love):

■ b**a**šᶜor[22] inno m**a** b**i**ddo‿yy**ā**-ni — *I feel that he doesn't want me.*

This last example above shows us that iyy**ā**- is followed by the 1st person attached pronoun -ni – **just as a verb is** – (not by -i).

To sum up:
The attached pronouns here are just the same as those added to the preposition w**ɑ**rɑ (**Book 1, page 73**), with the exception of the 1st person, i.e.,

iyy**ā**-ni, iyy**ā**-k, iyy**ā**-ki, iyy**ā**ʰ, iyy**ā**-ha, -na, -kom, -hom

Exercises

A. Translate into English:

1. b**i**ddo‿iᶜ**a**mmer b**ē**t‿ᵉjd**ī**d.
2. k**u**nna b**i**dna‿nᶜ**a**mmer d**ɑ̄**r la-'**i**bᵉn-na, j**i**bna bann**ā**y...
3. bass h**u**wwe b**i**ddo‿iᶜamm**e**r-ha la-ḥ**ā**lo.
4. '**ē**mta b**i**ddak‿ᵉtħ**ɑ**lleṣ š**u**ġlak?
5. l**i**ssa ma ħɑllɑṣn**ā**-š! b**i**dna‿nħ**ɑ**lleṣ b**u**krɑ.
6. ᵉmb**ā**reḥ samm**a**ᶜt-ni '**u**ġniye.
7. miš h**ā**y il-'**u**ġniye‿lli samm**a**ᶜt-ni‿yy**ā**ha.

---

21. Remember that in Arabic you have to say *Take the pictures that you want **them***. The word for *them* is feminine singular, in accordance with the rule you learned in **Lesson 25, Explanations 3**.

22. The verb š**a**ᶜɑr [y**u**šᶜor] means *to feel*, especially with reference to emotions
■ (rather than sensations), and šuᶜ**ū**r [2] means *feeling,emotion.* š**u** šuᶜ**ū**rak b**a**ᶜd **i**lli ṣ**ɑ̄**r? = *How do you feel after what happened* <what is your feeling after [that] which happened>?

8. is-sayy**ɑ̄**ra w**a**qqafat jamb b**ē**tna.
9. il-b**ɑ̄**ṣ biw**a**qqef h**ō**n?
10. n**a**ᶜam, '**i**za bᵉtaš**še**r-lo, l**ā**zem iw**a**qqef.

B. Complete the sentences

(Replace the English words with the appropriate expression in Arabic):

11. il-bann**ā**y (worked) mn**ī**ḥ, (they finished)‿š-š**u**ġᵒl q**a**bl‿iḍ-ḍ**u**hᵒr.
12. l**a**', l**i**ssa ([they] haven't finished), l**ā**zem <that they finish>.
13. '**a**na j**i**bᵉt (records)‿ᵉjd**ī**de, b**i**ddak tism**a**ᶜ-ha?
14. '**a**ywa, samm**e**ᶜ-ni (them)!
15. m**a** b**i**ddi **a**smaᶜ (songs) 'ajnāb**i**yye.
16. (He stopped) sayy**ɑ̄**rto jamb (the town hall).
17. l**ā**zem <that you signal> lal-b**ɑ̄**ṣ '**i**za b**i**ddak <that it stop>.
18. ma k**ā**n-f**ī**ʰ (room) fi-l-b**ɑ̄**ṣ, ᶜaš**ā**n h**ē**k[23] (it didn't stop).
19. k**u**ll (the passengers) n**i**zlu min it-t**a**ksi.
20. **A**rik '**a**fḍɑl (singer) ᶜ**i**ndi.

C. Translate into Arabic:

21. She hushed the child. She hushed him.
22. [On] what day did they travel?
23. The letter that youᵐ wrote <it>.
    The letter you wrote to me <that you wrote to-me it>.
24. The laborers worked from the morning until the evening.
25. The door of the office was closed.
26. I found all the doors[24] closed.
27. I heard a beautiful song.
28. What's the name of the song that we heard <it>.
29. Where are the letters that youᵐ brought…
    that you brought me <that you brought to-me them>?
30. I left the pictures on the table.
31. Youᶠ must finish your work before midday.

---

23. ᶜaš**ā**n h**ē**k means *that's why… / because of that…*See **Book 1, p. 33**.

24. Doors = bw**ā**b. See today's **Conversation.**

32. Yesterday we didn't work in the afternoon. We worked only in the morning.
33. Our neighbor wants to teach his son.
34. Do you^{m} want to complete your studies?
35. Do you^{f} want to complete your studies?
36. She wants to complete her studies.
37. She told me that she wants to complete her studies.
38. Afterwards her father wants her to work <wants to make her work> with him in the office.

il-y**ō**m, bik**a**ffi!

Of all the verbs in this lesson, try to remember the following, at least: w**a**qqaf, s**a**kkɑr, ḫ**ɑ**llɑṣ, together with the expression jibt-**i**llak‿iyy**ā**^{h} (*I brought it to you / I brought you it*). The next lesson will give you an opportunity to practice again what you have learned today.

d**a**rs s**a**b^{c}a u-^{c}išr**ī**n — 27

Lesson Twenty-Seven

Your first task for today is to repeat **out loud** the paradigms of n**a**zzal and k**a**mmal. Then you can take a look at a new text and meet some more verbs from the fa^{cc}al Form (f-2). They're no strangers to you, as you're already familiar with words derived from the same roots, and practicing this new Form will help you extend your vocabulary.

^{c}**i**ref	he knew
^{c}**a**rraf / ^{c}**ɑ**rrɑf	he informed / he let know he introduced / he made known
šu ^{c}**ɑ**rrɑfak?	How do you know <what made you know>?
^{c}ɑrr**ɑ**f-ni ^{c}ala 'ab**ū**^{h}	He introduced me to his father.
b**i**ddi a^c**a**rrfak ^{c}ala '**a**hli	I want to introduce you to my family.
bi^c**a**rref ^{c}ala ḥ**ā**lo	He introduces himself.
(To an interviewee on the radio:)	
m**u**mken‿et^c**ɑ**rref ^{c}ala ḥ**ā**lak?	Could you introduce yourself <possible you make known on yourself >?
ġ**ē**r	different; other
ġ**a**yyɑr	he changed
ġ**a**yyɑr '**i**smo	he changed his name
ġ**a**yyɑr f**i**kro	he changed his mind <his thought>
^{e}nš**ɑ**llɑ r**ɑ**ḥ‿etġ**a**yyer f**i**krak!	Hopefully, you'll^m change your mind!
^{e}nš**ɑ**llɑ r**ɑ**ḥ‿etġ**a**yyri f**i**krek!	Hopefully, you'll^f change your mind!
r**i**keb	he rode, he got on (a vehicle)
r**a**kkab	he gave (someone) a ride (on a bike, etc.); he assembled, put together (a machine)
rakk**e**b-ni!	Give me a ride (on your bike)!
r**a**kkab il-mot**ō**r	He put the engine together <assembled the engine>.
ḍ**i**ḥek	he laughed
ḍ**ɑ**ḥḥɑk	he made (someone) laugh
ḍɑḥḥ**ɑ**k-ni	he made me laugh

bal**ā**š‿ᵉnḍ**ɑ**ḥḥek in-n**ā**s ᶜal**ē**na	Let's not make fools of ourselves <no need that we make the people laugh at us>!
qar**ī**b	near
q**a**rrab / q**ɑ**rrɑb	he brought close[r] / he drew (something) up; he drew near / he approached
q**a**rreb iṭ-ṭ**ɑ̄**wle! *	Draw up the table <bring-near the table >!
badd**ī**-š aq**a**rreb iṭ-ṭ**ɑ̄**wle, l**ā**zem '**i**nte‿tq**a**rreb ᶜal**ē**ha.	I don't want to draw up the table, **you** should come closer to it.
ḫ**ɑ**bɑr	announcement; news item
ḫ**ɑ**bbɑr	he informed / he let (someone) know / he gave news
bass t**i**smaᶜ '**i**ši, ḫabb**e**r-ni!	The minute you[m] hear something, let me know!
bass t**i**smaᶜi '**i**ši, ḫabbr**ī**-ni!	The minute you[f] hear something, let me know!
law r**i**jeᶜ, kunt ḫɑbb**ɑ**rtak	If he'd come back, I would have let you know.
r**i**jeᶜ	he returned / he came back
r**a**jjaᶜ	he returned (something to someone / somewhere) he gave back; he put back
rajj**e**ᶜ-li l-ᵉkt**ā**b! *	Give me back the book!
rajj**a**ᶜto maḥ**a**llo	I put it back [in] its place.
rajjaᶜt-**i**llak‿iyy**ā**ʰ	I gave it back to you <I returned-to-you it>!

muš m**u**mken‿^{e}nr**a**jje^{c} it-tār**ī**ħ	We can’t turn back history <not possible that we
la-w**ɑ**rɑ!	return the history to behind>!
l**ē**š ’aħ**a**d^{e}t m**i**nni l-haw**i**yye?	Why did you take my identity card [away] from me?
rajj**e**^{c}-li‿yy**ā**ha,	Give it back to me,
’**ɑ**llɑ‿iħall**ī**k!	please <may God preserve you>!
f**ā**t [if**ū**t]	he entered
f**a**wwat	he brought in; he let in; he let through; he put (something) into (something)
fawwat-ni ^{c}ala‿m**a**tḥaf	He let me into the museum without
min ġ**ē**r-ma ’**a**dfa^{c}.	paying <without that I pay (subj)>.
’**i**za b**i**ddo‿if**ū**t, f**a**wwto!	If he wants to come in, let him in!
’**i**za b**i**d(d)-ha‿tf**ū**t, faww**e**t-ha!	If she wants to come in, let her in!
ġ**i**leṭ	he was wrong
ġ**ɑ**llɑṭ	he misled; he caused (someone) to make a mistake
’**u**skot! b^{e}tġ**ɑ**ll**e**ṭni fi l-^{e}ḥs**ā**b!	Be quiet, you’re making me get my sum wrong!
ħ**i**reb [y**i**ħrɑb][1]	it broke down; it was destroyed / ruined
ħ**ɑ**rrɑb	he damaged; he destroyed; he broke / he caused to break down
ṣ**ɑ**llɑḥ[2]	he repaired
aħad il-mot**ō**r ta‿iṣ**ɑ**llḥo,	He took the engine to repair <that he
ħ**ɑ**rrɑbo!	repair-it> [and] ruined it!
ba^{c}**a**tt‿il-b**a**dle lal-ħɑyy**ā**ṭ	I sent the suit to the tailor to repair
ta‿iṣɑll**e**ḥ-ha, ħɑrr**ɑ**b-ha.	<it> [and] he ruined it!
il-m**a**tal biq**ū**l:	According to the proverb <the proverb says>:
’**a**ja‿ikaḥḥ**e**l-ha, ^{c}am**ā**-ha[3]	He came to put kohl round her eyes <to kohl-her> [and] blinded her!
(’**i**ja la-ika**ḥ**ḥlo, ^{c}am**ā**^{h})	He came to put ointment in his eyes, and blinded him!

---

1. ħarb**ā**n means *broken, damaged, no good* (see **Lesson 16**). It is an adjective derived from the verb ħ**i**reb [y**i**ħrɑb] in accordance with the rule explained in **Lesson 19, Explanations 3**. it-telef**ō**n ħarb**ā**n means *The telephone is out of order.*

2. ṣ**ā**leḥ, ṣ**ā**lḥɑ^{f} means *good; suitable; valid.*

3. ku**ḥ**^{o}l means *kohl; eye ointment.* The proverb is well-known. The other two verbs it contains will be explained in future lessons.

ṣɑd**ī**q		friend
ṣ**ɑ̄**deq̈# → s**ā**deq[4]		right, truthful, honest
s**a**ddaq[4]		he believed (someone)
sadd**e**q-ni!	*	Believe me!
'**i**za m**a** b^{e}ts**a**ddeq, '**i**s'al ġ**ē**ri!		If you don't believe [me], ask someone else <someone other than me>! (See **Book 1, p. 67**)
ma saddaqt**ō**-š		I didn't believe him.
bɑṭ**ɑ̄**le		unemployment, idleness
b**ɑ**ṭṭɑl		he stopped
bɑṭṭ**ɑ**lt 'ar**ū**ḥ la-^{c}**i**ndo[5].	*	I stopped visiting him <going to at-him>.
sal**ā**me		safety; wellbeing; welfare
s**a**llam[6]		he greeted; he sent [his] regards; he delivered / handed over (himself, his weapons, etc.) / gave (himself) up
il-ḥ**a**mdi-lla^{h} ^{c}a-s-sal**ā**me[7]!	*	Welcome back <praise to God on the (your) safety>!
'ab**ū**y bis**a**llem ^{c}al**ē**k/-ki		My dad sends you$^{m/f}$ [his] regards.
sall**e**m-li ^{c}ala 'ab**ū**k!	*	Send my regards to your dad!
s**a**llem!		Regards (to all at home)!
(The answer is:)		
sl**e**mt / sl**e**mti![8]	*	You$^{m/f}$ too <be healthy and whole>!
sall**a**mto‿l-makt**ū**b		I delivered the letter to him.

---

4. In colloquial Arabic, the ṣ becomes s in these words, just as ṣund**ū**q̈# *box, chest* (literary Arabic) becomes sand**ū**q in everyday conversation.

5. This is one way of translating *no longer. I no longer visit him* is bɑṭṭ**ɑ**lt 'az**ū**ro <I've stopped visiting him>. *She's stopped talking / She no longer speaks* is b**ɑ**ṭṭɑlɑt t**i**ḥki. Note that the verb following b**ɑ**ṭṭɑl is in the subjunctive.

6. In other words, *handed over something to someone*. Its relationship with the root meaning seems to lie in the idea of handing something over safely.

7. This is commonly said to someone who has returned from a journey, or from hospital, etc.

8. From the verb s**i**lem [y**i**slam], which is used mainly in this sort of expression. Why is it sall**e**m-li in the previous sentence? Because the meaning is: *Send on my behalf / in my name; Do **me** this service.*

sallam ḥālo laš-šurṭα[9]	He gave himself up to the police.
sallem ḥālak!	Give yourself up!
sallmu!	Give [yourselves] up!
sallamu slāḥ-hom	They handed over their weapon[s].

[This section is not included on the recording]

dabbαr	he arranged / he put in order
bidabber ḥalo	He manages <he puts himself in order>.
dabber ḥālak!	Sort things out for yourself <arrange yourself>!
'ana badabber-lak‿iyyā-ha.	I'll arrange it for you.

Out of this long series of sentences, try to remember at least the ones marked with a star *, and repeat them out loud several times. Now you're ready to go on to the Explanations, where you'll meet the **verbal noun** and learn something about its important functions.

Explanations

1. The verbal noun (VN)

The verbal noun denotes an action, activity or state expressed by a verb, e.g., singing, as in *She likes singing.*

a. Forming the verbal noun

Every verb Form in Arabic has a related verbal noun that conforms to a fixed pattern. Only in f-1 is there more than one pattern, the most common being □a□□. Examples derived from verbs taught in Book 1 are: **ta**rk, **ḍα**rb, '**a**kl, **ma**n^c, and **da**f^c (which, in accordance with Rule [5], receive a helping vowel as an aid to pronunciation at the end of a sentence, e.g., **da**f^c = **da**f^{ec}). We'll content ourselves with two more f-1 patterns for today: □□**ī**□e, e.g., kt**ī**be – *writing*; and □u□**ū**□, e.g., du**ḫū**l – *entering*, derived from **da**ḫal$^{\#}$ [**yu**dḫol] meaning *to enter.*

Now we can move on to Form 2 verbs. **The verbal noun of f-2 invariably assumes the pattern** ta□□**ī**□ [2]. Let's look at verbal nouns derived from verbs you've just learned:

■ ġ**a**yyαr *he changed* taġy**ī**r *change*

9. š**ur**ṭα [2] means *police* in official Arabic, but bul**ī**s (from English *police*) is more commonly used in everyday conversation. *Police officer* is š**ur**ṭi or... w**ā**ḥad bul**ī**s.

rakkab	*he assembled*	tarkīb	*assembly, putting together*
qɑrrɑb	*he brought closer*	taqrīb	*bringing closer / together*
and consequently:		taqrīban	*approximately* (see p. 35)
ђɑrrɑb	*he destroyed*	takђrīb	*destruction*
sallam	*he handed over*	taslīm	*handing-over, delivery*
sajjal	*he registered, recorded*	tasjīl[10]	*registration, recording*

b. Using the verbal noun

Arabic uses the VN in the same way as English (e.g., *He prefers **talking** to **listening***), but also employs it in cases where English uses the infinitive of the verb (which Arabic does not possess). For example:

■ manaᶜ il-walad ᶜan 'akl‿il-laḥme — *He forbade the child to eat the meat.*

manaᶜ-ni min id-duђūl — *He prevented me from entering.*

ђɑllɑṣ (± min) tarkīb il-motōr — *He finished assembling the engine.*

mamnūᶜ‿id-duђūl — *No entry* <forbidden the entering>.

Note that in Arabic the verbal noun is usually preceded by the definite article il- except in the construct form where, as usual, the article appears only before the second of the two nouns, e.g., tarkīb il-motōr.

The verbal noun opens up new horizons for us and we'll revisit it at every stage of our studies and as each new verb Form is introduced, from Form 3 to Form 10. For today, it's enough to make a superficial acquaintance with it. If only you could learn everything in a single lesson – but you can't! You have to progress step by step. ᶜala fikrɑ (*by the way* <on a thought>), how do you say: *If only he had...we would have ...*? That's the next topic.

2. If only (it were so...., but ...) = law

Something like this came up in Book 1 (see **Lesson 13, Explanations 3**), but so far most of the conditional sentences we have encountered have started with 'iza (*if*). 'iza is used when it is possible for the condition to be met, for example, *If you know ...*(and you could easily know); *If you come tomorrow* ...(and you probably can).

---

10. See **footnote 18, page 28.**

But when speaking about a situation that does not exist, i.e., when "*If (only) ...*" can be followed by *"but that's not the case,"* the word used for *if* is l**a**w (pronounced as in "loud"). For example:

l**a**w q**a**l-li	*If (only) he had told me* (then)	(but he didn't!)
l**a**w ba^c^ref...	*If (only) I knew* (now)	(but I don't.)

These examples illustrate an important point: in Arabic it is easy to know which tense to use after l**a**w. The rule is simple:

– The **past tense** is used when the situation did not exist **in the past**.

– The **present-future tense** is used in relation to a theoretical situation that does not exist **in the present** (nor, apparently, in the future).

This rule applies to both the conditional clause and the main clause that expresses what would have happened *if* ..., but in the main clause it is usual to insert the auxiliary k**ā**n, k**u**nt... before the verb, as in the following examples:

Relating to the past:

■ l**a**w š**ā**f-ni, k**ā**n sa'**a**l-ni — *If he'd seen me* (then), *he would have asked me* (but he didn't see me).

l**a**w š**u**fto, k**u**nt qult-**i**llo — *If I'd seen him* (yesterday), *I would have told him.*

Relating to the present:

l**a**w ba^c^ref w**ē**no, k**u**nt b**a**s'alo — *If I knew* (now) *where he was, I would ask him.*

l**a**w b**a**qdɑr, kunt b**a**kteb — *If I could* (today, tomorrow) *I would write ...*

And as we like to set little brain-teasers for our students – or, more precisely, step in before a problem arises, we'll remind you of the expression kunt '**a**kteb (see **Lesson 22, Explanations 7**). What is the difference between kunt b**a**kteb and kunt '**a**kteb? The following sentences will demonstrate:

■ qab^e^l s**a**ne (s**i**ne^G^) — *A year ago*

kunt '**a**kteb la-'**i**mmi kull j**u**m^c^a — *I used to write to my mother every week.*

law b**a**qdɑr, — *If I could,*

kunt b**a**kteb la-ṣ**ɑ̄**ḥbi (h**a**llaq) — *I would write to my friend* (now).

– The first case (kunt '**a**kteb) uses the subjunctive to express the **habitual past tense**.

– In the second case (kunt b**a**kteb), the use of the present-future with the b-prefix denotes **a non-existent situation in the present** (*I would write, but I can't*).

By now you don't need to be told not to panic. You can be confident that we'll provide plenty of authentic examples of these differences.

Recently (in **Lesson 23**) we started a new section called "Getting to the root of it." It could also be called:

Root and branch

You've now reached the stage where you can start to play around with Arabic roots and discover their hidden treasures. Let's take n-ẓ-m, for example:

■	niẓ**ā**m	*order; regime*
	l**ā**zem ik**ū**n-f**ī**h niẓ**ā**m!	*There's got to be order!*
	in-niẓ**ā**m id-dimūqr**ā**ṭi	*the democratic regime / system*
	n**a**ẓẓam (f-2)	*to put in order / arrange / organize*
	m**ī**n bin**a**ẓẓem ir-re**ḥ**le?	*Who's organizing the trip?*
	tanẓ**ī**m[11] [2]	*organization* (*the act of organizing*)
	mun**a**ẓẓame [8]	*organization* (*group*) = passive participle, f sing = *organized*

Here is a verbal noun related to an adjective we learned in Lesson 21:

■	ḥorr – ḥ**a**rrar – taḥr**ī**r	*free – to free – liberation*
	mun**a**ẓẓamet it-taḥr**ī**r	*The (Palestine) Liberation Organization (PLO)*
	Palestinians shorten it to:	
	il-mun**a**ẓẓame	*The Organization*

We've started to dabble here in the vocabulary of politics, which we'll need in order to understand Arabic news broadcasts and TV interviews. It's too early for you to learn how to say *The United Nations,* because you haven't yet learned the Verb Form that enables you to express it in Arabic. ᶜala **fi**kra, we can already talk about *unification*!

■	w**ā**ḥed – wa**ḥ**ḥad (f-2)	*one – to unite*
	tawḥ**ī**d 'alm**ā**nya[12]	*[the re-]unification of Germany*
	...il-'alm**ā**niyat**ē**n	(or) *...of the two Germanies*

---

11. it-tanẓ**ī**m is the name of a group within the Palestinian Fatah (**Fa**teḥ) movement.

12. The reunification of Germany took place in 1990, when Book 2 of this course was first published in Hebrew! Today the talk is of tawḥ**ī**d 'U**ru**bba (*Europe*) in the EU.

Now it's time for you to practice expressing yourself with the wealth of vocabulary you've learned in this lesson.

Exercises

A. Translate into English:

1. ᶜɑrrɑfni ᶜala 'ahlo.
2. bidna‿tᶜɑrrfīna ᶜala 'ahlek.
3. bil-'awwal qāl: mā biddi! baᶜdēn ġayyɑr fikro.
4. 'uђti ġayyarat fikᵉr-ha. bɑṭṭɑlɑt‿ᵉtzūr-hom.
5. qul-lo‿iqarreb ᶜala‿š-šubbāk.
6. lāzem‿ᵉtrajjeᶜ-lo‿l-muftāḥ.
7. rajjaᶜt-illo‿yyāʰ ᵉmbāreḥ.
8. law‿ᵉᶜmelᵉt zayy-ma qult-illak, ma kān ṣār illi ṣār.
9. law kān ᶜindi mākinet‿ᵉḥsāb, kunt ђɑllɑṣᵉt min zamān.
10. ђɑlɑṣ! bɑṭṭɑlt 'alᶜab maᶜo!
11. law bākol‿ᵉktīr, kān bɑṭni būjaᶜni.
12. qabᵉl kunt 'ākol‿ᵉktīr, kān bɑṭni yūjaᶜni.

B. Complete the sentences

(Replace the English words with the appropriate expression in Arabic):

13. mīn 'ɑfḍɑl (Arab singer^{m}) ᶜindak?
14. (Play^{m} me <cause me to hear>) 'akam min 'uġniye, (then afterwards> baqul-lak.
15. (We played) 'aġāni la-ṣḥābna.
16. il-'aġāni illi (we played [to] them <that we played-them it^{f}>).
17. 'ayya sēᶜa (did you^{pl} finish)‿mbāreḥ?
18. 'iza biddak‿ᵉ ([to] go home), lāzem‿ᵉ (you finish) šuġlak.
19. baᶜdēn‿ᵉ(you$^{m\ sing}$ can)‿ᵉtrawweḥ.
20. lamma‿wṣelna‿l-mɑḥɑṭṭɑ, qult-illo: (Stop!)
21. wēn id-diskāt illi (you$^{m\ sing}$ brought <it>).
22. wēn id-diskāt illi (I brought you$^{f\ sing}$ <it>)?
23. biddo‿iᶜallem ibno, (he wants to enable him to study <to teach him>).
24. u-binto kamān, biddo (to teach her).

C. Translate into Arabic:

25. I liked this singer very much. He has a very nice voice <his voice very sweet>.
26. They're building new houses.
27. We want to enable my son to study <to teach my son>.
28. In the beginning I didn't understand, but the teacher helped-me-to-understand / explained [to] me.
29. He didn't understand what happened and I explained [it] to him.
30. Did you[m sing] close the door? – Not yet. – Close it! (**bāb** [m])
31. Latifa, did you close the door? – No, I didn't close it. – You must close it!
32. I've written to Munir. I've written him a letter. This is the letter I wrote him <that I wrote to him it>.
33. I've brought you[m sing] [some] disks (**disk** [2] [**diskāt**]); I want you to play me a song <one song>.
34. Which song do you[m sing] want? – Whichever you want <[that] which you-want it>.
35. He stopped the truck in front of our house.
36. He taught me [some] new words. – Which words did he teach you[m] <what the words that he taught you>?
37. Did he bring the book to the teacher? – Yes, he brought him a book.
38. When did he bring him it? – The day before yesterday.

d**a**rs tam**ā**nye u-ʿišr**ī**n

28

Lesson Twenty-Eight

It's time to go back to Form 1 of the verb (also known as f**a**ʿal), as we haven't yet described all the various sub-groups it contains. You're already familiar with several of these groups – verbs of the k**a**tab, n**i**zel, sh**ū**f, j**ī**b and n**ā**m types – and now it's time for you to meet Form 1 verbs whose 3rd root letter is -i. One of these is the verb ḥ**a**ka (*he spoke, he told*), whose root is ḥ-k-i. Even though the -i of the root doesn't appear in the past tense (in the 3rd person masculine singular it turns into an -a; in the 3rd person plural it vanishes altogether; and in the 1st and 2nd persons it turns into a long -**ē** – see the paradigm below), it's prominent in many other manifestations of the verb.
The paradigm of the verb ḥ**a**ka in the **past tense** is as follows:

I / you[m sing] spoke	ḥak**ē**t	ḥ**a**ka	*he spoke*
you[f sing] spoke	ḥak**ē**ti	ḥ**a**kat	*she spoke*
we spoke	ḥak**ē**na	ḥ**a**ku	*they spoke*
you[pl] spoke	ḥak**ē**tu		

Note that the long **-ē** appears in the 1st and 2nd persons only, and that the stress, which is on the first syllable in the 3rd person, "moves on" to the second syllable in the 1st and 2nd persons, as we've already seen with k**a**tab → kat**a**bt.

In the **present-future** and the **subjunctive** the -i of the root is present in all singular forms and in the 1st person plural. It vanishes, however, in the 2nd and 3rd person plural before the suffix -u:

b**a**ḥki	*I speak, I tell*	'**a**ḥki	*that I speak*
bt**i**ḥki	*you[m sing] speak / will speak*	t**i**ḥki	*that you[m sing] speak*
bt**i**ḥki	*you[f sing] speak / will speak*	t**i**ḥki	*that you[f sing] speak*
b[y]**i**ḥki	*he speaks / will speak*	y**i**ḥki	*that he speak*
bt**i**ḥki	*she speaks / will speak*	t**i**ḥki	*that she speak*
bn**i**ḥki (mn**i**-)	*we speak / will speak*	n**i**ḥki	*that we speak*
bt**i**ḥku	*you[pl] speak / will speak*	t**i**ḥku	*that you[pl] speak*
b[y]**i**ḥku	*they speak / will speak*	y**i**ḥku	*that they speak*

You'll have noticed that the forms for the 2nd person singular (*you*) are the same in both the masculine and the feminine. This represents a 12.5% saving in the number of forms you have to learn in this paradigm!

As expected, you will hear the form mniḥki (*we speak*) more often in Galilee; also, most people say biḥki / biḥku rather than byiḥki / byiḥku.

Here is a list of some other verbs in the same family:

rama [yirmi]	*to throw*	ġala [yiġli]	*to boil* (trans and intrans)
bana [yibni]	*to build*	ṭɑfɑ [yiṭfi][1]	*to turn off / extinguish*
mɑḍɑ [yimḍi]	*to sign*	ḍɑwɑ [yiḍwi][1]	*to light / turn on; to illuminate*

The active participle is:

rāmi, rāmye[f] [rāmyīn] = *thrower / having thrown.*

Example: 'ana māḍi means *I'm a signatory; I've signed* <I am having-signed>.

The passive participle is:

marmi (mermi), f marmiyye [marmiyyīn] = *thrown*

Further examples:

mabni (mebni) = *built*; mɑḍwi = *lit / on / turned on*; maġli = *boiled*

Vocabulary

majbūr[2]	forced, obliged	bil-mɑrrɑ	completely; [not] at all
ᶜāš [iᶜīš]	to live, be alive	'iṭfā'i ['iṭfā'iyye]	firefighter
ṭɑqṣ [2]	weather	jurṯūme [jarāṯīm]	germ, microbe
fāḍi	empty; vacant; free	wād [widyān]	valley, gully, *wadi*
il-ᶜīše [8]	lifestyle, way of life	ḥārɑ [8] [ḥārāt]	neighborhood, quarter
tɑfṣīl [2]	detail	nusḫa [2] [8] [nusaḫ]	copy (n)
ḥarīqa	fire, blaze	ᶜēn [eᶜyūn]	eye; spring (water source)
dawwɑr	to turn (f-2)	dawwɑr ᶜala	to look for

---

1. There is no need to remind you (but we will, nonetheless!) why some verbs have an -a while others have an -ɑ: "emphatic" consonants such as ḍ, ṭ and ṣ affect the pronunciation of the vowels around them. The -i, too, sounds more like *e* or even *o*: yiṭfi → yeṭfi, almost yoṭfi.

2) jabɑr [yujbor] = to force / compel. jabɑrūni = *They forced me / They made me do [it]*.

Conversation – Part 1

– btiḥki ᶜarabi?	– Do you speak Arabic?
– 'aywa, baḥki šwayy.	– Yes, I speak a little.
– u-aђūk, biḥki 'inglīzi?	– And your[m] brother, does he speak English?
– 'ā, ktīr‿emnīḥ! majbūr yiḥki.	– Yes, very well! He has to speak [it] <he's obliged to speak…>.
marato 'inglīziyye u-dāyman biḥku 'inglīzi maᶜ baᶜeḍ.	His wife's English and they always speak English together.
– kīf ? marato btiḥkī-š ᶜarabi?	– Why <how>? Doesn't his wife speak Arabic?
– wala kilme. bteᶜraf-š ᶜarabi bil-marra.	– Not a word! She doesn't know Arabic at all.
– ḥakēt maᶜha 'iši[3]?	– Have you spoken to her at all <something>?
– 'ā, ḥakēna sawa marrāt‿ektīre. bil-'inglīzi ᶜan‿eblād-ha,	– Yes, we've often talked together in English about her homeland < her country>,
ᶜan in-nās, kīf ᶜāyšīn hunāk.	about people [and] how they live there.
– šu ḥakat? šu ḥakat-lak ᶜan il-ᶜīše hunāk.	– What did she say? What did she tell you about life there?
– kull 'iši: kīf ᶜāyšīn fi 'ingeltra, fi-l-mudon[4] u-fi-l-q̈ura	– All sorts of things <every thing>: how they live in England, in the towns and the villages,

3. ši or 'iši at the end of a question means *perhaps / at all.*

4. madīne [mudon] = *town* and q̈arye [q̈ura] = *village*. The word balad, which is feminine, can mean either *town* or *village*, while blād (bilād#) – also feminine – means *state / country.* fi blād-na = *in our country / in our homeland.*

u-kīf iṭ-ṭaqṣ...	and what the weather's like…
– 'ēmta raḥ-tiḥkī-li	– When will you tell me
kull hāda bit-tafṣīl?	all this in detail?
– 'issa // halqēt muš fāḍi,	– [I'm] not free at the moment,
bass kamān sēᶜa	but in an hour's [time] I'll tell
baḥkī-lak kull 'iši biddak.	you everything you want.

– mā-lak ṣāfen?	– Why are you [so] preoccupied?
mā-lak sāket?	Why are you so quiet?
'iḥki[5]!	Say something <speak>!
qūl šū ṣār maᶜak.	Tell [me] what's wrong with you <what has happened with you>.
íḥkī-li‿l-quṣṣa kull-ha.	Tell me the whole story!
– šu biddi aḥkī-lak, ya zalame?	– What can I tell you, man?
ṣaᶜeb, ṣaᶜeb! 'afḍal niḥki ᶜan	[It's] hard, hard! Better that we talk about
'iši tāni 'aw nuskot bil-marra.	something else, or don't say anything at all!

– futᵉt ᶜa-l-bēt u-ḍawēt.	– I went into the house and turned on [the
yaᶜni biddi aḍwi,	light]. That's to say, I wanted <I want>
fišš kahraba.	to turn [it] on – no electricity!
jibᵉt qandīl u-ḍawēto.	I brought an oil lamp and lit it.
baᶜdēn rijᶜat il-kahraba, ḍawat.	Then the electricity came back [on] and there was light <[it] illuminated>,
ṭafēt il-qandīl.	[so] I turned off the oil lamp.
– lēš ṭafētīʰ? ma teṭfī-hō-š[6]!	– Why did you turn it off? Don't turn it off!
ђallīʰ[7] maḍwi, 'iḥtiyāṭ[8].	Leave it on, [as a] precaution.

---

5. Remember that the imperative is formed by replacing the ti- of the 2nd person subjunctive with 'i-
- tiḥki (*that you speak*) → 'iḥki = *speak!* m/f
- tirmi (*that you throw*) → 'irmi = *throw!* m/f

6. -hō-š?? This new style of suffix will be discussed in **Explanations 2** below.

7. ђalli! is the imperative of a verb you haven't learned yet. You'll make its partial acquaintance in **Explanations 5** in Part 2, below.

8. iḥtiyāṭ = *precaution.* The word for *army* is jēš, and jēš il-iḥtiyāṭ means *reserves / reserve forces.*

– il-jirān miš fil-bēt.	– The neighbors aren't home.
– ^{e}mbala, 'iza ḍāwyīn[9],	– Yes, they are. If there's a light on <if [they're] illuminating>
ma^{c}nāto[10] humme fi-l-bēt.	that means they're at home.
lamma biṭla^{c}u, biṭfu‿ḍ-ḍaww[11].	When they go out, they turn off the light.
or b^{y}eṭla^{c}u, b^{y}eṭfu...	

---

kānat il-lamba maḍwiyye	The lamp was on <lit>.
'aja[12] Yūsef ṭafā-ha.	[Along] came Yusef [and] turned it off.
ṣār fī^{h} ḥarīqa fi ḥāret-na	A fire broke out in our neighborhood.
'ajat[13] il-'iṭfā'iyye ṭafū-ha.	The firefighters came and put it out.
'iḍwi – 'iḍwī-ha!	Turn on – Turn + it^{f} on! / Light + it^{f}!
'iṭfi – 'iṭfī-ha!	Turn off – Turn + it^{f} off! / Put + it^{f} out!

šūf! il-bēt hadāk mabni	Look, that house is built
fi-l-wād. 'amma ^{c}ādatan	in the valley. But
fi hādi‿l-manṭiqa[14], l-^{e}byūt	in this area the houses are usually built
mabniyye ^{c}ala rūs l-^{e}jbāl.	on the hilltops <on the heads of the hills>.

---

9. ḍāwi (active participle) = *having-lit*; 'ana ḍāwi = *I've turned on...*

10. See below, **Explanations 3.**

11. lamma biṭla^{c}u reminds us of the rule in **Lesson 23, Explanations 3**: this is a habitual action, and the present-future tense is used after lamma. However, if we want to say *When you go out, turn off the light* (i.e., a one-time action) we use the subjunctive: lamma tiṭla^{c}, 'iṭfi‿ḍ-ḍaww. When iḍ-ḍaww (*the light*) occurs at the end of the sentence, we don't hear the doubled -w. However, in a phrase like ḍaww il-qamar (*moonlight*) the doubling is heard. The word nūr#, which you encountered in the phrase *morning of light* in **Book 1, p. 8**, also means *light* but it is borrowed from the literary language, and is used only in certain specific phrases like ṣabāḥ in-nūr.

12. 'ija // 'aja ('ijat // 'ajat) means *he came* (*she came*). We'll learn this verb soon (in Lesson 30).

13. Why is the verb in the feminine singular? See below, **Explanations 1**.

14. manṭiqa [manāṭeq] means *area / region*. il-manāṭeq il-muḥtalle = *the occupied territories*. Arabic-speaking Israelis refer to them as il-manāṭeq. We'll learn the accompanying adjective (actually a passive participle) on another occasion.

Explanations - Part 1

1. byūt mabniyye and other curious phenomena

In **Lesson 25, Explanations 3** we saw how the expression *new houses* was translated into Arabic as byūt jdīde (i.e., a masculine plural noun followed by an adjective in the feminine singular), and in this lesson we have another example: byūt mabniyye. The rule is that any plural noun **that does not designate human beings** requires a feminine singular verb / adjective; this also applies to all attached pronouns that refer back to the noun.
The same rule applies to nouns that denote a **group of people** (e.g., in-nās = *the people*, l-ewlād = *the children*). In this case, too, the verb is in the feminine singular, especially when it **precedes** the noun:

rāḥat in-nās / in-nās rāḥu	*The people went*
ṣārat l-ewlād turkoḍ	*The children started to run*

That is why, in today's **Conversation**, the word *firefighters* is preceded by a feminine singular verb, but followed by a plural one:

'ajat il-'iṭfā'iyye ṭafū-ha. *The firefighters came and put it out.*

However, we've already seen that nouns denoting human beings are followed by an **adjective in the plural**: nās ṭayybīn (*good people*), il-jirān mabsūṭīn (*the neighbors are pleased*), talāmīz šāṭrīn (*good students*), etc. In urban speech the plural is the same for masculine and feminine nouns; in rural speech' however, there is a separate feminine plural form:

banāt ḥilwīn = *pretty girls* (in rural speech they are usually banāt ḥilwāt)
ḫawāti mitjaw(w)zīn = *My sisters are married* (in rural speech: mitjawwzāt)

There is, however, one instance in which townies and country people speak the same way: when a noun designating a human female is followed by an adjective whose feminine singular ending is -iyye. In this case the feminine plural ending is always -iyyāt, in both town and country.

fatāh ᶜarabiyye	*an Arab girl*	fatayātᶜarabiyyāt	*Arab girls*
fatāh yahūdiyye	*a Jewish girl*	fatayāt yahūdiyyāt	*Jewish girls*

But we say bāṣāt ᶜarabiyye (*Arab[-owned] buses*), because we're not talking about human beings.

To sum up, remember these examples:

b**ē**t‿ᵉjd**ī**d	by**ū**t‿ᵉjd**ī**de
r**ɑ̄**ḥat in-n**ā**s	in-n**ā**s r**ɑ̄**ḥu
ewl**ā**d šɑ̄ṭr**ī**n	
ban**ā**t ḥilw**ī**n / ḥilw**ā**t	
fatay**ā**t ᶜɑrɑbiyy**ā**t	

2. We didn't see him – ma šufnā-h**ō**-š

In the **Conversation** you encountered the sentence ma tiṭfī-h**ō**-š, which means *Don't turn it off / Don't put it out!* (depending on whether you're talking about an electric light or a fire). You will recall from **Book 1, p. 72** that biz**ū**ru (*they visit*) → bizūr**ū**ʰ (*they visit **him***). Now let's take a look at the three expressions below:

b**ɑ**ṭfi	bɑṭf**ī**ʰ	ma bɑṭfī-h**ō**-š
I turn off	*I turn it off*	*I don't turn it off*

Back in **Book 1**, on **p. 69**, we said that the final -h that means *him* after a verb ending in a vowel was silent – but we added that it would come in useful in the future. This -h is the remnant of the suffix -hu used in literary Arabic, where yazūr**ū**hu means *they visit him.* In colloquial speech, when the sentence is negated by adding -š, the *u* sound "comes back to life." We can sum this up in the following formula:

(ā/ī/ū)ʰ + -š = -h**ō**š

Here are a few examples:

š**u**fna	šufn**ā**ʰ	ma šufnā-h**ō**-š
we saw	*we saw him*	*we didn't see him*
š**u**fti	šuft**ī**ʰ	ma šuftī-h**ō**-š
you[f sing] *saw*	*you*[f sing] *saw him*	*you*[f sing] *didn't see him*
ṭ**ɑ**fɑ	ṭɑf**ɑ̄**ʰ	ma ṭɑfɑ̄-h**ō**-š
he turned off	*he turned it off*	*he didn't turn it off*

3. ya**ᶜ**ni, ma**ᶜ**na …

You learned the first of the words above way back in Lesson 2, and now it's time to investigate its origins. The word ᶜ**a**na [y**e**ᶜni] belongs to the group of verbs we're studying today, and so it conjugates like ḥ**a**ka; it means *to mean / indicate / intend,* e.g., šu bʸ**e**ᶜni b-hal-kal**ā**m? = *what does he mean by that*

<what does he mean with this speech>? The word yaᶜni is the literary Arabic form of the colloquial bʸeᶜni (*he / it means*), and it is the equivalent of English expressions like *that's to say..., in other words...* and *I mean....* šū yaᶜni? = *What does [that] mean?*

The word maᶜna [maᶜāni], which means *meaning, significance, sense*, comes from the same root. With the attached pronouns it can also take the form maᶜnā- / maᶜnāt-, e.g.,

■ hal-kilme, smeᶜt-ha, bass ma baᶜref šu maᶜnāt-ha.
This word – I've heard it, but I don't know what it means <what [is] its meaning>.
'iza qāl hēk, maᶜnāʰ ma biddō-š.
If he said that <thus>, *it means* <its meaning [is]> *that he doesn't want [to].*
muš maᶜnāto inno rafaḍ.
It doesn't mean <its meaning [is] not> *that he refused.*

Before we take our leave of this root, let's look at one more sentence, which will teach you a very useful new word:

hal-kilme ᶜindha ᶜiddet maᶜāni.
This word has a number of meanings <this word, at it a number of meanings>.

The word ᶜidde, when used in the construct form (ᶜiddet), means *several / a number of*, especially when discussing abstract concepts. ᶜidde is used in educated speech, unlike kam / 'akam (see **Book 1, p. 102**).

■ kam marra / ᶜiddet marrāt# — *several times*
fīʰ ᶜiddet mašākel. — *There are a number of problems.*

Exercises – Part 1

A. Translate into English:

1. bteᶜraf 'ēš ђakū-li fi-l-maktab?
2. 'ana majbūr 'aḥkī-lek il-quṣṣa min 'awwal-ha.
3. šū ᶜam-biḥki? muš fāhem kalāmo.
4. il-qandīl kān meḍwi, lēš ṭafētīʰ?
5. 'iḥki šwayy‿ešwayy ᶜašān 'afham.
6. law kān-fīʰ kahraba mbēreḥ, kunt ṭafēt il-qandīl.
7. law fīʰ kahraba halqēt, kunt baṭfīʰ.
8. ђod ir-rādyo, ṣallaḥt-illak‿iyyāha.

9. hiyye ᶜam-(b)tiḥki maᶜo, maᶜnāto bʸeᶜrafu bɑᶜᵉḍ.
10. bɑṭṭɑl yiḥki maᶜi, zaᶜlān minni, mbayyen.

B. Complete the sentences

(Replace the English words with the appropriate expression in Arabic):

11. biḥki maᶜ 'aħūʰ, bass (he doesn't speak) maᶜ 'uħto.
12. 'aywa, (he stopped) yiḥki maᶜha.
13. ḥakā-li (what [had] happened) bit-tɑfṣīl.
14. u-hiyye, šu ḥakat? – (She told me) quṣṣɑ ġarībe.
15. kīf (the weather) ᶜin(d)kom?
16. šu (do you mean) lamma bᵉtqūl "ᶜindkom"?
17. ᶜindkom, yaᶜni fi-l-jalīl (= *in Galilee*).
18. (Close$^{m\ sing}$) iš-šubbāk, fīʰ mɑjrɑ hawa w-il-qandīl inṭɑfɑ[15].
19. šuftu l-ᵉmᶜallem? – la', ma (we haven't seen-him) -š.
20. lāzem (you speak^{pl}) maᶜ il-mudīr fi ([the] end [of]) iš-šahᵉr.

C. Translate into Arabic:

21. Why are you building your house there, on the hill?
22. Why don't you build it here, next to our house?
23. What are you saying (at the moment)[16]?
24. Now I'm free. Sit down$^{f\ sing}$ here and tell me stories.
25. Can't you$^{m\ sing}$ hear <you don't hear> what I'm saying?
26. I want to tell you$^{m\ sing}$ a joke[17].
27. The joke you told me <it> – I heard it yesterday.
28. The firefighters put out the fire. People <the people> brought water to put out the fire.
29. Shall I turn off the oil lamp[18]? No, don't turn it off.
30. She doesn't have to tell him everything.

---

15. Do you remember Form 7 of the verb (infaᶜal), which we talked about in Lesson 26? The verb ṭɑfɑ means *to put out / extinguish,* and inṭɑfɑ (Form 7 of the same root) means *to get put out / to be extinguished.* 'immi ṭɑfɑt in-nɑ̄r = *My mother put out the fire*, while in-nɑ̄r inṭɑfɑt = *The fire was put out.* Note that the word for *fire* is feminine in Arabic.

16. To convey the notion of "at the moment," use the prefix ᶜam- before the present-future tense.

17. nukte [2] [8]. See Lesson 18.

18. In Arabic, literally: [Is it necessary that] I turn off the lamp? See **Book 1, p. 72, footnote 4**.

Conversation – Part 2

– mīn rama hal-ḥajar?	– Who threw that stone?
ya Najīb, lēš ramēt ḥajar?	Najib, why did you throw a stone?
ḍarab^{e}t fī^{h} iš-šubbāk	You hit the window with it
u-kasart lōḥ il-qazāz[19]!	and broke the window pane!
– la', muš ana!	– No, it wasn't me <no, not I>!
yaᶜni Mūsa qal-li	That's to say, Musa told me,
'irmi ḥajar ᶜa-l-ḥēṭ	"Throw a stone at <on> the wall,
u-ana‿t-tāni biddi armi ḥajar	and I'll throw a stone too
ta‿nšūf mīn 'ašṭar.	so that we can see who does it better <so that we see who is cleverer>."
– walla[20], 'intu šāṭrīn tnēnāt-kom!	– Boy, you're a clever pair <you're clever the two of you>!
šūf šu‿ᶜmeltu!	Look what you've done!
hēk id-dinya: il-wāḥad b^{y}eᶜmel	That's the way of the world: someone
'iši muš‿^{e}mnīḥ u-baᶜdēn	does something bad then he lays
b^{y}irmi‿l-mas'ūliyye ᶜala ġēro.	the blame on <throws the responsibility onto> someone else.

---

19. Literally <the glass board>; lōḥ [lwāḥ] means *board / plank. Glass* = qazāz (in literary Arabic: zujāj#). *Two window panes* = lōḥēn qazāz.

20. w- before a noun sometimes indicates an oath: w-allāh(i)# = *By God!* Some people prefer not to take God's name in vain, but most speakers don't really consider the shortened form walla to be an oath.

– daww**a**rt ᶜala‿š-šāk**ū**š ma laq**ē**t**ō**-š[21]. – ’**a**na laq**ē**to m**a**rmi fi-z-zb**ā**le.	– I looked for the hammer, [but] I couldn’t find it. – I found it thrown in the rubbish / the trash.
– laq**ē**na‿l-jar**ɑ**yed marm**i**yye ᶜala‿l-’**ɑ**rḍ.	– We found the newspapers thrown on the ground.
– l**ā**zem t**i**ġli‿l-m**ɑ**yy. f**ī**ha jaraṯ**ī**m, yaᶜni makrub**ā**t	– You’ve got to boil the water. There are germs in it, that’s to say, microbes.
– b**a**ᶜref, ġal**ē**t-ha / ṣ**e**rt ġāl**ī**-ha[22]. ’**a**na b**a**šrɑb bass m**ɑ**yy maġl**i**yye.	– I know, I’ve already boiled it. I drink only boiled water.
– mɑḍ**ē**t il-makt**ū**b.	– I’ve signed the letter.
– ṭ**ɑ**yyeb, w**ē**n iṭ-ṭ**ɑ**lɑb?	– OK, where’s the application?
– hiyy**ā**ʰ // h**a**yyo h**ō**n, f**ī**ʰ t**a**lat n**u**saẖ.	– Here it is. There are three copies.
– l**ā**zem t**i**mḍi ᶜala kull n**u**sẖa. ’**i**mḍi h**ō**n, t**a**ḥᵉt.	– You must sign each copy. Sign here, at the bottom <below>.

Explanations - Part 2

4. There are people who think… The vanishing relative pronoun

In English we often drop the words *that / which / whom*, etc. from a sentence. We can say either:

the man ***whom*** *I saw* or *the man I saw*

the table ***that*** *she bought* or *the table she bought*

with no difference in meaning whatsoever.

However, we cannot always do this. The word *who* cannot be dropped in the same way:

the man who came yesterday does not mean the same thing as *the man came yesterday.*

In Arabic, too, the relative pronouns (*that / which / who / whom*, etc., all of which translate into Arabic as illi) are often dropped, but the rules that govern this are quite different from those of English.

---

21. For details of this verb see below, **Explanations 5a.**

22. We know that the adjective ġ**ā**li means *dear*. But ġ**ā**li is also the active participle of the verb ġ**a**la, which means *to boil*; ’**a**na ġ**ā**li = *I’ve already boiled...*

If you look back at today's Conversation, you'll notice that the phrase kull '**i**ši b**i**ddak, which we can translate into English as either *everything you want* or *everything that you want*, does not include the word illi (*that*). However, when we say in Arabic *the man I saw yesterday / the man whom I saw yesterday* (=iz-z**a**lame illi š**u**fto‿mb**ā**reḥ), we have to say illi. Why is this?

When the noun that precedes the words *that / which / who / whom* is indefinite (i.e., when we are talking about ***a*** *man* or *men,* not about ***the*** *man* or ***the*** *men*), the word illi is **not used**. Compare the following sentences:

■ ji**b**^{e}t l-^{e}kt**ā**b illi laq**ē**to fi-š-š**ā**re^{c}.	*I brought* ***the book*** *that I had found in the street.*
ji**b**t‿^{e}kt**ā**b laq**ē**to fi-š-š**ā**re^{c}.	*I brought* ***a book*** *that I had found in the street.*

Now we can translate the sentence that serves as a title for this section of the Explanations – but first we have to mention that the Arabic for *think* is f**a**kkɑr (no surprises here: this is a Form 2 verb from the same root as the word f**i**k^{e}r, which means *thought*). Let's compare the following sentences:

■ in-n**ā**s illi bif**a**kkru inno '**a**na mɑr**ī**ḍ	***The people*** *who think that I'm ill...*
f**ī**^{h} n**ā**s bif**a**kkru inno '**a**na mɑr**ī**ḍ	*There are* ***people*** *who think that I'm ill.*

We'll come across many similar examples in the future. In the meantime the exercises will give you an opportunity to practice applying this rule, which will eventually become second nature. (Yes, we say this the whole time, but it doesn't hurt to repeat it yet again!)

5. Two verbs with which you are (vaguely) familiar: l**a**qa and ḫ**a**lla

a. l**a**qa

These verbs might be familiar, but they have their own special peculiarities! You have met the word laq**ē**t (*I found*) and now it's time to learn the rest of the paradigm in the past tense, as it conjugates like ḥ**a**ka. Read out loud:

laq**ē**t, laq**ē**ti, l**a**qa, l**a**qat, laq**ē**na, laq**ē**tu, l**a**qu

What an excellent opportunity this gives you to practice what you learned in **Explanations 2** of this lesson! Let's compare:

■ laq**ē**na,	laqēn**ā**^{h}	ma laqēnā-h**ō**-š
we found	*we found him*	*we didn't find him*

Why did we talk about learning the paradigm in the **past tense**? Because in the subjunctive and the present-future this verb conjugates like Form 3, which you have not yet learned (it's on the menu for Book 3).

b. ƕalla

■ We encountered this verb in the expressions '**α**llα iƕallī-lak ewlādak (see **Book 1, p. 100, footnote 11**) and'**α**llα iƕallīk! (Lesson 27); its imperative form (ƕ**a**lli! = *leave! / let!*) appears in Part 1 of the Conversation earlier in this lesson. Today we're going to talk about the paradigm in the past tense only.

Although the conjugation of ƕ**a**lla resembles that of ḥ**a**ka, you can tell it's a Form 2 verb because the second root letter (-l-) is doubled. ƕ**a**lla means *to leave; to let / allow; to make (someone do something).* At the beginning of Lesson 26 we reassured you that all Verb Forms – from f-2 all the way to f-10 – conjugate **in the past** like Form 1. This means that the past tense of ƕ**a**lla follows the same pattern as that of ḥ**a**ka. Let's see:

■ ƕ**a**lla‿l-b**ā**b maft**ū**ḥ — *He left the door open.*
ƕ**a**llat l-ewl**ā**d if**ū**tu — *She let the children come / go in.*
ƕall**ē**to y**e**ṭlα[c] . — *I let him go out.*
h**ā**da ƕall**ā**-ni af**a**kker inno… — *This made me think that…*
ƕallēn**ā**[h] ik**a**mmel š**u**ġlo — *We let him get on with his work.*

Those of you feel like doing exercises production-line style are invited to take **all the verbs** you've learnt from the very beginning of the course and put them in the subjunctive after every conceivable form of the verb khalla. For example:

■ ƕall**ā**-ni / ma ƕallān**ī**-š — *He let me / He didn't let me…*
ƕallēn**ā**[h] / ma ƕallēnā-h**ō**-š — *We let him / We didn't let him…*

All in all, there are 94 possibilities multiplied by approximately 100 verbs = around 10,000 possible sentences. If you add the auxiliary verb **kān** to the beginning of the sentence (after a conditional clause of the *If I knew / If I had known…* type – see **Lesson 27, Explanations 2**), you can construct sentences like the following:

l**a**w…, k**ā**n ƕall**ā**-ni af**ū**t — *If…, he would have let me come in.*

This gives you 2 x 10,000 = 20,000 interesting sentences. If the mere thought
■ has given you a headache, ƕ**o**du ḥ**a**bbet 'asbir**ī**n u-r**ū**ḥu n**ā**mu!

Exercises - Part 2

A. Translate into English:

1. il-mαyy maġliyye? – ’α, ’immi ġalat-ha.
2. ma ɧallā-nī-š ’aḥki, sakkat-ni.
3. il-muftāḥ kān fi-l-jārūr. – ^{c}ašān hēk ma laqā-hō-š.
4. law‿e^{c}refe^{t} ’ana, kunt laqēto.
5. lēš ma ɧallū-kī-š‿etfūti ^{c}a-l-maktab?
6. dawwaru ^{c}ala‿l-^{c}ilbe, ma laqū-hā-š.
7. ɧallat il-walad yeṭlα^{c} la-ḥālo.

B. Complete the sentences

(Replace the English words with the appropriate expression in Arabic):

8. wēn ([is] the application <the request>)? – hayyo, ’ana mα̅ḍi (it).
9. ya Jamīle, wēn (did you find) ‿l-jarīde?
10. ’ana (searched for it) fi kull il-bēt, (I didn’t find it).
11. ’ana ma ba^{c}ref iz-zalame (who spoke) ma^{c}ak.
12. bte^{c}rαf wāḥad (who speaks)[23] ’almα̅ni?
13. ’aɧūk ’aɧad (the hammer).
14. bukrα birajje^{c} (it to you$^{m\ sing}$ – *please mark where the stress falls here!*)

C. Translate into Arabic:

15. He told me: Sign the application. I signed it.
16. There are children there who are playing next to the house.
17. I know the man who let him <come> in.
18. I know a man who’s looking for work.
19. And I know someone who’s looking for workers.
20. I want to introduce you$^{m\ sing}$ to him.
21. She signed the letter.
22. He let him in, then he let him <go> out.

---

23. wāḥad = *anyone*, i.e., not a specific person. See **Explanations 4,** particularly page 139, before you translate this.

dars tis^{c}a u-^{c}išrīn

29

Lesson Twenty-Nine

Just as the verb katab has a “cousin” nizel, which resembles it in many ways, so, too, the verb ḥaka has a close relative, whose features also resemble those of nizel: nisi, which means *to forget.* You will remember that nizel loses its first vowel (-i) in the 1st and 2nd person of the past tense: nizel → nzelt, nzelna, etc. The same thing happens to nisi. Let’s compare:

I / you$^{m\ sing}$ forgot	n|sī|t	ni|si	*he forgot*
you$^{f\ sing}$ forgot	n|sī|ti	ni|syat	*she forgot*
we forgot	n|sī|na	ni|syu	*they forgot*
you^{pl} forgot	n|sī|tu		

The present-future and subjunctive of nisi are similar (though not identical) to those of ḥaka:

bansa	*I forget*	’ansa	*that I forget*
btinsa	*you$^{m\ sing}$ forget*	tinsa	*that you$^{m\ sing}$ forget*
btinsi	*you$^{f\ sing}$ forget*	tinsi	*that you$^{f\ sing}$ forget*
b^{y}insa	*he forgets*	yinsa	*that he forget*
btinsa	*she forgets*	tinsa	*that she forget*
bninsa (mninsa^{G})	*we forget*	ninsa	*that we forget*
btinsu	*you^{pl} forget*	tinsu	*that you^{pl} forget*
b^{y}insu	*they forget*	yinsu	*that they forget*

While in ḥaka the final syllable of the present-future and subjunctive is -i (apart from the forms for *you^{pl}* and *they*, of course, because of the -u ending that “overwhelms” the -i, as you have already seen), in verbs like nisi the final syllable is in most cases -a. Let’s compare:

■ ḥaka → yiḥki nisi → yinsa

There are, however, a number of irregular verbs that do not obey this rule, e.g., miši (*to walk; to go*), and biki (*to cry / weep*).

Past, conjugates like nisi	**Subj.**, conjugates like yiḥki
mšīt… miši… mšīna… mišyu	’amši, timši… yimšu
bkīt… biki… bkīna… bikyu	’abki, tibki… yibku

The **active participle** resembles that of ḥaka:

nāsi, f nāsye [nāsyīn / nāsīn] = *having forgotten*

The verb biqi [yibqa], which means *to stay / remain*, is another example:

Its **active participle** is bāqi = *remaining / having remained.* il-bāqi = *the remainder / the rest*; il-bāqīn = *those that remain / the rest (of the people) / the others.*

To accustom your ear (and your tongue) to these verbs, conjugate biki **out loud** in both the present-future and the subjunctive:

bkīt, bkīti, biki, bikyat, bkīna, bkītu, bikyu

(b)abki, (b)tibki (b)yibki (b)tibki (b)nibki (b)tibku (b)yibku

We suggest that you repeat this exercise with the verb miši. If you agree, you can say māši! (*OK! / Fine!*) <it goes>.

Vocabulary

riḍi [yirḍɑ]	to agree; to be pleased / be satisfied[1]		
ġili [yiġla]	to go up in price / become more expensive		
jamāᶜa [8] [-ᶜāt]	group, gang (of friends), "guys"		
bil-kād	scarcely, barely, hardly	biqi [yibqa]	to stay / remain
siyāse [2] [8]	policy; politics	bidi [yibda]	to begin
ribi[2]	to grow up, be brought up	qiri [yiqra]	to read
dōrɑ [2] [-rɑ̄t]	turn; course[3]	biki [yibki]	to cry
riwāye [2] [-yāt]	story; novel	kubbāye [-yāt]	glass

1. See **Explanations 3.**

2. You will hear the verb ribi in Galilee. However, the f-5 verb from the same root is more commonly used, i.e., trabba [yitrabba]. We'll discuss this verb in Book 3, but you already know how to conjugate it in the past tense (just like ḥaka), e.g., *I grew up / I was raised* = trabbēt.

3. When people want to say *course* (e.g., *Hebrew course, sewing course, handicrafts course,* etc., i.e., a cyclical course of study) they tend to use the literary Arabic form of the word = dawrɑ#. You are familiar with the f-2 verb dawwɑr. The f-1 verb from this root is dɑ̄r [idūr] = *to revolve / turn* (intrans). il-ᶜajal bidūr = *the wheel turns*; il-'ɑrḍ bᵉtdūr ḥawl‿iš-šams = *The earth revolves around the sun.*

Conversation

– ’**a**na‿rb**ī**t fi b**a**lad‿ᵉzġ**ī**r.	– I grew up in a small village.
bt**e**ᶜref Jam**ī**l ’**i**bn‿il-ḫɑyy**ɑ̄**ṭ?	Do you know Jamil, the tailor’s son?
ᵉrb**ī**t ’**a**na wiyy**ā**h [4]	He and I <I and him> grew up
fi had**ī**k il-b**a**lad.	in that village.
ᵉrb**ī**na s**a**wa, u-baᶜd**ē**n‿ᵉbq**ī**t	We grew up together, then I stayed in
’**a**na fi-l-q**ɑ**rye, u-h**u**wwe r**ɑ̄**ḥ	the village and he went somewhere else
la-ġ**ē**r maḥ**a**ll, ’**ɑ**bṣɑr w**ē**n.	<to another place>, I don’t know where.
– u-**u**ḫtak?	– And your sister?
– ’**u**ḫti r**i**byat ᶜind s**ī**di u-s**i**tti [5]	– My sister grew up with my grandfather and
b**a**ᶜᵉd-ma m**ā**tat ’**i**mmi.	grandmother after my mother died,
u-b**i**qyat ᶜ**i**ndhom laḥ**a**dd il-y**ō**m.	and she’s still with them <she remained with them until today>.
– Y**ū**sef !	– Yusef !
– n**a**ᶜam [6]!	– Yes!
– q**u**l-li: bt**e**ᶜref t**i**qrɑ ᶜ**ɑ**rɑbi?	– Tell me, do you know [how] to read
– n**a**ᶜam, b**a**qrɑ šw**a**yy.	Arabic? – Yes, I [can] read a bit.
– qr**ī**t [7] il-jar**ī**de?	– Have you read the newspaper?
– ᵉqr**ī**t bass il-ᶜanaw**ī**n [8].	– I’ve only read the headlines.
– ’**a**na‿qr**ī**t-ha k**u**ll-ha, ma	– I’ve read all of it <I read it, all-of it> [and]
fīh**ā**-š ’**i**ši. h**ā**da k**u**llo siy**ā**se...	there’s nothing in it! It’s all politics…

---

4) Here’s another use of the particle -iyy**ā**-: ’**a**na w-iyy**ā**-k = *you and me*; *you and I* <I and you>.

5) The word s**a**yyed means *master*, and s**a**yyide means *lady*. These words (which shorten to s**ī**d and s**i**tt), with the addition of the appropriate attached possessive pronoun, are also used to mean *grandfather* and *grandmother* respectively, alongside the “proper” terms j**i**dd [jd**ū**d] and j**i**dde [jidd**ā**t].

6) n**a**ᶜam is another (and more polite) way of saying ’**a**ywa / ’**ɑ̄**, the more commonly used words for *yes*. You can also use n**a**ᶜam (with a rising intonation: n**a**ᶜám?) to mean *what? / pardon?* when you haven’t heard exactly what someone has said to you, and would like them to repeat it. You say n**a**ᶜàm! (with a descending intonation) to reply when someone calls your name, as is the case here.

7) qr**ī**t can be pronounced either qᵉr**ī**t or ᵉqr**ī**t.

8) ᶜunw**ā**n / ᶜinw**ā**n [ᶜanaw**ī**n] means *address* (i.e., where one lives) and also *headline* and *title (of a book)*.

’**u**ḫti b^{e}tf**ɑ**ḍḍel riwāy**ā**t!	My sister prefers novels!
mb**ā**reḥ q**i**ryat riw**ā**ye	Yesterday she read a novel,
w-il-y**ō**m kam**ā**n	and today, too,
ᶜam-(b)t**i**qrɑ riw**ā**ye t**ā**nye.	she’s reading another novel.
b**i**dyat iṣ-ṣ**u**b^{o}ḥ	She started in the morning
u-n**i**syat šu**ġ**^{o}l-ha.	and forgot [about] her work.
y**ā** M**a**ryam, šu ᶜam-t**i**qri?	Hey, Maryam, what are you reading?
miš s**ā**mᶜa... Maryam!	She can’t hear <doesn’t hear>… Maryam!
– š**ū** f**ī**^{h}? ᶜam-b**a**qrɑ riw**ā**ye,	– What’s up? I’m reading a novel,
m**a** aḥl**ā**-ha!	it’s so beautiful!
– ’**a**na kam**ā**n b**i**ddi aqr**ɑ̄**-ha.	– I’d like to read it too.
– ṭ**ɑ**yyeb, b**a**ᶜ^{e}d-ma aḫ**ɑ**lleṣ,	– Fine, when I’m finished <after I finish>
babᶜ**a**t-lak‿iyy**ā**-ha	I’ll send it to you^{m}
maᶜ ’aḫ**ū**y l-^{e}zġ**ī**r.	with my little brother.
– ṭ**ɑ**yyeb, bass ma tins**ī**-š!	– OK, but don’t forget!
– ’**a**nsa[9]? k**ī**f ’**a**nsa?	– Forget? How can I forget?
’**a**na b**i**ddi‿yy**ā**k tiqr**ɑ̄**-ha	I want you to read it and tell me what you
u-tq**u**l-li šu f**i**krak ᶜ**a**nha.	think of it <your opinion of it>.
– ’aḫ**ū**ki b^{y}**e**ᶜrɑf y**i**qrɑ?	– Does your brother know how to read?
– bil-k**ā**d y**e**ᶜrɑf ḥarf**ē**n tal**ā**te,	– He just about <hardly> knows two [or]
ma by**e**ᶜrɑf kull l-^{e}ḥr**ū**f	three letters. He doesn’t know all
/ k**u**ll il-’**a**ḥrof [10].	the letters.
bass š**ɑ̄**ṭer, qaw**ɑ̄**m biṣ**ī**r y**e**ᶜrɑf.	But he’s bright! He’ll learn fast <immediately he will become he knows>.
– ya w**a**lad, j**i**b-li kubb**ā**yet m**ɑ**yy,	– Hey, kid, bring me a glass of water,
’**ɑ**llɑ y**i**rḍɑ ᶜal**ē**k![11]	please <God will be pleased with you>!
ma ’**a**šṭɑro!	How smart he is!

---

9. Subjunctive: *[How can it be] that I forget?*

10. ḥ**a**rf [’**a**ḥrof / ḥur**ū**f or ḥr**ū**f [3]] = *letter (of the alphabet).*
il-’**a**ḥrof il-ᶜɑrɑb**i**yye = *the Arabic letters.*

11. This expression of encouragement is used when asking a service of someone – *If you do this, God will be pleased with you.* See **Explanations 3.**

– l**a**mma s**i**me^c^ il-ђ**ɑ**bɑr	– When he heard the news.
ṣ**ɑ̄**r y**i**bki.	he started to cry
m**ɑ**rɑto kam**ā**n ṣ**ɑ̄**rat t**i**bki.	His wife began to cry, too.
qult-**i**lhom: bal**ā**š t**i**bku!	I told them: “Don’t cry!
’**a**wwal ’**i**ši b**i**dna‿ntalfen[12]	First of all we’ll phone
lal-must**a**šfa;	the hospital. It may not be true
b**a**lki‿l-ђ**ɑ**bɑr muš mɑẓb**ū**ṭ...	<perhaps the news [is] not true>.”

– q**a**b^e^l š**a**h^e^r ṣ**ɑ̄**r-fī^h^ intiђāb**ā**t[13]	– A month ago there were elections
u-min y**ō**m-ha[14] ġ**i**lyat il-ђ**u**ḍrɑ.	and since then vegetables have gone up in
u-kull ši ṣ**ɑ̄**r ġ**ā**li.	price and everything has become expensive.

---

12) You can either “hit a phone [call]” (see Lesson 25) or use this verb, which has a 4-letter root. See **Explanations 5.**

13) intiђāb**ā**t – don’t let this long and inscrutable-looking word frighten you off. Just think of an English-language student faced with “mouthfuls” like *extraordinariness* and *indistinguishability*! Let’s break it down into its component parts. The verb *to choose; to vote* is n**a**ђab (n**ā**ђeb = *voter*) or int**a**ђab (f-8 of the same root), whose verbal noun is intiђ**ā**b. If we add the plural suffix **-āt** we get intiђāb**ā**t. We’ll come back to this when we learn about f-8 of the verb.

14) min y**ō**m-ha means literally *since its day* (i.e., *since the day the incident mentioned took place*). You can also say min sā^c^**e**t-ha <since its hour>, i.e., *since then.* This is a good moment to tell you that the “official” word for *hour* is s**ā**^c^a, as we can see from the foregoing expression. In colloquial speech, however, most people say s**ē**^c^a.

– h**ɑ̄**! h**ā**da ’**i**ši maᶜr**ū**f:	– Oh, it’s a well-known thing:
qabl‿il-intiḫāb**ā**t kull ši‿rḫ**ī**ṣ	before elections everything’s cheap,
u-baᶜd**ē**n kull ši bʸ**i**ġla.	and afterwards everything goes up in price.
– h**ē**k is-siy**ā**se, ya jam**ā**ᶜa.	– That’s politics, guys!

– k**ī**f iš-š**u**ġᵒl ᶜ**i**ndak? m**ā**ši?	– How’s work with you^{m}? OK?
– y**a**ᶜni, iš-š**u**ġᵒl w**ā**qef	– So-so. Work’s not going so well <work is standing>.
u-**a**na q**ā**ᶜed[15]!	And I’m sitting [around doing nothing]!
u-k**ī**f ᶜ**i**n(d)kom?	How’s by you^{pl}?
– ᶜ**i**n(d)na, m**ā**ši‿l-ḥ**ā**l.	– With us things are OK <the situation goes>.

– ’**ē**mta b**i**dyat il-ḥ**a**fle?	– When did the party start?
– r**ɑ**ḥ-t**i**bda baᶜd nuṣṣ s**ē**ᶜa.	– It’s going to begin in half an hour.
– bd**ī**t bil-ᶜ**a**mal w**i**lla l**i**ssa?	– Have you started work yet, or not <you started with the work or not yet>?
– l**a**’, r**ɑ**ḥ-’**a**bda b**u**kra.	– No, I’m going to start tomorrow.
– ᵉnš**ɑ**llɑ.	– God willing.

(fi l**u**ᶜbe)	*While playing a game:*
fi ’**a**wwal d**ō**rɑ bd**ī**na min	The first time round <in the first turn> we
il-yam**ī**n, h**a**llaq r**ɑ**ḥ-n**i**bda	started from the right. Now we’re going
min iš-šm**ā**l, y**a**ᶜni	to start from the left, in other words
b**i**dna nibda f**ī**k / maᶜ**ā**k[16].	we’ll start with you^{m}.

Explanations

1. How (nice / beautiful)!

When we admire something, we use the following formula in Arabic:
ma + comparative adjective + attached pronoun: ma + ’**a**jmal + -o /-ha.
For those of you who have forgotten what a **comparative adjective** is: it is the

---

15) Anyone who is not working (because he or she is unemployed, on holiday or celebrating a religious festival) is said in Arabic to be *sitting*. il-yah**ū**d bʸ**u**qᵒᶜdu fi y**ō**m is-s**a**bt = *Jews don’t work on Saturdays.*

16) The word maᶜ has the alternative form maᶜ**ā**-; the attached pronouns used with it are the same as those used after w**ɑ**rɑ (see **Book 1, p. 73**): maᶜ**ā**y, maᶜ**ā**-k /-ki, etc.

adjectival form that in English either ends in -er (*bigg**er**, small**er**, thinn**er**, fatt**er**, nic**er***, etc.) or is preceded by the word *more* (***more** beautiful, **more** extreme, **more** docile*, etc.); see **Book 1, p. 102**.

■ Here are a few examples with words you already know:

š**ā**ṭer (cp = '**ɑ**šṭɑr)	*clever, skilful, quick*
ma '**ɑ**šṭɑr-ak!	*How clever you^m are!*
ma '**ɑ**šṭɑr-o	*How clever he is!*
ma 'ɑšṭ**ɑ**r-ha!	*How clever she is!*
ḥ**i**lu (cp = '**a**ḥla)	*beautiful, handsome; nice; sweet*
m**a** 'aḥl**ā**-ki!	*How beautiful you^f are!*
m**a** 'aḥl**ā**^{h} !	*How handsome he is!*
m**a** 'aḥl**ā**-ha!	*How beautiful she is!*

il-q**e**rd fi ᶜ**ē**n '**i**mmo ġaz**ā**l

Beauty is in the eye of the beholder

<the monkey in the eye of his mother [is] a gazelle>.

q**a**wi (cp = '**a**qwa)	*strong*
ma‿aqw**ā**-k (= maqw**ā**k)!	*How strong you^m are!*
ma‿aqw**ā**-ki (= maqw**ā**ki)	*How strong you^f are!*

A number of the examples above will remind you of a rule you have already learned: after a vowel the glottal stop (') weakens or drops (we say min 'ab**ū**y, but la-ab**ū**y), and so you will hear people say ma-**ɑ**šṭɑr-ak, etc.

Note how closely the stress follows the rules you have already learned:

he wrote	*he wrote it^m*	*he wrote it^f*
k**a**tab	k**a**tabo	kat**a**b-ha
'**ɑ**šṭɑr	ma **ɑ**šṭɑro	ma ɑšṭ**ɑ**r-ha
cleverer	*how clever he is*	*how clever she is*

he put out / extinguished	*he put it[m] out*	*he put it[f] out*
ṭαfα	ṭαfᾱh	ṭαfᾱ-ha
'aḥla	ma‿aḥlāh	ma‿ahlā-ha
more beautiful / handsomer	*how handsome he is*	*how beautiful she is*

In accordance with these rules we say (note where the stress falls):

■ *This bread is very good,* / *taste it [and see] how good it is!*
hal-ђubez ṭαyyeb‿ektīr[17] dūqo[18], ma αṭyαbo!
hal-jibne ṭαyybe‿ktīr, dūq-ha, ma αṭyαb-ha!
This cheese is very tasty, / *taste it [and see] how good it is!*

2. On boiling, and on rising prices…

In the previous lesson we learned the word ġala (*to boil*, trans / intrans), while in this lesson we encountered its cousin ġili. We can well understand that rising prices make the blood boil, and perhaps this explains the answer to the following question:

■ – kīf il-ʿīše hunāk? – nᾱr!
– *What's life like there? – Fire!* (meaning that things are very expensive).

The water boiled	*Vegetables got dearer*
il-mαyy ġalat	il-ђuḍrα ġilyat
il-mαyy‿ebtiġli	il-ђuḍrα btiġla
The water boils	*Vegetables are getting dearer*

We have already seen that two types of verb – ḥaka and nisi – have active participles that resemble each other: rᾱmi / nāsi, and so you should not be

---

17. The word ṭαyyeb means *good, kind; tasty* and also *alive.* You will hear people ask 'abūk baʿdo // lissāto ṭαyyeb? = *Is your father still alive?*

18. In literary Arabic and rural speech this word is pronounced d̲āq [id̲ūq] = *to taste.* d̲awq / d̲ōq means *taste* (both *the sense of taste* and *[good] taste*). In urban speech the d̲ sound is pronounced like a *d* in the verb and like a *z* in the noun! (We described a similar phenomenon in **Book 1, p. 97, footnote 9.**) biddi adūq = *I want to taste*; ma-lō-š zōq! = *he's got no taste!* When you talk about the taste of food, however, you must use the word ṭαʿem or ṭαʿme. hal-ђubez ma-lō-š ṭαʿme = *this bread's tasteless*, and ṭαʿemto / ṭαʿmet-ha = *its taste* (m / f).

surprised to discover that ġ**ā**li is the active participle of both verbs in the table above. In Part 2 of the Conversation in Lesson 28 we came across the word ġ**ā**li used in the sense of *having boiled*, but you will meet it more frequently in its other meaning of *dear* <having gone up in price>, i.e., *expensive*.

3. Unoccupied and pleased

This is an appropriate time to mention two more verbs and their active participles:

a) f**ā**ḍi (*empty, vacant; free, unoccupied*) is the active participle of f**i**ḍi [y**i**fḍɑ], which means *to empty* (intrans); *to become free / have time [for]*.

■ '**i**ssa fḍ**ī**t = *I'm free now* <I've become free>; bass t**i**fḍɑ / t**i**fḍi^{f} = *as soon as you're free*; il-b**ā**ṣ b^{y}**i**fḍɑ = *The bus empties*; il-qann**ī**ne f**ā**ḍye = *The bottle's empty*.

b) r**ā**ḍi (*satisfied, pleased; in agreement [with]*) is the active participle of r**i**ḍi

■ (r**e**ḍi) [y**i**rḍɑ]. 'ab**ū**k muš r**ā**ḍi ᶜ**a**nnak = *Your father's not pleased with you*; ma‿rḍ**ī**t-^{e}š = *I didn't agree* (i.e., *I wasn't satisfied / pleased [with the proposal]*).

4. Sleeping – or just lying down?

In **Lesson 23, footnote 6** we said that n**ā**yem "means *asleep* or just *lying down*" (in the latter sense it can also be used of objects). Now we can be more precise when we want to talk about someone who is actually sleeping, and use the verb ġ**i**fi [y**i**ġfa] (*to fall asleep*); ġf**ī**t means *I fell asleep / I dropped off*. The active participle, ġ**ā**fi, means *asleep*.

■ laq**ē**to ġ**ā**fi, fayy**a**qto means *I found him asleep [and] woke him up* (f**a**yyaq = *to wake up* [trans], f-2).

5. Verbs with four root letters (quadriliteral verbs)

Some Arabic verbs, such as t**a**lfan and t**a**rjam, have four root letters (t-r-j-m) instead of three. They conjugate like f-2 verbs (i.e., like k**a**mmal), e.g.,

bat**a**rjem	*I translate*	^{e}mt**a**rjam	*translated* (past part.)
talf**a**nt	*I telephoned*	bit**a**lf^{e}nu	*they telephone*
		bit**a**l^{e}fnu	

The two options for the 3rd person plural above remind us of the alternative forms b^{y}**i**kt^{e}bu / b^{y}**i**k^{e}tbu, and here, too, the second alternative is preferable. You can also drop the ^{e} altogether, if the word can easily be pronounced without it – e.g., bit**a**rjmu. We'll come back to this point when we meet other members of the "quadriliteral club."

Exercises

A. Translate into English:

1. rɑ̄ḥat‿tnām u-ġifyat ᶜala ṭūl (immediately).
2. ṣɑ̄ru yiḥku ᶜan il-intiḫābāt u-nisyu šuġᵒl-hom.
3. biddi aqrɑ‿l-jarīde.
4. jib-li‿yyā-ha, biddi aqrɑ̄ha.
5. ᶜam-baqrɑ ktāb.
6. šu ᶜunwān l-ᵉktāb illi ᶜam(b)tiqrɑ̄ʰ?
7. 'ēmta bidkom tibdu bil-ᶜamal?
8. bidyat tiġsel, bass 'ijat // 'ajat jɑ̄ret-ha,
9. ṣɑ̄ru yiḥku maᶜ bɑᶜeḍ u-ma ḫɑllɑṣɑt il-ġasīl.
10. ma ᶜalēš, bᵉtḫɑlleṣ bukrɑ.
11. law‿btiqrɑ ᶜɑrɑbi, kunt bajib-lak riwāyāt ᶜɑrɑbiyye.

B. Complete the sentences

(Replace the English words with the appropriate expression in Arabic):

12. dāyman (I forget)‿d-dars.
13. 'iza basmaᶜ nukte, baᶜdēn (I forget it).
14. 'iza hēk, rɑḥ-aḥkī-lak (the joke) kamān mɑrrɑ.
15. wēn l-ᵉktāb? – (She forgot it^{m}) fi-l-maktab.
16. (We forgot)‿nsakker il-bāb.
17 (I began) 'akteb maktūb, bass ma ([didn't] finish it) -š.
18. 'ayya sēᶜa (does... begin) il-ḥafle bukrɑ?
19. bʸeᶜmal 'aġlɑ̄ṭ, 'ana basɑlleḥ-lo (them).
20. law (you'd told me), kunt jibt-illak (it^{f}).

C. Translate into Arabic:

21. There's a picture here – how beautiful it^{f} is!
22. I forgot to bring (ajīb) the newspaper; bring it to me <bring to me it^{f}>, please!
23. Everyone <all the people> read the announcement / advertisement[19] in the street. I read it^{m}, too.

---

19. *Advertisement / announcement* = 'iᶜlān ['iᶜlānāt].

24. My wife has taken the newspaper. She wants to read it.
25. Yusef went and I was left alone. Don't$^{\text{m sing}}$ go! Stay$^{\text{m sing}}$ here with me!
26. Do you$^{\text{m sing}}$ know the Arabic letters?
27. I know two or three letters <two letters, three>, no more.
28. After his father died <after died his-father> he left the village.
29. When are there going to be (biṣ**ī**r-f**ī**^{h}) elections?
30. He wants to manage to finish before noon.
31. As soon as the party starts, I'm going home.
32. In this course (*see footnote 3*) there are Arab girls and Jewish girls.

How do country children cry?

Children cry in the same way all over the world – but in the countryside people talk about it in a slightly different way: once again there is a difference in how the vowels are pronounced. Instead of saying b**i**ki, b**i**qi and q**i**ri in the **past**, they usually say b**a**ka, b**a**qa and q**ɑ**rɑ, which all conjugate like ḥ**a**ka (see Lesson 28). Here are a few examples:

I read = qɑr**ē**t *she cried* = b**a**kat *we stayed* = baq**ē**na

It's time for you to learn a commonly used popular saying. Of someone who hurts someone else, then tries to depict himself as the victim, we say:

■ ḍɑr**ɑ**b-ni u-b**a**ka, sab**a**q-ni w-išt**a**ka, which means *He hit me and cried, he took precedence over me [with the judge] and complained.* The final verb here belongs to f-8, and comes from the root š-k-y.

In f-1, i.e., š**a**ka [y**i**ški] min, it means *to complain of; to suffer from*: il-mɑr**ī**ḍ b^{y}**i**ški min w**a**ja^{c} fi ḍ**ɑ**hro = *The patient complains of a pain in his back.*

dars talātīn

30

Lesson Thirty

The time has come to devote a few pages to a verb that conjugates in its own highly individual way. It's a word you hear all the time, and one you'll be using constantly – the verb *to come*. Like those we've studied in the preceding lessons, this verb, too, bears a certain resemblance to **nisi** – though some of its features are all its own!

■ ('e)jīt	*I / you^m sing^ came*	'ija // 'aja	*he came*
('e)jīti	*you^f sing^ came*	'ijat // 'ajat	*she came*
('e)jīna	*we came*	'iju // 'aju	*they came*
('e)jītu	*you^pl^ came*		

You can choose whichever form you prefer – **jīt** (without 'e), **'aja** (with **'a**-), etc. – but you'd do well to learn the other forms, too, so that you can identify them when you hear others using them.

Here is the conjugation in the present-future and the subjunctive:

■ bāji	*I come / I will come*	'āji	*that I come*
btīji	*you^m/f sing^ come / will come*	tīji	*that you^m/f sing^ come*
bīji	*he comes / will come*	yīji	*that he come*
btīji	*she comes / will come*	tīji	*that she come*
bnīji	*we come / will come*	nīji	*that we come*
btīju	*you^pl^ come / will come*	tīju	*that you^pl^ come*
bīju	*they come / will come*	yīju	*that they come*

The first syllable is generally long (**ā** in the 1st person singular, **ī** in the other persons), though speakers in some areas shorten it. It also shortens when the negative particle -š is added, in accordance with the rule you have already learned [17]: ma bijī-š = *he doesn't come; he won't come.*

■ **The active participle** is jāy, f jāy[1] or jāye [jāyīn].

mnēn (or min wēn) jāy? = *Where have you been / Where have you come from?*

---

1. In other words, just like the masculine. In colloquial Arabic the ending **-āye** is often shortened to **-āy**, e.g., *mirror* = mrāye or mrāy. We'll see further examples of this in the future.

When is this active participle used and what does it mean? Don't forget that the active participles of verbs of **motion** (*to go, to go up, to come down,* etc., see **Lesson 23, Explanations 1**) denote an action taking place at this very moment:

huwwe r**ɑ̄**yeḥ	*he's going* (now)	bir**ū**ḥ	*he goes* (habitually); *he will go*
huwwe j**ā**y	*he's coming* (now)	b**ī**ji	*he comes* (habitually); *he will come*

You've already learned the imperative of this verb – an adopted child with no resemblance to its parents: taᶜ**ā**l, f taᶜ**ā**li! pl taᶜ**ā**lu! See **Book 1, p. 67, Explanations 4**.

taᶜ**ā**l la-h**ō**n! means *come here!*
(When people speak fast, this is reduced to **ta**ᶜ-la-h**ō**n!)

Vocabulary

r**ɑ**'y[2] ['ɑr**ɑ̄**']	opinion	mɑђṣ**ū**ṣ[5]	special
(i)st**a**nna[3]	he waited	s**i**ker [y**i**skɑr]	to get drunk
sl**ū**k [2]	behavior	š**ɑ**ђṣ[6] [2] ['ašђ**ɑ̄**ṣ]	person, individual (n)
bakk**ī**r[4]	early	š**ɑ**ђṣi [2]	personal, individual (adj)

---

2. You will also hear people say r**ɑ̄**y. It's not easy to pronounce the form r**ɑ**'y when it stands alone, but it usually occurs in phrases such as šu r**ɑ**'yak? = *what's your opinion? / what do you think?* r**ɑ**'y‿il-mud**ī**r (r**ɑ**'–yil–mud**ī**r) means *the boss's opinion* and ir-r**ɑ**'y‿il-ᶜ**ā**mm = *public opinion* <the general opinion>.

3. You'll learn this irregular verb later on, but in the meantime you can guess that it conjugates, partially at least, like ḥ**a**ka. In the past, for example, *I waited* = (i)stann**ē**t. In the Conversation we'll encounter the imperative form st**a**nna! = *wait*[m sing], whose feminine form is st**a**nni! and plural st**a**nnu! – no surprises here.

4. When a guest gets up to go, the host says bakk**ī**r! = *it's still early* (i.e., *it's not time to go yet, stay a bit longer*).

5. The root ђ-ṣ-ṣ denotes individuality and particularity. The words ђ**ɑ̄**ṣṣ and ђuṣ**ū**ṣi mean *special / particular* and ђ**ɑ̄**ṣṣatan / ђuṣ**ū**ṣan means *specially / especially / particularly*; mɑђṣ**ū**ṣ means *especially; deliberately*.

6. The word šɑђṣ**i**yye means *personality*, in both the social and psychological senses. *His personality* = šɑђṣ**ī**to, *her personality* = šɑђṣiyy**e**t-ha [10]. The adverb šɑђṣ**i**yyan means *personally.*

Conversation

– '**a**hlan wa-s**a**hlan, k**ī**f il-ḥ**ā**l?	– Hello, how are things <welcome, what's the situation>?
mn**ī**ḥ‿illi j**ī**t bakk**ī**r il-y**ō**m.	It's good you came early today,
b**i**ddi aḥk**ī**-lak '**i**ši	I want to tell you something
u-**a**smaᶜ šu r**ɑ**'yak.	and hear what your opinion [is].
– tf**ɑ**ḍḍɑl, '**i**ḥki, '**a**na j**ī**t	– Go ahead <please>, tell [me]. I've come
mɑḥṣ**ū**s ḥ**a**tta **a**smaᶜ	especially to hear your news
šu f**ī**ʰ ᶜ**i**ndak 'ɑḫb**ɑ̄**r.	<what there-is at you news>.
– ṭ**ɑ**yyeb, '**i**smaᶜ! '**a**wwal‿mb**ā**reḥ	– OK, listen! The day before yesterday
'aj**ā**-ni makt**ū**b min '**i**bᵉn ᶜ**a**mmi	I got <came to me> a letter from my
biq**ū**l inno 'aj**ā**ʰ w**a**lad[7].	cousin telling me he'd had a son.
– mabr**ū**k!	– Congratulations!
– '**ɑ**llɑ‿ib**ā**rek f**ī**k!	– Thank you <God bless you>.
– šu '**i**smo?	– What's his name?
– '**i**smo... st**a**nna...	– His name… wait…
w**ɑ**llɑ, r**ū**ḥ min b**ā**li[8]!	heavens, it's slipped my mind!
ᶜala kull ḥ**ā**l	In any case,
'**a**ja ᶜala b**ā**li ar**ū**ḥ az**ū**ro.	it occurred to me [to go] to visit him.
mb**ā**reḥ kunt b**i**ddi **ɑ**ṭlɑᶜ	Yesterday I wanted to leave the house,
min il-b**ē**t w**i**lla[9] j**ā**ye m**ɑ**rɑto.	and suddenly his wife appeared!
qult-**i**lha: "mabr**ū**k m**ā** j**ā**-kom!"[10]	I said to her, "Congratulations on the baby" <blessed [be] what came [to] you>!
q**ā**lat: "'**ɑ**llɑ ib**ā**rek f**ī**k!"	She said, "Thank you" <God bless you>.

7. See below, **Explanations 1**.

8) You're familiar with the expression d**ī**r b**ā**lak! which means *watch out / be careful!* For more information on this multi-functional word see **Explanations 2**.

9) w**i**lla or '**i**lla u-... = *and there [he / she / it] was!* ma fat**a**ḥt il-b**ā**b w**i**lla‿l-mud**ī**r w**ā**qef = *I'd just opened the door and there was the boss standing [right there]* <I hadn't opened = I'd barely opened the door, and there….>

10) mabr**ū**k is what you say to people who announce a happy event concerning themselves or their family (especially a birth or a marriage), or to someone wearing a new garment. To the parents of the newborn you say *blessed [be] what has come to you.* On the use of m**ā** meaning *what* in the sense of *that which,* see **Lesson 22, Explanations 6c**. Here the initial 'a- of '**a**ja has dropped, as it also often tends to do in negative sentences: ma-j**ā**-š = *he didn't come / he hasn't come.*

sa'alt-ha kīf ḥāl il-walad	I asked her how the baby was and how
u-kīf jōz-ha, ṣārat tibki!	her husband was. She began to cry!
u-ṣārat tiḥki ᶜanno,	And she began to talk about him,
kīf‿ᵉslūko,	how he was behaving <how his behavior
qālat:	[was]>, [and] she said,
"kull yōm bijī-ni sakrān."	"Every day he arrives <to me> drunk."
– harām[11]!	– Shame [on him]!
– bteᶜᵉrfo (bteᶜrafo)	– Do you know my cousin
la-'ibᵉn ᶜammi[12]?	<my uncle's son>?
– smeᶜᵉt ᶜanno, bijūz šufto marra,	– I've heard about him, I may have seen him once <it's possible I saw him once>,
bass ma baᶜrafō-š šaḫṣiyyan.	but I don't know him personally.
– walla, muš ᶜēb[13] il-wāḥad	– Really, isn't it a disgrace for someone
yiskar hēk u-yuṣrof kull il-maṣāri	to get drunk like that and spend all [his]
badāl-ma‿ijīb-ha ᶜa-l-bēt[14]?	money instead of taking it home?
– kull-ma bāji la-ᶜindak	– Whenever I come to see you
fīʰ ᶜindak 'aḫbār muš‿ᵉmnīḥa.	you've got bad news!
– šu bidna neᶜmal?	– What can you do <what shall we do>?
in-natīje[15], biddo yitrek-ha.	The long and the short of it <the result> is, he wants to leave her.

---

11. The root ḥ-r-m indicates a moral or religious prohibition. ḥarām = *forbidden, prohibited*, and ḥarām! here means *shame [on him]!* The word ḥarīm means *women's quarters*, which are off-limits to strangers, and also *female members of a [Muslim] family*. It is, of course, the origin of the English word *harem*. The root ḥ-r-m likewise indicates *sanctity*: ḥaram = *holy place; sanctuary*, and il-ḥaram iš-šarīf <the noble sanctuary> = *the Temple Mount* (in Jerusalem).

12. Literally: *You know him [I'm referring] to my cousin?* This construction is designed to emphasize a word that refers to someone or something already indicated by an attached pronoun. We say *Do you know him?* then we indicate exactly whom we mean.

13. il-wāḥed / il-wāḥad <[the] one> = *one / someone*, when making a generalization. Used in much the same way as the English *one* or the less formal *you* in such sentences as *When you see things like that you start to wonder… / When one sees things like that one starts to wonder…*

14. maṣāri is a plural noun, originally used to designate Egyptian coins. Rule 13 applies to it, and so the attached pronoun referring back to it is in the feminine singular (-ha).

15. See **Lesson 19, footnote 3.**

qāl biddo yīji la-^{c}indi‿lyōm.	He said he wanted to come and see me today.
– ba^{c}do // lissa ma-jā-š[10]?	– Hasn't he come yet?
– la', ba^{c}do // lissa. 'iza bīji, rɑḥ-aqul-lo kil^{e}mtēn‿^{e}nḍɑ̄f[16]!	– No, not yet. If he comes, I'm going to give him a piece of my mind <say to him two clean words>!
– (i)nšɑllɑ btinjaḥ u-b^{y}irja^{c}-^{e}lha u-bibɑṭṭel yiskɑr!	– Let's hope you succeed and he goes back to her and stops drinking <getting drunk>.
– (i)nšɑllɑ!	– Let's hope [so]...
– lāzem arɑwweḥ, ^{c}an 'iznak[17].	– I have to go home, excuse me.
– 'iznak ma^{c}āk! ma^{c} is-salāme[18]!	– Feel free! Take care!
– 'ɑllɑ‿isal(l)mak!	– You too <may God keep you well>!

Explanations

1. He came to me

You will have already noticed that the verb **'aja** (**'ija**[G]) behaves rather differently from the English verb *come*: in English we say *he came **to** me*, while in Arabic we can say 'ajā-ni <he/it came me>, with an attached pronoun indicating a direct object.

The verb **'aja** + attached pronoun can also be used to describe the arrival of a **letter,** an **invitation** or even a **newborn baby**! And while we're on the subject of children, please note that there is a gender difference when we're talking about new parents: the newborn child *comes* to the father, while the mother *brings* him / her [into the world]; see **Book 1, p. 63, footnote 3**. To sum up (this time we're using the **'ija** form, just for a change):

---

16. In some cases the adjective that qualifies a plural noun designating an inanimate object likewise appears in the plural (rather than in the feminine singular, as Rule 13 decrees). This can happen when objects are numbered, as here. We'll come across additional examples of this later.

17. 'izn (in literary Arabic 'iḏn) = *permission.* ma^{c}ak 'iz^{e}n? means *Do you have permission / Are you allowed to?* The guest is asking for permission to leave, and his host replies *You're free to go / You don't need permission* <the permission is with you = *in your hands*>.

18. See **Book 1, p. 56.**

■	'ij**ā**^{h} w**a**lad	*He had a son*	j**ā**bat w**a**lad	*She gave birth to a son*
	'**i**jato b**i**nt	*He had a daughter*	j**ā**bat b**i**nt	*She gave birth to a daughter*

As we pointed out in our explanation of š**ā**fu → šāf**ū**^{h} (*they saw; they saw him*) and ṭ**α**fα → ṭαf**ᾱ**^{h} (*he extinguished; he extinguished it*) it is only the shift in the position of the stress that enables us to differentiate between '**i**ja and 'ij**ā**^{h}, as the final –^{h} is barely heard. Foreign learners of colloquial Arabic find it hard at first to distinguish between the sentences below:

■	'**i**ja w**a**lad	*A boy came / arrived.*
	'ij**ā**^{h} w**a**lad	*He had a boy.*
	'**a**ja makt**ū**b	*A letter arrived.*
	'aj**ā**^{h} makt**ū**b	*He got a letter* <came [to]-him a letter>.
	'**i**za b**ī**ji makt**ū**b	*If a letter arrives...*
	'iza bij**ī**^{h} makt**ū**b	*If he gets a letter...*

Or, in the 1st and 2nd person, just for a change:

'aj**ā**-k w**a**lad	*You had a son*	'aj**ā**-ni w**a**lad	*I had a son*
'**a**jat-ak b**i**nt	*You had a daughter*	'aj**a**t-ni b**i**nt	*I had a daughter*

Although all this may seem obvious, it's a good idea to practice it – **out loud** of course – with the new verb you've just learned.

■ **2.** dīru bālkom!

You're already familiar with the word **bāl**, which means *mind*, from the expression **dīr bālak** (*be careful / watch out* <turn your mind>!) – see **Book 1, p. 87**.

The verb **dɑ̄r** [idīr] means *to turn* (trans) / *direct*, and, by extension, *to manage.* A **mudīr** (*manager*) is the person who gets things going, turns them in the proper direction, etc. For example:

■ – mīn bidīr il-mustašfa? – il-mudīr.
– Who manages the hospital? – The manager.

And with the word **bāl**:

■ dɑ̄r bālo = *He was careful.*
ma dirt-eš bāli = *I wasn't paying attention / I didn't notice; I wasn't careful*

Here are a few more expressions using the word **bāl**:

■ 'aja ᶜala bāli / ᶜa-bāli
It occurred to me <[it] came on my mind>.
rɑ̄ḥ min bāli — *It slipped my mind.*
šu‿lli jāb hāda ᶜala bālak?
What made you think of that <what brought that on your mind>?
hāda šāġel[19] bāli — *That worries me / It's on my mind.*
la tišġel bālak! — *Don't worry* <don't occupy your mind>!
mašġūl il-bāl — *preoccupied* <busy-of mind>
'iza biddo hēk, 'inte šu ᶜa-bālak?
If that's what he wants, what do you care <if he wants thus, what [is] on your mind>?
ṭūl[20] – ṭawīl — *length – long*
ṭɑwwɑl f-2 — *to lengthen* (trans); *to last / take [a long] time*
ṭɑwwel bālak / ṭɑw(w)li bālek!
Be patient / Have patience <lengthen your mind>!

---

19. **šaġal** [yišġel] = *to occupy [one's mind], to preoccupy / worry* (trans). The Form 2 verb **šaġġal** means *to employ.* **bišaġġel talatīn ᶜāmel** = *He employs 30 workers.*

20. **ṭūl** = *length*; **qaddēš ṭūlo?** = *How long is it* <how much its length>? **ṭūl is-sane** = *all year long / all year round.* **ṭūl il-lēl** = *all night long.* **ṭūl in-nhɑ̄r** = *all day long* The verb **ṭɑwwɑl** means *to lengthen*; *to last,* e.g., **rɑḥ-iṭɑwwel‿ektīr?** = *Will it take a long time* <will it last much>?

3. Next week + the days of the week

Today's lesson will provide you with everything you need to be able to talk about the days of the week in both the **past** and the **future** tenses.

Let's start with the verb mαḍα [yimḍi / yimḍα^{G}], which means *to pass*, where time is concerned. You don't need to be told that it conjugates like nisi and that its active participle is mᾱḍi, f mᾱḍye. Now it's time to learn the days of the week and expressions like *last Thursday, next week,* etc.

yōm il-ḥadd // yōm il-'aḥad	*Sunday*
yōm it-tᵉnēn	*Monday*
yōm it-talāta	*Tuesday*
yōm il-'arbᶜa (il-'arbaᶜa)	*Wednesday*
yōm il-ḫamīs	*Thursday*
yōm il-jumᶜa	*Friday* <the day of assembly>
yōm is-sabt	*Saturday*
il-jumᶜa‿l-mᾱḍye[21]	*last week*
il-jumᶜa‿lli fātat[22]	*last week*
il-jumᶜa‿l-jāy(e)	*next week*
yōm il-ḫamīs il-mᾱḍi	*last Thursday*
yōm il-ḫamīs il-jāy[23]	*this [coming] Thursday*

It's a good idea to recite the list above out loud along with the recording. If you don't manage to learn all these terms straight away, at least you now know where to find them (you can also use the word index at the end of this book).

---

21. Or il-'usbūᶜ il-mᾱḍi.

22. You are familiar with the verb fāt [ifūt] in the sense of *to go in*, but its basic meaning is *to pass* (yet another word that means *to pass* – one day we'll list them all), and the Arabic equivalent of the English expression *last* [*month / year*] etc. is illi fāt <that has passed>. The expression 'illi fāt māt <what has passed is dead> means *It's water under the bridge.*

23. At the beginning of the week we say in English *this Tuesday / this Wednesday*, etc. to refer to days in the same week. In Arabic, however, we say il-jāy <the coming…>.

Exercises

A. Translate into English:

1. '**a**hlan! mn**ē**n j**ā**y?
2. '**a**na j**ā**y min is-s**ū**q.
3. b**i**ddak / b**i**ddek t**ī**ji ma^c**ā**y?
4. b**id**kom t**ī**ju ma^c**ā**na?
5. '**a**ywa, bn**ī**ji '**i**za f**ī**^{h} b**ɑ̄**ṣ.
6. '**i**za ma btīj**ū**-š, b^{e}nr**ū**ḥ la-ḥ**ā**lna.
7. bass yīj**ī**-ni ђ**ɑ**bɑr, baq**u**l-lak.
8. min w**ē**n '**a**jat il-mɑṣ**ɑ̄**ri[24] h**ā**y?
9. l**ā**zem t**i**nzal ^{c}a-l-m**aw**qaf il-j**ā**y.
10. l**ē**š ma‿'^{e}jītū-š‿^{e}mb**ē**reḥ?
11. ma‿'^{e}jīn**ā**-š li'**a**nno k**ā**n-fī^h š**i**ta.

B. Complete the sentences

(Replace the English words with the appropriate expression in Arabic):

12. il-y**ō**m (I came) laḥ**ā**li. – l**ē**š? '**a**ђ**ū**ki (didn't come) ma^c**ā**ki?
13. l**a**', ma qid**e**r-š / ma q**i**dr^e-š (come) ma^c**ā**y.
14. (We've come)‿nz**ū**rkom u-nis'**a**lkom '**ē**mta r**ɑ**ḥ-(you come) '**i**ntu la^c**i**n(d)na.
15. min y**ō**m-ha (he stopped) y**ī**ji ^{c}a-l-m**a**ktab.
16. l**a**w j**ī**t (last week) k**u**nna ђɑll**ɑ**ṣna‿š-š**u**ġol.
17. l**a**w ђall**ū**ni (go out) kunt r**u**ḥ^{e}t '**a**na kam**ā**n.

---

24. See **footnote 14**.

18. law b**i**smaḥ il-mud**ī**r, (I'd go home) h**a**llaq.
19. k**ī**f (did it occur to you) t**ī**ji fi-l-l**ē**l (see **Lesson 18, footnote 8**)?
20. '**a**ja y**ō**m il-ḫam**ī**s (last).
21. sm**e**ᶜna (that you'd had a) w**a**lad, mabr**ū**k!
22. (I received) makt**ū**b min '**u**ḫti.
23. bᵉtq**ū**l inn-ha r**ɑ**ḥ-(she [will] come) iš-š**a**hr‿il-j**ā**y 'in š**ɑ̄**' ɑll**ɑ**h.

C. Translate into Arabic:

24. When did you$^{\text{m sing}}$ come here last time?
25. Who came this morning <today the morning>? The postman (il-b**u**sṭɑji) came and brought a letter for you$^{\text{m sing}}$.
26. He always comes at one o'clock.
27. Tomorrow you$^{\text{m sing}}$ don't have to come <not necessary that you come> early...
28. because we haven't finished the job yet. Come in the afternoon.
29. It occurred to me to visit him, do you$^{\text{m sing}}$ want to come with me?
30. I was [just] talking about him (ᶜ**a**nno), and there he was standing in front of me.
31. A lot of people came. – Did the neighbors come too? – No, they'll come tomorrow.
32. We heard you$^{\text{m sing}}$ had had a son, congratulations! – Thank you!
33. My sister's given birth to a daughter. – Congratulations!
34. We've got to finish before he comes (see **Book 1, p. 32** in the **Conversation**).

A few nawāder[1] in conclusion

The further you progress in your studies and the more Arabic you hear spoken, the more you will find that what you've learned so far in this course can be put to practical use in all areas. At the same time, however, you'll realize that not all Arabic speakers talk precisely like those on the recordings, and that not everyone speaks "by the book." Why is this?

We could say, jokingly, that they didn't have the benefit of using this course!

Or, more seriously, we may remind you that colloquial speech is fluid and variable. Transliteration in this book attempts to reflect urban pronunciation, as this is the form of speech expected of non-native speakers of Arabic (naturally, this limitation does not apply to a foreigner who has lived for a long period in a particular village or among Bedouin, and has integrated to the point of becoming "one of them"). Different accents are heard in different parts of the country, and sometimes even within the same area, and it's impossible to survey the speech habits of the entire population and discover precisely how each individual pronounces every one of the thousand words you've learned so far. For example, people living in the same area – and sometimes even the same individual – will say r**a**ma or r**ɑ**mɑ, m**a**drase or m**a**drasa, etc., and, even though most people may say ṭull**ɑ̄**b, you'll always find someone who says ṭull**ā**b. As we didn't want to encumber you with a multiplicity of possible forms, we've supplied only those that seemed to us most widely used.

Despite our remarks above on the fluidity of the spoken language, we recommend that learners try to stick to the forms given in the book, just to be on the safe side. Most words have only one accepted pronunciation, and carefully distinguishing between -a and -ɑ, for example, will enable your listeners to understand precisely which word you intend.

The same applies to rules and the use of certain expressions. When asked how they express themselves in a particular context, native speakers will often provide an answer that they consider desirable, elegant or logical – rather than what they actually say. With regard to Rule 13, for example, even native Arabic speakers are sometimes in doubt as to whether they should use the plural or the

---

1. n**ā**drɑ [naw**ā**der] = *amusing anecdote / curious tale* (n**ā**drɑ literally means *rare*[f]).

feminine singular (we'll come back to this problem in Book 3). The question "How do you say that?" can disconcert native speakers, who are unaccustomed to a close examination of their routine speech habits.

It's rather like the story of the bearded man who was asked if, when he slept, he tucked his beard underneath the sheet or left it on top. He hesitated before replying: "On top of the sheet…? No, actually, I think… underneath. Well, I'll take note of what I do tonight, and I'll let you know tomorrow."

I once asked an Arab friend from Nazareth, a very reliable language informant of mine for many years, if children in his area addressed their fathers as yā-bα! as I had heard youngsters doing in the Western Galilee village of Tarshiha 25 years previously; or if they preferred the term bᾱbα, as I had been told that year in Jerusalem.

He replied without hesitation: "bᾱbα? mᾱmα? People who use those terms have been influenced by the West. We say yā-bα!" Soon after, I happened to call him at home to consult him on another linguistic matter, and his son, who answered the telephone, said: "I'll get him." Then I heard his voice calling out: "bᾱbα!".

And while we're on the subject of "word-hunting," here are a few more nawāder :

I gathered the material for my Hebrew-Arabic dictionary from live conversations and recordings, as I wanted it to contain only expressions that I'd heard first-hand, rather than things copied from other books. Although the material I collected provided the translations for most of the Hebrew words and phrases in the dictionary, there were, of course, gaps – words or expressions I'd never chanced across before. One problem was the plurals, which I wanted to check for each noun individually, even though there are rules that govern plural formation (you'll learn them soon). My list already contained the masculine and feminine singular forms of the word *hunchback* – but what was the plural? Were the forms I'd found in other books in use in our area, too? I asked an elderly man how he said *hunchbacks* in Arabic. He looked surprised, hesitated for a moment, then replied with a smile: "I've never seen five people with humps together all at once!"

It can happen the other way round, too. I knew that the bubbles in fizzy drinks were referred to as faqāqīᶜ, and, naturally, I wanted to add the singular form to the dictionary. When I asked a teacher from Nazareth how to refer to a single one of these bubbles she replied: "But… there are always a lot of them together." A native speaker can grow old without ever hearing the singular or plural form of certain words. Incidentally, according to the rules, the singular of faqāqīᶜ can be either fuqqāᶜa (as in literary Arabic) or fuqqēᶜa (or something similar). But even informants willing to risk an answer usually hesitate slightly before replying. A friend of mine who heard the bubble story remarked that a spirit level contained only a single bubble... walla fikra! I waited for an opportunity, then one day I saw an Arab builder standing at the traffic lights on the other side of the road, holding a spirit level. When he drew level with me, I asked him what the thing in the middle of his instrument was called. His eyes widened in surprise as he replied, "hāda? hāda hawa!" (*That? That's air!*) So my research is still incomplete, and you are invited to join in: any one of you who hears the word *bubble* in the course of normal conversation in colloquial Arabic (not in response to a question, as that can be tricky), will be rewarded with a fizzy drink with lots of bubbles in it.

On another occasion I wanted to know how to say *to cheat* and *a cheat* in the context of a game. I asked a boy in the Western Galilee village of Tarshiha: "What do you call a boy who cheats when playing a game?" He replied disdainfully: "I say ya‿ḥmār (*you ass*)!"

One final nādra to demonstrate the pitfalls that lie in wait for the word-hunter. While searching for a new informant to provide me with information on the colloquial speech current in the Jerusalem area, I was introduced to a woman who had been born in the city. After a number of initial questions, I remarked that it was odd that she had responded with words characteristic of the Galilee dialect (which resembles colloquial Lebanese speech), rather than that of Jerusalem. "Ah, yes, that's very possible," she said. "My father's from Lebanon and my maternal grandmother came from Syria. Our neighbors in Jerusalem used to say to us: 'You've got a special way of talking.'" People who move from one country to another continue to maintain their original speech patterns, at least partially. I hardly need add that after this conversation I started looking for another "more Jerusalemite" source of information.

That's enough for now. We wanted to provide a little entertainment for our students who have stuck it out this far, and show them that presenting an accurate snapshot of the current state of a colloquial dialect is no simple matter. It's like trying to photograph a small child so brimming with vitality that he or she is constantly in motion: the reality will always be much more interesting than the photograph!

Key to the Exercises

Here are the solutions to the exercises. When you finish each lesson compare your answers (the written ones, of course) with the key below. After you've corrected any mistakes, read the amended text out loud.

Lesson 16

1. This book is full of stories.
2. There are three boxes here, [and that's] enough.
3. But where are the lids?
4. There's one lid here, but where are the rest?
5. What size is this box?
6. Tell me what size the room is <how much size [is] the room>.
7. There's no room for him here.
8. Yes [there is], there's plenty of room <much space>.
9. He doesn't want to go without me.
10. In that case <if so> we'll go without you.
11. We visit one another.
12. Some <part> of the boxes have no lids <[are] without lid>.
13. The children go in one after the other.

14. il-qannīne malāne / malyāne.
    The bottle is full.
15. il-mɑṭbɑẖ wiseẖ il-yōm.
    The kitchen is dirty today.
16. lōn il-bāb 'aḥla min lōn iš-šubbāk.
    The color of the door is nicer than the color of the window.
17. il-yōm il-fil^{e}m kān 'ɑṭwɑl min‿^{e}mbāreḥ.
    Today the film was longer than yesterday.
18. lāzem ijību 'aflām haqṣɑr minšān l-ewlād.
    They should put on <necessary [that] they bring> shorter films for the children.

19. biddi ġurfe 'akbɑr.
20. bidna 'akbɑr ġurfe.
21. hāt ^{c}ulbe 'azġɑr.
22. hādi luġɑ hay(y)ne.
23. mā fī^{h} luġɑ hayne, kull luġɑ ṣɑ^{c}be lal-'ajāneb.
24. btiḥki luġɑ 'ajnabiyye?
25. la', baḥki bass ^{c}ɑrɑbi.

Lesson 17

1. 'ana baġsel u-inti btiġ^{e}sli.
2. 'uskot 'inte, u-inti kamān 'us^{o}kti!
3. ya walad, lāzem tudros; ya‿ulād, lāzem tud^{o}rsu.
4. Ask for as much as you want.
5. Children, write the lesson, study hard <well>!
6. Bring the box so we can see what's inside <so we see what there is in its heart>.
7. Sit here beside me!
8. Don't sit <not good that you sit> here, there's a draft.
9. Don't leave the boy on his own!
10. il-mɑrɑ btiḥmel il-jɑrrɑ ^{c}ala rɑ̄s-ha; btiḥmel-ha.
    The woman carries the pitcher on her head; she carries it.
11. ya Maryam, 'it^{e}rki hal-bint u-ta^{c}āli la-hōn!
    Maryam, leave that girl alone and come here!
12. hiyye 'azġɑr minnek, 'it^{e}rkī-ha!
    She's smaller than you, leave her alone!
13. lēš qimt il-ġɑṭɑ?
    Why did you remove the lid?
14. baqīm il-ġɑṭɑ. – lēš b^{e}tqīmo?
    I'm removing the lid. – Why are you removing it?
15. biddak 'aqīm il-^{c}ilbe min hōn?
    Do you want me to remove the box from here?
16. l-ewlād buḍ^{o}rbu bɑ^{ce}ḍ.
    The boys hit one another.
17. biddi asboq is-sayyɑ̄rɑ illi quddām-na.
    I want to overtake the car that's in front of us.
18. fī^{h} sayyɑ̄rɑ quddāmi, biddi asboq-ha.
    There's a car in front of me. I want to overtake it.
19. jību‿l-^{c}ulbe, biddi ašūf šū fī^{h} b-qal^{e}b-ha.
20. ya Kāmle, 'ik^{e}tbi la-'immek!
21. 'ēš biddak 'akteb?
22. 'aḫbɑ̄r min il-bēt.
23. rūḥ la-ḥālak / rūḥi la-ḥālek!
24. ya ulād, ma trūḥū-š / la trūḥu la-ḥālkom!
25. mīn 'ɑṭwɑl wāḥad, Kāmel willa Nabīl?
26. humme qadd bɑ^{ce}ḍ-hom.

27. mbāreḥ is-sandūq kān fi nafs il-maḥall.
28. jib^{e}t talāte kīlo: lāzem kull wāḥad ijīb qaddi.

Lesson 18

1. Today the lesson is not hard.
2. Yes it is! I listened to the recording and didn't understand.
3. If you don't listen to the recording again and again <more and more>, you won't understand <not possible that you understand>.
4. Can you tell me when there's a bus?
5. I can't tell you.
6. No-one here can tell you.
7. This bed is good. I slept well.
8. I can say that I slept well.
9. Do you want to sleep in the afternoon?
10. No, thank you, I can't sleep in the daytime.

11. ma sme^{c}t-^{e}š kalāmak.
    I didn't hear what you said.
12. fi 'awwal id-dars ma‿fhemt-^{e}š,
    At the beginning of the lesson I didn't understand,
    bass hallaq bafham kull kilme.
    but now I understand every word.
13. 'iza bakteb‿^{e}ktīr, bat^{c}ab.
    If I write a lot, I get tired.
14. 'ēmta birja^{c} 'abūk, il-yōm willa bukrα?
    When's your father coming back – today or tomorrow?
15. lamma basma^{c} nukat, bαḍḥαk.
    When I hear jokes, I laugh.
16. sim^{c}u‿l-quṣṣα, bass ma fihmū-š wala kilme.
    They heard the story but they didn't understand a word.
17. iš-šuġ^{o}l kān hayyen (G: kān‿^{e}hwayyen), ma‿t^{c}ebnā-š.
18. banzal kull yōm, bass il-yōm ma‿qdert-^{e}š.
19. ma‿qdert-^{e}š tinzal?
20. mαẓbūṭ, ma‿qdert-^{e}š 'anzal.
21. jāri qal-li innak‿^{e}ḍḥek^{e}t.
22. mαẓbūṭ ^{e}ḍḥek^{e}t, kull in-nās ḍeḥku, muš bass 'ana.
23. 'iza biddak‿^{e}tnām, btiqdαr‿^{e}tnām ^{c}in(d)na.

24. ’iza biddek‿ᵉtnāmi, btiqdɑri‿tnāmi fōq, fīʰ farše.
25. lamma banām, ma basmaᶜ-š wala ’iši.
26. lamma bᵉtrūḥ ᶜa-l-quds, ᶜind mīn bᵉtnām?
27. hal-mɑrrɑ nimᵉt ᶜind‿ᵉṣḥɑ̄b.
28. lāzem nismaᶜ it-tasjīl kamān mɑrrɑ.

Lesson 19

1. Did you hear the joke?
2. No, let’s hear it <say, that we see>.
3. We want to laugh too (and he’s already laughing).
4. OK, listen first, then you’ll laugh.
5. Get off here. The next stop is very far [away].
6. I understand a few words in the sentence.
7. How should I do [it]?
8. Watch <see> how I do [it] , and do the same as me <like me>.
9. Your brother was angry with you. Why?
10. Because I made a mistake and we lost money.
11. How much did **you** lose? Did you lose a lot?
12. Well, not less than him.
13. Go backwards, reverse, reverse, stop!
14. wēn l-ewlād? – ṭelᶜu la-fōq.
    Where are the kids? – They went upstairs <to above>.
15. bteᶜrɑf ’inte inno ’ana‿l-ђasrɑ̄n.
    You know that I’m the loser.
16. ’ēmta birjaᶜ min iš-šuġᵒl?
    When does he come back from work?
17. hal-mɑrrɑ ma‿ђsernā-š‿ᵉktīr.
    This time we didn’t lose much.
18. mɑẓbūṭ, ’ana‿ġleṭᵉt, bass humme kamān ġelṭu.
    [That’s] right. I made a mistake but they, too, were wrong.
19. ’irjaᶜ la-wɑrɑ, fīʰ maḥall.
    Go backwards / Back up, there’s room.
20. ’iza bteṭlɑᶜi, ђodi hāda la-fōq.
    If you’re going up, take this up.
21. ’ēš‿ᵉbteᶜmali‿ṣ-ṣubᵒḥ?
22. bɑṭlɑᶜ maᶜ ’uђti, bᵉnrūḥ ᶜa-s-sūq u-bnirjaᶜ ᶜa-l-bēt.

23. bteᶜrɑf tirkab ᶜa-l-busuklēt / baskalēt?
24. lamma bᵉtrūḥ ᶜala‿š-šuġᵒl, wēn‿ᵉbtinzal?
25. ᶜādatan banzal hōn.
26. ma rijᶜū-š‿ᵉmbāreḥ; in-natīje, ẖserna yōm.
27. il-bisse nāmat bɑrrɑ.
28. kīf? ᵉmbēreḥ kānat juwwa.
29. mɑẓbūṭ, bass il-walad fataḥ il-bāb w-il-bisse ṭelᶜat la-bɑrrɑ.
30. kull yōm il-bisse bteṭlɑᶜ u-baᶜdēn‿ᵉbtirjaᶜ ᶜa(la)-l-mɑṭbɑẖ.

Lesson 20

1. Make an effort <all your effort> if you want to succeed.
2. Bring the knife!
3. What do you want to do with it?
4. Please, bring me the recording, I want to hear it again.
5. You owe him 200 shekel[s], so he tells <told> me.
6. On the contrary! He's wrong!
7. He owes me 300 shekel[s].
8. Mum, I don't want to sleep, I want to play a bit longer.
9. OK, here's your doll. Play with it.
10. Come [here], we want to play a new game.

11. 'iᶜmal jahdak (juhdak) 'iza biddak tinjaḥ.
    Make an effort if you want to succeed.
12. jīb‿is-sikkīne!
    Bring the knife!
13. šu biddak teᶜmel fīha?
    What do you want to do with it?
14. min fɑḍlak, jib-li‿t-tasjīl, biddi asmaᶜo kamān mɑrrɑ.
    Please bring me the recording, I want to hear it again.
15. 'ilo ᶜindak mītēn šēkel, hēk qal-li.
    You owe him 200 shekel[s], so he tells <told> me.
16. bil-ᶜaks! huwwe ġɑlṭɑ̄n!
    On the contrary! He's wrong!
17. 'ana biddi minno talat mīt šēkel.
    He owes me 300 shekel[s].
18. ya mɑ̄mɑ, biddī-š anām, biddi alᶜab kamān‿ᵉšwayy.
    Mum, I don't want to sleep, I want to play a bit longer.

19. ṭαyyeb, hayy il-luᶜbe tabaᶜek, 'ilᶜabi fīha!
OK, here's your doll. Play with it.

20. taᶜāl, bidna nilᶜab luᶜbe jdīde.
Come [here], we want to play a new game.

21. 'ilak nafs / nefs tākol (tōkol) 'iši hallaq?

22. la', ma-lī-š nafs!

23. 'ilek ђāṭer teṭlαᶜi maᶜi 'issa?

24. la', ma-lī-š ђāṭer αṭlαᶜ baᶜd‿iḍ-ḍuhᵒr.

25.'iza hēk, rūḥi nāmi!

26. wαllα fikrα.

27. wēn il-mαṣāri? – fi juzdāni.

28. bass il-mαṣāri miš 'ilak!

29. ᵉmbala! il-mαṣāri 'ili, miš 'ilak!

30. jībi‿l-qalam w-ikᵉtbi fīʰ!

31. wēn il-ġαṭα tabaᶜ il-ᶜilbe hāy?

32. il-ᶜulbe hōn, bass wēn il-ġαṭα tabaᶜ-ha?

33. najaḥna! – 'aywa, bass il-fαḍᵉl 'ilo.

Lesson 21

1. What's your dialect like <how your dialect>? [Is it] like the Egyptian dialect?
2. No, our dialect is the Palestinian dialect.
3. Whose car is this <a) this the car-of whom; b) to whom this car>?
4. That's my brother's car.
5. Is the car his or the manager's?
6. No that's his car.
7. But he has another car.
8. Yes, he has two cars. Lucky him!
9. Give [me] your [driving] license.
10. He has three brothers and he lives with his brothers.
11. Why didn't you bring your identity card?

12. hal-mαrrα ma 'aђad ruђᵒṣto maᶜo.
This time he didn't take his license with him.

13. ᶜazamtu Yūsef ᶜala‿l-ᶜaša?
Did you invite Yusef to dinner?

14. n**a**^{c}am, ^{c}azamn**ā**^{h}.
    Yes we did <we invited him>.
15. il-f**a**rše k**ā**nat fi-l-q**u**rne.
    The bed was in the corner.
16. is-sayy**ɑ̄**rɑ d**a**hsat il-w**a**lad.
    The car ran over the boy.
17. qɑṭ**ɑ**^{c}t iš-š**ā**re^{c} h**ō**n.
    I crossed <cut> the road here.
18. qɑṭ**ɑ**^{ce}t š**a**qfet ḫ**u**b^{e}z.
    I cut a slice of bread.
19. j**ī**b haw**ī**tak u-haw**i**yyet m**ɑ**rɑtak kam**ā**n.
    Bring your identity card and your wife's identity card, too.
20. niyy**e**t-na k**ā**nat‿^{e}mn**ī**ḥa.
21. l-ewl**ā**d b**i**qdɑru‿in**ā**mu fi-l-ġ**u**rfe h**ā**di, h**ā**di ġurf**e**t-hom.
22. f**a**rštak '**ɑ**ṭwɑl min farš**e**t-ha.
23. b**i**dna n**i**^{c}zem (n**e**^{c}zem) Y**ū**sef ^{c}a-l-ġ**a**da.
24. b**i**ddi **a**^{ce}zmo.
25. h**u**q^{c}od hun**ā**k fi-l-q**u**rne.
26. 'iḫw**e**t-na fi ġurf**e**t-hen // -hom.
27. '**i**qṭɑ^{c}i šaq^{e}ft**ē**n, š**a**qfe '**i**lek u-š**a**qfe '**i**li.
28. ṣ**e**ḥḥti mn**ī**ḥa, il-ḥ**a**mdu lill**ā**h!
29. il-y**ō**m il-mɑr**ī**ḍ ma ^{c}ind**ō**-š hɑr**ɑ̄**rɑ.
30. ^{e}fh**e**m^{e}t kull '**i**ši. – niyy**ā**-lak!

Lesson 22

1. At first it was easy, then it got harder.
2. [It's] cold today.
3. [That's] right, it's cold outside but not in the room.
4. If you open the window, it'll get cold in the room, too.
5. When he was a boy, he didn't know how to write,
6. but now <today> he can write well.
7. A year ago, I understood very little,
8. but now I understand more.
9. Ten years ago, he only had two daughters,
10. [but] now he has five children.
11. Yesterday I told him: I haven't got any. Today he asked me again for the same thing.

12. Before the war there were 200 [of them], today there are 500 [of them] <they became 500>.
13. Two days ago he went out of the house and didn't come back. I don't know what's become of him.
14. My mother fell on the steps [and] broke her arm. – I hope she's better soon <her health>!

15. fi-l-bidāye kān hayyen, baᶜdēn ṣār 'ɑṣᶜɑb. = 1, above.
16. bard il-yōm! = 2, above.
17. 'iza btiftaḥ iš-šubbāk biṣīr bard fi-l-ġurfe kamān. = 4, above.
18. lamma kān walad ma kān yeᶜref / yeᶜrɑf yikteb, = 5, above.
19. 'amma‿l-yōm ṣār yikteb‿ᵉmnīḥ. = 6, above
20. lissa ma rijeᶜ, 'ɑbṣɑr šu ṣār maᶜo.
    He hasn't come back yet! I don't know what's happened to him.
21. 'immi wiqᶜat ᶜa-d-daraj, kasrɑt 'īd-ha.
    My mother fell on the steps [and] broke her arm.
22. l-ewlād ṣāru yurᵒkḍu.
    The children / boys began to run.
23. fi-l-bidāye kān ṣɑᶜᵉb, hallaq ṣār 'ahwan.
24. ᵉmbāreḥ ma kān fīʰ (ma kan-š fīʰ) bɑnḍōrɑ.
25. smeᶜᵉt ṣār fīʰ bɑnḍōrɑ.
26. id-doktōr fɑḥɑṣak? / fɑḥɑṣak id-doktōr?
27. 'aywa, fɑḥɑṣ-ni.
28. biddi afḥɑṣɑk / -ṣek.
29. id-doktōr qāl (± inno) biddo yifḥɑṣo.
30. kān biddo‿iṣīr doktōr / ṭɑbīb.
31. lāken 'abūʰ qal-lo: la', bᵉtṣīr muḥāmi.
32. hāda‿t-tamrīn ṣɑᶜᵉb, bikaffi, rūḥ nām / rūḥi nāmi!
33. 'ā, ṣār il-waqt!

Lesson 23

1. Mahmud, where are you going? – To the office,
2. and where are you going? – I'm going to the office, too.
3. I saw them walking <going> together.
4. Where's the girl? – I saw her going up[stairs].
5. [That's] right. I went up and found her asleep.
6. Good morning, children! What? You're still asleep?! Get up quick!

7. When she saw me, she realized she had to come down.
8. She’s still upstairs. I [can] hear her voice.
9. No, she came down a long time ago.
10. The shop is open from morning until noon.
11. Yes, I saw him sitting in his shop.
12. I went to the neighbors’ [and] found them sitting in the yard.
13. Don’t sit on the chair, it’s broken.

14. š**u**fto q**ā**^{c}ed b**ɑ**rrɑ.
    I saw him sitting outside.
15. k**ā**nat q**ā**^{c}de fi ġ**u**rf**e**t-ha.
    She was sitting in her room.
16. is-sand**ū**q h**ā**da maks**ū**r, j**ī**b ġ**ē**ro!
    This box is broken, bring another one!
17. ’**a**na ṣert k**ā**teb hal-makt**ū**b.
    I’ve written this letter.
18. ma‿^{c}r**e**ft-^{e}š inno h**ā**da mamn**ū**^{c}.
    I didn’t know that was forbidden.
19. k**ā**n ḥ**ā**mel š**a**nta zġ**ī**re.
    He was carrying a small suitcase.
20. h**ā**y ṣ**ū**rti u-**a**na w**a**lad.
    That’s a picture of me when I was a boy / child.
21. ṭ**e**l^{c}at min il-b**ē**t u-h**i**yye ḥ**ā**mle w**a**lad‿^{e}zġ**ī**r ^{c}ala **ī**d-ha.
    She went out of the house carrying a small boy / child in her arms.

22. laq**ē**t il-b**ā**b maft**ū**ḥ – laq**ē**t il-muft**ā**ḥ maks**ū**r.
23. q**u**lt la-J**ō**n: ’**e**ṭlɑ^c! mb**a**yyen ma f**i**hm-^{e}š, h**ā**da ġar**ī**b, muš f**ā**hem š**u** ṣ**ɑ̄**r;
24. qāl**ū**-li inno b^y**i**fham ^{c}**ɑ**rɑbi, l**ē**š ma ṭ**e**le^c?
25. mb**a**yyen f**i**hem inno l**ā**zem y**e**ṭlɑ^c la-f**ō**q, li’**a**nno qult-**i**llo : ’**e**ṭlɑ^c!
26. m**ɑ**rrɑ t**ā**nye, q**u**l-lo: ’**e**ṭlɑ^c la-b**ɑ**rrɑ!
27. mɑẓb**ū**ṭ, h**u**wwe f**ō**q. ya J**ō**n, ’**i**nzal qaw**ɑ̄**m!
28. ’**a**na š**ā**yef / š**ā**yfe ’**u**ḫtak ṭ**ɑ̄**l^{c}ɑ min il-b**ē**t.
29. š**u**ft il-muḫt**ɑ̄**r ṭ**ɑ̄**le^c min b**ē**to.
30. š**u**f^{e}t ^{c}umm**ā**l m**ā**rq**ī**n fi-š-š**ā**re^c.
31. iṭ-ṭull**ɑ̄**b ṭ**e**l^{c}u min ^{c}**i**nd il-mud**ī**r.
32. il-mud**ī**r is-s**ā**beq ^{c}az**a**m-ni ^{c}a-l-ġ**a**da. – ’**a**na kam**ā**n ma^{c}z**ū**m ^{c}**i**ndo.
33. qadd**ē**š‿^{e}tn**ē**n fi tal**ā**te? – ma baqd**ɑ**r-š ’aq**u**l-lak, mākint‿^{e}l^e-ḥs**ā**b (m**ā**kinet l^e-ḥs**ā**b) fi-l-m**a**ktab.

Lesson 24

1. I wanted to eat the meat [but] I found the dog had eaten it.
2. The girl always gets a good mark / grade.
3. Have you taken the medicine today?
4. You need to take two tablets in the morning and [one] tablet after dinner.
5. Umm Saleh, what are you doing? – I'm doing the laundry.
6. And then what will you do?
7. I'll hang out the laundry on the line.
8. Abu Mazen, what are you doing (just now)? – I'm writing an article.
9. The newspaper will publish my article.
10. You should go to the neighbors and offer them your condolences.

11. z**i**ᶜlat minno, kt**ī**r '**a**ħad ᶜala ħ**ɑ̄**ṭro.
    She was angry at him [and] he was very hurt.
12. b**i**ddi ar**ū**ḥ '**ā**ħod‿ᵉb-ħ**ɑ̄**ṭ**e**r-hen // -hom.
    I want to go to offer condolences to them.
13. w**ē**n l-ewl**ā**d? š**u** ᶜ**ā**m-bʸ**e**ᶜmalu?
    Where are the children? What are they doing (just now)?
14. laq**ē**t-ha m**ā**kle k**u**ll il-f**u**sdoq.
    I found she'd eaten all the peanuts.
15. ṣ**ɑ**r-lak zam**ā**n t**ā**rek il-b**ē**t?
    Is it long since you left the house?
16. '**i**mmi b**i**d(d)ha ᶜamal**i**yye.
    My mum needs an operation.
17. ᶜ**ā**datan m**ā** fīʰ ṣuᶜūb**ɑ̄**t.
    Usually there are no difficulties.

18. w**ē**n il-l**a**ḥme‿(i)lli k**ā**nat ᶜala‿ṭ-ṭ**ɑ̄**wle? – il-b**i**sse 'akl**a**t-ha.
19. w**ē**n il-l**a**ḥme‿lli j**i**bt-ha mb**ā**reḥ? – ma ḥad**ā**-š 'ak**a**l-ha.
20. b**i**nti '**a**ħdat ᶜal**ā**me mn**ī**ḥa fi-l-m**a**drase.
21. q**ā**l**a**t-li: b**ɑ̄**bɑ, 'aħ**a**dᵉt ᶜal**ā**me mn**ī**ḥa! bt**e**ᶜref il-ᶜal**ā**me‿lli 'aħ**a**dt-ha?
22. ħod l-ᵉkt**ā**b ᶜa-l-m**a**drase.
23. ma ᶜ**i**nd**ī**-š maḥall fi-š-š**a**nta. b**ā**ħdo m**ɑ**rrɑ t**ā**nye.
24. l**ā**zem t**ā**ħod (t**ō**ħod) had-d**a**wa qabl‿il-ġ**a**da.
25. qadd**ē**š '**a**ħad m**a**ᶜak w**a**qᵉt?
26. l-ewl**ā**d ᶜam-b**i**lᶜabu fi-š-š**ā**reᶜ.
27. ᵉzᶜ**e**lᵉt min b**i**nti, qult-**i**lha: '**u**sᵒkti!

28. ktīr 'aħdat ᶜala ħāṭer-ha.
29. kam mɑrrɑ lāzem 'āħod ('ōħod) had-dawa u-ēmta?
30. bass ḥab(b)tēn baᶜd‿il-ġada.
31. qul-lo yōħod fusdoq qadd-ma biddo.
32. dāyman bʸiġlɑṭ. 'akīd rɑḥ-yiġlɑṭ kamān mɑrrɑ.

Lesson 25

1. What time did you arrive?
2. We arrived early.
3. My parents arrived in the afternoon.
4. Ask your mum where it hurts <what hurts her>.
5. We phoned the doctor.
6. The minute you arrive, phone me!
7. The doctor said: It's not good to take much of that medicine!
8. That's why my stomach was aching!
9. I used to take three tablets every day.
10. My dad knows nice stories.
11. 'abūy kān yeᶜref quṣɑṣ ḥilwe.
    My dad used to know nice stories.
12. 'aħūy kān yuḍrob-li telefon / telefōn mɑrrtēn fi-š-šahᵉr.
    My brother used to phone me twice a month.
13. bass rijeᶜ, 'ana tarakt‿il-bēt.
    The minute he came back, I left the house.
14. smeᶜna biddo ibīᶜ sayyārto.
    We heard he wants to sell his car.
15. katab kalimāt 'uħrɑ, bass 'ana ma dirt-ᵉš bāli.
    He wrote different <other> words, but I didn't notice.
16. il-kalimāt illi katab-ha.
    The words he wrote.
17. lamma futᵉt ᶜa-l-ġurfe, il-walad kān ᶜam-bilᶜab.
    When I entered the room, the boy was playing.
18. lamma kunna zġār, kunna nilᶜab fi-š-šāreᶜ.
    When we were small, we used to play in the street.

19. h**ō**n f**ī**^{h} maš**ā**kel‿^{e}kt**ī**re.
    There are many problems here.
20. f**ī**^{h} hun**ā**k sanad**ī**q maks**ū**rɑ.
    There are broken boxes there.
21. '**a**yya s**ē**^{c}a‿wṣ**e**ltu? – ^{e}wṣ**e**lna‿s-s**ē**^{c}a s**i**tte.
22. b**ū**ja^{c}ek r**ɑ̄**sek? ɧ**o**di ḥ**a**bbet 'asbir**ī**n.
23. '**a**wwal kunt 'ab**ī**^{c} bɑnḍ**ō**rɑ. il-y**ō**m bab**ī**^{c} sayyɑ̄r**ɑ̄**t.
24. ṣ**e**rt '**a**^{c}ref ('**a**^{c}rɑf) kalim**ā**t‿^{e}kt**ī**re.
25. b^{y}**e**^{c}rɑf luġ**ā**t 'ajnab**i**yye.
26. '**ē**š il-luġ**ā**t illi bte^{c}r**e**f-ha?
27. il-kalim**ā**t illi bafh**a**m-ha.
28. '**i**bni b**i**jma^{c} ṭɑw**ɑ̄**be^{c}. – '**a**na kam**ā**n, l**a**mma kunt‿^{e}zġ**ī**r, kunt '**a**jma^{c} ṭɑw**ɑ̄**be^{c}.
29. h**i**yye bt**u**ɧod ḥ**a**bbe kull y**ō**m. mb**ē**reḥ ġ**i**lṭɑt, '**a**ɧdat ḥab(b)t**ē**n.
30. q**a**b^{e}l / '**a**wwal k**ā**nat t**ō**ɧod '**a**rba^{c} ḥabb**ā**t.

Lesson 26

1. He wants to build a new house.
2. We wanted to build a house for our son, [and] we brought builders …
3. But he wanted to build it himself.
4. When will you / do you want to finish your work?
5. We haven't finished yet! We'll finish tomorrow.
6. Yesterday you played me a song.
7. This isn't the song you played me.
8. The car stopped outside <next to> our house.
9. Does the bus stop here?
10. Yes, if you signal to it, it has to stop.
11. il-bann**ā**y išt**a**ġalu mn**ī**ḥ, ɧ**ɑ**llɑṣu‿š-š**u**ġ^{o}l q**a**bl‿iḍ-ḍ**u**h^{o}r.
    The builders worked well. They finished the work before noon.
12. l**a**', l**i**ssa ma ɧɑllɑṣ**ū**-š, l**ā**zem iɧ**ɑ**l(l)ṣu.
    No, they haven't finished yet. They've got to finish.
13. '**a**na jib^{e}t isṭiwɑ̄n**ā**t‿^{e}jd**ī**de, b**i**ddak tism**a**^{c}-ha?
    I brought [some] new records. Do you want to hear them?
14. '**a**ywa, samm**e**^{c}ni‿yy**ā**-ha!
    Yes, play me them.

15. ma biddi asma^c 'aġāni 'ajnabiyye.
    I don't want to hear foreign songs.
16. waqqaf sayyɑ̄rto jamb il-baladiyye.
    He stopped his car beside the town hall.
17. lāzem‿^{e}t'aššer lal-bɑ̄ṣ,'iza biddak (± inno) iwaqqef.
    You've got to signal to the bus if you want it to stop.
18. ma kān fī^h maḥall fi-l-bɑ̄ṣ, ^{c}ašān hēk ma waqqaf-^{e}š.
    There was no room on the bus, so it didn't stop.
19. kull ir-rukkāb nizlu min it-taksi.
    All the passengers got out of the taxi.
20. 'Arik 'ɑfḍɑl muṭreb ^{c}indi.
    Arik is my favorite singer.
21. sakkatat il-walad. sakkatato.
22. 'ayya yōm sāfaru?
23. il-maktūb illi katabto. il-maktūb illi katabt-illi‿yyā^h.
24. il-^{c}ummāl ištaġalu min iš-šub^{o}ḥ lal-muġreb.
25. bāb il-maktab kān‿^{e}msakkɑr.
26. laqēt kull l^e-bwāb‿^{e}msakkɑrɑ.
27. sme^{ce}t 'uġniye ḥilwe.
28. šu 'ism‿il-'uġniye illi sme^{c}nā-ha?
29. wēn il-makatīb illi jibt-ha / ... illi jibt-illi‿yyā-ha?
30. tarakt‿iṣ-ṣuwɑr ^{c}ala‿ṭ-ṭɑ̄wle.
31. lāzem‿^{e}tḫɑl(l)ṣi šuġlek qabl‿iḍ-ḍuh^{o}r.
32. mbāreḥ ma‿štaġalnā-š ba^{c}d‿iḍ-ḍuh^{o}r. štaġalna bass iṣ-sub^{o}ḥ.
33. jɑ̄rna biddo i^{c}allem 'ibno.
34. biddak‿^{e}tkammel ^{c}ilmak / dirɑ̄stak?
35. biddek‿^{e}tkammli ^{c}ilmek / dirɑ̄stek?
36. bid-ha‿tkammel ^{c}il^{e}m-ha / dirɑ̄set-ha.
37. qālat-li inno bidha‿tkammel dirɑ̄set-ha.
38. ba^{c}dēn 'abūha biddo išaġġel-ha ma^{c}o fi-l-maktab.

Lesson 27

1. He introduced me to his family.
2. We want you to introduce us to your family.
3. At first he said: I don't want [to]! Then he changed his mind.

4. My sister changed her mind [and] stopped visiting them.
5. Tell him to go to <approach> the window.
6. You’ve got to give him back the key!
7. I gave it back to him yesterday.
8. If you’d done what I told you, it <what happened > wouldn’t have happened.
9. If I’d had a calculator, I would have finished a long time ago.
10. [We’re] finished! I’ve stopped playing with him.
11. If I ate a lot, my stomach would hurt <me>.
12. Once I used to eat a lot and my stomach would ache.

13. m**ī**n ’**ɑ**fḍɑl mu**ṭ**reb ᶜ**ɑ**rɑbi ᶜ**i**ndak?
Who is your favorite Arab singer?
14. samm**e**ᶜni ’ak**a**m min ’**u**ġniye, baᶜd**ē**n baq**u**l-lak.
Play me a few songs, then I’ll tell you.
15. samm**a**ᶜna ’aġ**ā**ni la-ṣḥ**ɑ̄**bna.
We played songs to our friends.
16. il-’aġ**ā**ni illi sammaᶜn**ā**-hom‿iyy**ā**ha.
The songs we played to them.
17. ’**a**yya s**ē**ᶜa ђɑll**ɑ**ṣtu‿mb**ā**reḥ?
What time did you finish yesterday?
18. ’**i**za b**i**ddak‿ᵉtr**ɑ**wweḥ, l**ā**zem‿ᵉtђ**ɑ**lleṣ š**u**ġlak.
If you want to go home, you’ve got to finish your work.
19. baᶜd**ē**n‿ᵉbt**i**qdɑr‿ᵉtr**a**wweḥ.
Then you can go home.
20. l**a**mma‿wṣ**e**lna‿l-mɑḥ**ɑ**ṭṭɑ, qult-**i**llo: w**a**qqef!
When we arrived at the bus stop, I said to him: Stop!
21. w**ē**n id-disk**ā**t illi j**i**bt-ha?
Where are the disks (CDs) you brought?
22. w**ē**n id-disk**ā**t illi jibt-**i**llek‿iyy**ā**ha.
Where are the disks I brought you?
23. b**i**ddo‿iᶜ**a**llem **i**bno, b**i**ddo iᶜ**a**l(l)mo.
He wants to enable his son to study, he wants to enable him to study.
24. u-b**i**nto kam**ā**n, b**i**ddo iᶜall**e**m-ha.
<And> he wants to enable his daughter to study, too.

25. hal-mu**ṭ**reb‿ᵉkt**ī**r ᶜaj**a**b-ni. ṣ**ō**to kt**ī**r ḥ**i**lu.
26. biᶜ**a**mmru by**ū**t‿ᵉjd**ī**de.
27. b**i**dna‿nᶜ**a**llem ’**i**bᵉn-na.
28. bil-’**a**wwal ma‿fh**e**mt-ᵉš, bass l-ᵉmᶜ**a**llem fahh**a**m-ni.
29. ma‿f**i**hem-š / ma f**i**hm-ᵉš ’**i**lli ṣ**ɑ̄**r u-**a**na fahh**a**mto.

30. sakkɑrt il-bāb? – lissa. – sakkro!
31. ya Lɑṭīfe, sakkɑrti‿l-bāb? – la', ma sakkɑrtō-š. lāzem‿ᵉtsakkrīʰ.
32. katabᵉt la-Munīr. katabt-illo maktūb.
hāda‿l-maktūb illi katabt-illo‿yyāʰ.
33. jibt-illak diskāt, biddi‿tsammeᶜ-ni 'uġniye (± waḥade).
34. 'ayya 'uġniye biddak? – 'illi biddak‿iyyā-ha.
35. waqqaf it-tender quddām bēt-na.
36. ᶜallam-ni kalimāt‿ᵉjdīde. 'ēš il-kalimāt illi ᶜallamak‿iyyāha?
37. jāb l-ᵉktāb lal-ᵉmᶜallem? – 'aywa, jab-lo ktāb.
38. 'ēmta jab-lo‿yyāʰ? – 'awwal‿ᵉmbēreḥ.

Lesson 28 – Part 1

1. Do you know what they told me at the office?
2. I must tell you the story from the beginning.
3. What's he talking [about]? I don't understand him <his speaking>.
4. The oil lamp was lit. Why did you turn it off?
5. Speak very slowly so I [can] understand.
6. If there had been electricity yesterday, I would have turned off the oil lamp.
7. If there were electricity now, I would turn it off.
8. Take the radio. I've repaired it for you.
9. She's talking to him (now), that means they know one another.
10. He's stopped talking to me. He's angry with me, apparently.
11. biḥki maᶜ 'aḫūʰ, bass ma biḥkī-š maᶜ 'uḫto.
He speaks to his brother, but he doesn't speak to his sister.
12. 'aywa, bɑṭṭɑl yiḥki maᶜha / maᶜāha.
Yes, he stopped talking to her.
13. ḥakā-li illi ṣɑ̄r bit-tɑfṣīl.
He told me in detail what had happened.
14. u-hiyye, šu ḥakat? – ḥakat-li quṣṣɑ ġarībe.
And what did **she** say? She told me a strange story.
15. kīf iṭ-ṭɑqṣ ᶜin(d)kom?
What's the weather like by you?
16. šu btiᶜni lamma bᵉtqūl "ᶜindkom"?
What do you mean when you say: "By you"?
17. ᶜindkom, yaᶜni fi-l-jalīl.
By you, I mean, in Galilee.

18. s**a**kker iš-šubb**ā**k, f**ī**^{h} m**ɑ**jrɑ h**a**wa w-il-qand**ī**l inṭ**ɑ**fɑ.
    Close the window. There's a draft and the oil lamp has gone out.
19. š**u**ftu l-^{e}m^{c}**a**llem? – l**a**', ma šufnah**ō**-š.
    Have you seen the teacher? – No, we haven't seen him.
20. l**ā**zem t**i**ḥku ma^{c} il-mud**ī**r fi '**ā**ḫer iš-š**a**h^{e}r.
    You've got to speak to the manager at the end of the month.

21. l**ē**š‿^{e}bt**i**bni b**ē**tak hun**ā**k, ^{c}a-l-j**a**bal / ^{c}a-j-j**a**bal?
22. l**ē**š ma btibn**ī**-h**ō**-š h**ō**n, jamb b**ē**tna?
23. š**ū** ^{c}am-(b)t**i**ḥki?
24. '**i**ssa '**a**na f**ɑ̄**ḍi, h**u**q^{oc}di h**ō**n w-iḥk**ī**-li q**u**ṣɑṣ.
25. muš s**ā**me^{c} šu ^{c}am-b**a**ḥki?!
26. b**i**ddi aḥk**ī**-lak n**u**kte.
27. in-n**u**kte‿lli ḥak**ē**t-ha, sm**e**^{c}t-ha‿mb**ā**reḥ.
28. il-'iṭf**ɑ̄**'**i**yye ṭ**ɑ**fu‿l-ḥar**ī**qa. in-n**ā**s j**ā**bu m**ɑ**yy ḥ**a**tta y**i**ṭfu‿l-ḥar**ī**qa.
29. '**ɑ**ṭfi‿l-qand**ī**l? – l**a**', ma tiṭf**ī**h**ō**-š.
30. muš l**ā**zem tiḥk**ī**-lo k**u**ll '**i**ši.

Lesson 28 – Part 2

1. Is the water boiled? – Yes, my mother boiled it.
2. He didn't let me speak, he shushed me / told me to keep quiet!
3. The key was in the drawer. – That's why he couldn't find it!
4. If **I** had known, I would have found it.
5. Why didn't they let you go into the office?
6. They looked for the box [but] didn't find it.
7. She let the boy go out on his own.

8. w**ē**n iṭ-ṭ**ɑ**lɑb? – h**a**yyo, '**a**na m**ɑ̄**ḍi ^{c}al**ē**^{h}.
   Where's the application? Here it is. I've signed it.
9. ya Jam**ī**le, w**ē**n laq**ē**ti‿l-jar**ī**de?
   Jamila, where did you find the newspaper?
10. '**a**na daww**a**rt ^{c}al**ē**ha fi k**u**ll il-b**ē**t, ma laqēt-h**ā**-š.
    I searched for it all over the house [but] I didn't find it.
11. '**a**na m**a** ba^{c}ref iz-z**a**lame illi ḥ**a**ka m**a**^{c}ak.
    I don't know the man who spoke to <with> you.
12. bt**e**^{c}rɑf w**ā**ḥad by**i**ḥki 'alm**ɑ̄**ni?
    Do you know [any]one who speaks German?

13. 'aḫ**ū**k '**a**ḫad iš-šāk**ū**š.
Your brother took the hammer.
14. b**u**kra birajj**e**ᶜ-lak‿iyy**ā**ʰ.
Tomorrow he'll return it to you <he'll return to-you it>.
15. q**a**l-li: '**i**mḍi ᶜala‿ṭ-ṭ**ɑ**lɑb, mɑḍ**ē**to / mɑḍ**ē**t ᶜal**ē**ʰ.
16. f**ī**ʰ hun**ā**k ul**ā**d ᶜam-b**i**lᶜabu jamb il-b**ē**t.
17. b**a**ᶜref iz-z**a**lame illi ḫall**ā**ʰ‿if**ū**t.
18. b**a**ᶜref z**a**lame bid**a**wwer ᶜala šu**ġ**ol.
19. u-**a**na b**a**ᶜref w**ā**ḥad bid**a**wwer ᶜala ᶜumm**ā**l.
20. b**i**ddi aᶜ**a**rrfak ᶜal**ē**ʰ.
21. m**ɑ**ḍɑt il-makt**ū**b / m**ɑ**ḍɑt ᶜa-l-makt**ū**b.
22. f**a**wwato u-baᶜd**ē**n ḫall**ā**ʰ yeṭlɑᶜ.

Lesson 29

1. She went to bed and fell asleep immediately.
2. They started to talk about the elections and forgot their work.
3. I want to read the newspaper.
4. Bring me it. I want to read it.
5. I'm reading a book (just now).
6. What's the title of the book you're reading?
7. When do you want to start the job?
8. She started to do the laundry, but her neighbor came [round].
9. They started to talk to each other, and she didn't finish the washing.
10. Never mind! She'll finish tomorrow.
11. If you could read Arabic, I would bring you Arabic novels.
12. d**ā**yman bansa‿d-d**a**rs.
I always forget the lesson.
13. '**i**za b**a**smaᶜ n**u**kte, baᶜd**ē**n bans**ā**-ha.
If I hear a joke, I forget it right away <afterwards>.
14. '**i**za h**ē**k , r**ɑ**ḥ-aḥk**ī**-lak in-n**u**kte kam**ā**n m**ɑ**rrɑ.
If that's how it is <if so>, I'll tell you the joke again!
15. w**ē**n l-ᵉkt**ā**b? – n**i**syato fi-l-m**a**ktab.
Where's the book? – She left it <forgot it> in the office.
16. (ᵉ)ns**ī**na‿ns**a**kker il-b**ā**b.
We forgot to shut the door.
17. bd**ī**t '**a**kteb makt**ū**b, bass ma ḫɑllɑṣt**ō**-š.
I began to write a letter, but I didn't finish it.

18. ’**a**yya s**ē**^{c}a bt**i**bda‿l-ḥ**a**fle b**u**krɑ?
    What time does the party begin tomorrow?
19. b^y**e**^{c}mal ’aġl**ā**ṭ, ’**a**na baṣɑll**e**ḥ-lo‿yy**ā**ha.
    He makes mistakes [and] I correct them for him.
20. l**a**w qult-**i**lli, k**u**nt jibt-**i**llak‿iyy**ā**^{h}.
    If you’d told me, I would have brought you it.
21. f**ī**^{h} h**ō**n ṣ**ū**rɑ, m**a**-aḥl**ā**ha!
22. ns**ī**t ’ajīb il-jarīde, j**i**b-li‿yy**ā**ha, ’**ɑ**llɑ‿iḫall**ī**k!
23. k**u**ll in-n**ā**s q**i**ryu (q**a**ru)‿l-’i^{c}l**ā**n fi-š-š**ā**re^c, ’**a**na kam**ā**n‿^{e}qr**ī**to.
24. m**ɑ**rɑti ’**a**ḫdat il-jar**ī**de, b**i**d(d)ha tiqr**ā**-ha.
25. Y**ū**sef r**ū**ḥ u-**a**na‿bq**ī**t la-ḥ**ā**li. ma‿tr**ū**ḥ-^{e}š! ’**i**bqa h**ō**n m**a**^{c}i!
26. bte^{c}rɑf il-’**a**ḥrof il-^{c}ɑrɑb**i**yye?
27. b**a**^{c}ref (b**a**^{c}rɑf) ḥarf**ē**n tal**ā**te, muš ’**a**ktɑr.
28. b**a**^{c}d-ma (b**a**^{ce}d-ma) m**ā**t ’ab**ū**^{h} t**a**rak il-q̈**ɑ**rye.
29. ’**ē**mta biṣ**ī**r-fī^h intiḫāb**ā**t?
30. b**i**ddo y**i**lḥaq iḫ**ɑ**lleṣ q**a**bl‿**i**ḍ-ḍ**u**h^{o}r.
31. bass b**i**bda‿l-ḥ**a**fle, ’**a**na bar**a**wweḥ (± ^{c}a-l-b**ē**t).
32. fi-d-d**a**wrɑ h**ā**y / fi h**ā**di‿d-d**a**wrɑ f**ī**^{h} fatay**ā**t ^{c}ɑrɑbiyy**ā**t u-fatay**ā**t yahūdiyy**ā**t.

Lesson 30

1. Hello! Where have you been / Where have you come <are you coming> from?
2. I’ve come from the market.
3. Do you want to come with me?
4. Do you want to come with us?
5. Yes, we’ll come if there’s a bus.
6. If you don’t come, we’ll go on our own.
7. As soon as I get news, I’ll tell you.
8. Where did this money come from?
9. You need to get off at the next stop.
10. Why didn’t you^{pl} come yesterday?
11. We didn’t come because it was raining.
12. il-y**ō**m j**ī**t laḥ**ā**li. – l**ē**š? ’**a**ḫ**ū**ki ma-j**ā**-š ma^c**ā**ki?
    Today I came on my own. – What? Didn’t your brother come with you?
13. l**a**’, ma qid**e**r-š / ma q**i**dr^e-š y**ī**ji ma^c**ā**y.
    No, he couldn’t come with me.

14. jīna‿nzūrkom u-nis'alkom 'ēmta rαḥ-tīju 'intu laᶜin(d)na.
We've come to visit you and to ask you when **you're** going to come to us.
15. min yōm-ha bαṭṭαl yīji ᶜa-l-maktab.
Since then he's stopped going to the office.
16. law jīt il-jumᶜa‿lli fātet, kunna ђαllαṣna‿š-šuġol.
If you had come last week, we would have finished the work.
17. law ђallūni αṭlαᶜ, kunt ruḥᵉt 'ana kamān.
If they had let me go out, I would have gone too.
18. law bismaḥ il-mudīr, kunt barawweḥ hallaq.
If the manager allowed [me], I would go home now.
19. kīf 'aja ᶜa-bālak tīji fi-l-lēl? (see **Lesson 18, footnote 8**)
Whatever were you thinking of <how did it come to your mind>, to come at night?
20. 'aja yōm il-ђamīs illi fāt.
He came last Thursday.
21. smeᶜna 'ajā-k ('ijā-kᴳ) walad, mabrūk!
We heard you'd had a [baby] boy. Congratulations!
22. 'ajā-ni maktūb min 'uђti.
I got a letter from my sister.
23. bᵉtqūl inn-ha rαḥ-tīji iš-šahr‿il-jāy 'in šᾱ' αllαh.
She says she's coming next month, hopefully.
24. 'ēmta jīt la-hōn 'āђer mαrrα?
25. mīn 'ija‿l-yōm iṣ-ṣubᵉḥ // mīn 'aja‿l-yōm iṣ-ṣubᵒḥ?
– 'aja‿l-busṭαji u-jāb maktūb minšānak.
26. dāyman bīji is-sēᶜa waḥade.
27. bukrα miš lāzem tīji bakkīr,
28. li'anno ma ђαllαṣnā-š iš-šuġᵒl. taᶜāl baᶜd‿iḍ-ḍuhᵒr.
29. 'aja ᶜa-bāli azūro, biddak tīji maᶜi / maᶜāy?
30. kunt ᶜam-baḥki ᶜanno willa hū wāqef quddāmi.
31. 'ajat nās‿ᵉktīr. – il-jirᾱn kamān 'aju? – la', bīju bukrα.
32. smeᶜᵉt 'ajāk walad, mabrūk mā jā-kom! – 'αllα‿ibārek fīk!
33. 'uђti jābat binᵉt. – mabrūk!
34. lāzem‿ᵉnђαlleṣ qabᵉl-ma yīji.

Index of Vocabulary and Rules

Notes:

16 = Lesson 16

21-2 = Lesson 21, footnote 2.

24-e-4 = Lesson 24, Explanations 4.

The ᶜ, which has no English equivalent, appears in this list as the first letter of the alphabet. For example, the word maᶜqūl will appear earlier in the list than the word mablaġ.

ᶜ

ᶜād̲ [yaᶜūd̲] 18-17
ᶜadad 23-16
ᶜafwan 24-4
ᶜaks 20
ᶜalāme 24
ᶜālem 23 root p.82
ᶜam- 24-e-6
ᶜamaliyye 24-e-6
ᶜamɑ̄r 24-e-3
ᶜamɑ̄ra 24-e-3
ᶜāmel 23-e-1c
ᶜammāl = ᶜam- 24-e-6
ᶜammɑr 26
ᶜamūd 25
ᶜan 17-e-2
ᶜana 28-e-3
ᶜɑrɑbi 16-e-1
ᶜarrɑf 27
ᶜāš [iᶜīš] 28
ᶜaša 21
ᶜatīq 16-8
ᶜazam 21
ᶜazīz 21-e-2
ᶜēb 17-8
ᶜēn [ᶜyūn] 28
ᶜibrɑ̄ni 16-e-1
ᶜibri 16-e-1
ᶜiddet 28-e-3
ᶜilbe 16
ᶜilm 23 root p.82
ᶜiref 18-3
ᶜīše 28
ᶜubrɑ̄ni 16-e-1
ᶜulbe 16
ᶜunwān 29-8

A

'aᶜlam p.82
'aᶜūd̲u billāh 18-17
active participle 23-e-1
'afḍal 26-16
'ahamm 16
'ahl 27
'aħad ≠ misek 24-e-1
'aħad 24
'aħad ᶜala ħɑ̄ṭro 24-e-2
'aħad b-ħɑ̄ṭro 24-e-2

'aḫaff 16
'āḫar 25-e-4
'āḫer 18-e-2, 25-e-4
'aḫīr 25
'aḫrāni 25-e-4
'aja 30
'ajāʰ walad 30-e-1
'ajnabi 16
'akal 24-1
'akīd 19, 23-5
'āle 23-2
'ɑllɑ yirḍɑ... 29-11
'almɑ̄nya 27
'amma 22-20
'ana wiyyāʰ 29-4
'aqall 16
'asbirīn 24-e-7
'aswad 20-2
'aššɑr 26
'ašyā', 'ašya 25
'aw 18-14
'awāᶜi 16
'awwal 18-e-2
'awwalan 19-e-2
-āy / -āye 30-1
'azᶜal 26

B

bᶜīd 17-e-2
bāᶜ 25
bɑᶜḍ 16-e-4
bɑ̄bɑ p.164
badāl-ma 30
baka 29
bakkīr 30-4
bāl 25, 30-e-2
balā-y, balā-k 16-e-3
balad, blād 28-4
baladiyye 23
balāš 16-e-3
balki 17
ballaš 26
bana 28
bɑnḍōrɑ 24-e-7
bɑnṭɑlōn 16-10
baqa 29
bard 22
barīz 25-7
barrɑ̄d 24
bass *just as* 25-6
bɑṣɑl 20-e-3
bɑṭṭɑl 26, 27-5
bɑṭṭɑniyye 23
bidi 29
biki 29
bil-kād 29
bil-mɑrrɑ 28
binni 20
biqi 29
bizᵉr 24-e-7
blokk 26
bōsṭɑ 23
b-surᶜa 17-5
bulīs 21
bunni 20
byūt‿ᵉkbīre 25-e-3
byūt mabniyye 28-e-1

C

comparative 16

D

dahas / dahak 21
dāq [idūq] 29-18
dūr [idīr] 30-e-2
dūr [idūr] 29-3
dūr bālo 25
daraj 22-2
daraje 22
dawa 23
dawle 21
dawra 29-3
dawwar (ᶜala...) 28
dāyme 24-e-3
days of the week 30-e-3
dear 21-e-2
dinya 22-8, rule 19
dirūse 26-18
dōle 21
dōra 29-3
dukkān 23-21

D̲

d̲ = d / z 29-18

Ḍ

ḍāᶜ [idīᶜ] 20-5
ḍaḥḥak 27
ḍawa 28
ḍaww 28-11
ḍiḥek 18-2
ḍuhᵒr 18
ḍumme 19-17

E

ending -āy / -āye 30-1
evening 18-e-1

F

f-2 26
fa- 23
faḍel 20-8
fūḍi 28
fahham 26
faḥaṣ 22
fakkar 28-e-4
falasṭīn 21-24
faqad 23-22
faqīr 22-15
fūr 24
farše, faršet 21
fāt 30-22
fatayāt ᶜarabiyyāt 28-e-1
fawwat 27
fāyde 25
fi / b- 20-e-4
fiᶜel 19-18
fiᶜlan (feᶜlan) 18, 25
fiḍi 29-e-3
fihem 18
fišel, fašal 20
fiten 18
fiyye, fīk... 17-e-4
flān 24-17
forms of the verbs 26
fusdoq / fustoq 24-10
future 24-e-6

Ġ

ġād 17
ġada 21

ġala 28
ġɑlɑṭ 25-10
ġāli 21-e-2, 28-22
ġɑllɑṭ 27
ġɑlṭān 19-e-3
ġani 22-15
ġɑ̄r 24-14
ġarb 18-e-1
ġarbi 18-e-1
ġarīb 18-e-1
ġɑṭɑ 16
ġayyɑr 27
ġazāl 29
ġider 18-1
ġifi 29-e-4
ġileṭ 19
ġili 29-e-2
ġurfe 16

H

hadāk 16
hadīk 16
hadīk il-yōm 16-e-5
hadiyye 20
hadlāk 16-3
hadolāk 16-3, 16-e-5
hadōk 16-3
halqadd 17-e-3
hana 21-21
hawiyye 21
hayyen 16
hazze 22
hō-š 28-e-2
hwayyen 16, p.4

Ḥ

ḥabas 21
ḥabbe 24-e-7
ḥab[e]l 17
ḥable 24
ḥadīd 25
ḥaka 28
ḥamal 17
ḥammal 26
ḥɑ̄rɑ 28
ḥɑrɑ̄m 30-11
ḥɑrɑm (il- – iš-šarīf) 30-11
ḥɑrɑ̄rɑ 21, 22-1
ḥarf 29-10
ḥarīm 30-11
ḥarīqa 28
ḥɑrrɑr 27
ḥasab 19-e-1
ḥɑẓẓ 21-21
ḥēṭ 26-12
ḥikme 22-e-2
ḥilu 19-16
ḥilwiyyāt 19-16
ḥmɑ̄r p.165
ḥmɑrr 26, f-9
ḥorr 27
ḥorriyye 21
ḥsāb 19-e-1

ḫ

ḫabbɑr 27
ḫɑ̄f 24-2
ḫafīf 16
ḫāl 25
ḫāle 21

ḫalla 28-e-5
ḫɑllɑṣ 26
ḫarbān 27-1
ḫɑrrɑb 27
ḫasrɑ̄n 19-e-3
ḫɑ̄ṣṣɑtan 30-5
ḫaṭa 19-15
ḫɑ̄ṭer 20-10, 20-e-3c
ḫazāne 16
ḫazaq 26-e-2b, 26-19
ḫazzaq 26-e-2b
ḫēṭ 17
ḫileṣ 19
ḫireb 27
ḫiser 19, 19-e-3
ḫod 16
ḫuḍrɑ 25
ḫuṣūṣi, ḫuṣūṣan 30-5
ḫuz^{o}q 26-19

I

'i^{c}lān 29-19
'ib^{e}nha ≠ misek-ha 24-e-4
'īd 22-21
'id̲n 30-17
if only, if it were 27-e-2
'iḥmɑrr 26, f-9
'iḥtiyɑ̄ṭ 28-8
'iḫwe 21-e-3
'ili ^{c}alēk 20-e-3c
'ili, 'ilak 20-e-3c
'illa u- 30-9
'illi fāt 30-e-3
illi vanishing 28-e-4
il-wāḥed 30-13
immediate present 24-e-5
imperative 17-e-1, 19-e-5
imtiḥān 20
infataḥ 26, f-7
'ingeltra 28
'inglīzi 28
intiḫābāt 29
ista^{c}mal 26, f-10
istanna 30-3
isṭiwɑ̄ne 26, 26-15
...iši? 28-3
ištaġal 26, f-8
ištaka 29 p.152
'iṭfɑ̄'i 28
'izn, 'iz^{e}n 30-17

J

jā = 'aja 30-10
jabɑr 28-2
jah^{e}d 20
jamā^{c}a 29
jām^{c}a 20
jɑrrɑ 17-e-1
jɑrrɑ̄r 16
jārūr 16
jnūn 17
juh^{o}d 20
jumle 19
jurt̲ūme 28
juzdān 20

K

ka^{c}ke 21-10
kaḥḥal 27
kahrɑbɑ 28

kalām 18
kamaš 24
kammal 26
kamše 24
kāteb 23
kēks 21-10
ketto 21-10
kilme 18
kīlo 16-e-2
-kī-š 17 p.20
kuḥol 27-3
kuter(-ma) 18 p.25
kūz 16-14

L

la- (I'm referring to)   30-12
lahje 21-1
laḥme 24
lɑmbɑ 28
lamma + subj 22-e-3
laqa 28-e-5
laqēt 23-9
lɑṭīf 20-12
law 20, 27-e-2
lē 22-13
lēl 18-8
liᶜeb 20
liḥeq 26
lōḫ 28-19
lsān 19
luᶜbe 20-4
luġa 16, 21

M

mᶜallem 22
ma meanings 22-e-6

ma 'ɑšṭɑro! 29-e-1
maᶜā- 29-16
maᶜāš 17
maᶜna 19
maᶜnāʰ / maᶜnāt- 28-e-3
madīne 28-4
mɑḍɑ 28
mūḍi 30-e-3
mah-ma 22-e-6c
maḫṣūṣ 30-5
majbūr 28
malān 16
malyān 16
māneᶜ 23-15, 23-e-1
mɑnṭiqa 28-14
mɑq̈ɑle 24-19
mɑrɑti, mart- 21 p.51
mɑrrɑ (bil-) 28
mas'ūl, mas'ūliyye 23-10
mɑṣūri fem 30-14
māši ل-hāl 29
mawqaf, mawq̈ef 19, 26-14
mešwɑ̄r 20-3
misek 18, 24
miši 29
mit'akked 23-5
mitᵉr 16-e-2
miyye fi-l-miyye 20
mlabbase 24
moḥḥ 22-6
motōr 27
mrɑ̄y 30-1
mu- 26-3
muᶜallem 26-3
muḍde 22, 25

muġreb 18
muḥāmi 22-24
muḫālafe 24-16
mulk 23
munaẓẓame 27
mustaqbal 19
mustawa 23-11
muš + active participle 23-e-1
muškile 22-7
mušwār 20-3
muṭreb, muṭribe 26

N

naᶜam 29-6
nafs 20-10
najaḥ, najāḥ 20
nām 18-4
nūr 28-15
našar 24-20
nāšef 23-e-1d
natīje 19-3
nāyem 23-6, 29-e-4
naẓẓam 27
nefs 20-10
nhār 18-8
nisi 29
niyyā-lak 21-21
niyye 21
nizel 18
niẓām 27
nukte 18
numbers 16-e-2
nūr 25-12, 28-11
nusḫa 28

O

one another 16-e-4

P

Paris 25-7
passive participle 23
past participle 23
people (who) 28-e-4
plural
 – → *fem sing* 28-e-1
 – *foreign words* 26-7
 – □u□□ā□ 23-e-1c

Q

qaᶜad 17-2
qāᶜed 29-15
qabel-ma 22-18
qadaḥ 26-e-2b
qadd 17-e-3
qaddaḥ 26-e-2b
qalb 16-9, 17-e-4
qām [iqīm] 16-9
qamar 28-11
qandīl 28 p.131
qara 29
qarrab 27
ǫarye 25, 28-4
qatle 24-15
qaṭaᶜ 21
qawi 17-4
qazāz 28-19
qider 18-1
qird 29
qiri 29
quadriliteral 29-e-5
qudeḥ 26-19
qult-illi 20-e-1
qurne 16

quwwe 21-e-3, 21-27
qyās 16

R

rɑ'san 25
rɑ'y 30-2
rafa^c 23
rɑḥ- 24-e-6
rajja^c 27
rakan 25
rākeb 26-13
rama 28
rɑ̄s 17-19, 24
rawwaḥ 26
rɑ̄y 30-2
ribi 29-2
riḍi 29-e-3, 29-11
rije^c 18
rikeb 19, 26-13
riwāye 29
ruḫṣɑ 21

S

sā^ca, sā^cet-ha 29-14
sā'eq 17-3
sabaq 17
sābeq 23-e-1
saddaq 27
sādeq 27-4
safɑr 18
sāfɑr 26, f-3
saḥab 21-9
sāken [sukkān] 23-16, 23-e-1c
sakkɑr 26
sakkat 26
sakrɑ̄n 21
salāme 21-13, 27
salāmtak 21-13
sallam 26
salle 16
samake 17-18
samma^c 26
sandūq 17
sɑnṭi 16-e-2
sāq 17-3
sayyɑ̄ra 17
sayyed 29-5
sīd 29-5
siker 30
silem 27-8
sime^c 18
sitt 29-5
siyāse 29
slūk 30
sta^cmal 26
stanna 30-3
subjunctive 19-e-6, 22-e-5, 26-e-1
suffix -an 19-e-2
suffix -ān 19-e-3
sūq 19 Exercises
sur^ca 17-5
swāqa 21

Ṣ

ṣɑb^er 16-14
ṣɑ̄fen 28
ṣɑḥīḥ 16
ṣɑḥu 22-9
ṣɑ̄leḥ 27-2
ṣɑnṭi 16-e-2
ṣɑ̄r 19-6, 22-e-1
ṣɑrɑf 26-17
ṣɑrrɑ̄f 26-17

ṣeḥḥa 21-6
ṣōt 23
ṣuᶜūbe 24
ṣūrα 23
ṣyᾱḫ 24

Š

šabᶜān 24-5
šaġal 30-19, 30-e-2
šaġġal 30-19
šαḥṣ 30-6
šαḥṣi 30
šαḥṣiyye 30-6
šaka 29 p.152
šakαr 24-4
šākūš 28, p.138
šamsiyye 21
šαns 21-21
šaqfe 21
šay' 25
šēkel 16-e-2
šibeᶜ 24
šireb 23
šita 22-3
šmāl 29
štaġal 26 f-8
štaka 29 p.152
šufēr 17
šukran 24-4
šurṭα, šurṭi 27-9

T

taᶜāl 30
tabaᶜ 20-e-2
tafṣīl 28
taḥrīr 27 root p.125
take (to-) 24-e-1
taklīf 24
taksi 26
talᵉj 24-8
talfan 29-e-5
tallāje 24, 24-8
tamīn 23-22
tamrīn 16, 22-25
tānyīn 17-9
tαnẓīm 27, root p.125
tarjam 29-e-5
tarkīb 27-e-1
tartīb 26
tasjīl 18-18, 27-e-1
tawḥīd 27 root p.125
telefōn / telefon 25
that, those 16-e-5
tiᶜeb 18
tilmīz 18
tnēnāt- 28 p.137
tqaddam 26
tqūrαb 26
tqīl 16
trabba 29-2
trakk 26-7
trēn 25
tult 25

Ṯ

ṯāniyan 19-e-2

Ṭ

ṭαbᶜan 16
ṭαbeᶜ 19-e-2

U

u-... while, as (he was) 23-e-3
'uġniye 26

W

w-... while, as (he was) 23-e-3
waᶜad 25
wād 28
wāḥed (il-) 30-13
waḥḥad 27, root p.125
wajaᶜ 25
wājeb 24-4
wala 18-19
wαllα 20-13, 28-20
wāqef 29
waqqaf 26
waraqa 25
warše 26-10
wasaḫ 16-13
wαsαṭ, wαsṭ 21-8
wijeᶜ 25-1
willa and suddenly 30-9
wiqeᶜ 22-4, 25, 25-e-2
wiseḫ 16-13
wiṣel 25
wiyyā- 29-4

Y

yā... yā... 18-14
yā-bα 19-11, 21-22, p.164
yamīn 29
ya-mmα 19-11, 21-22, p.164
yarēt 22-e-5
yiterku 17
yōm 18-8
yōm-ha 29-14
yyā- 26-e-3

Z

zaᶜal 19
zaᶜlān 19-19, 19-e-3
zakαr 26-e-2a
zakkαr 26-e-2a
ẓbāle 17-e-2, 28 p.138
zhūr 19
ziᶜel 19-19, 19-e-3
ziheq 21-e-1, 21-26
zōq 29-18
zujāj 28-19

Ẓ

Rules Indicated by a Number Inside a Square

A word marked with a number inside a square – such as $\boxed{5}$ or $\boxed{13}$ – behaves in accordance with the rule indicated by that number (see below). Examples:

– A word marked with the number $\boxed{2}$ begins with a sun letter (see **Book 1, p. 10**). So, when you see, for example, š**i**ta $\boxed{2}$, you will realize that you have to say iš-š**i**ta and not il-š**i**ta (*the rain; the winter*).

– Similarly: q**a**b^{e}l $\boxed{5}$ behaves like b**i**nt / b**i**n^{e}t, which means that we use the form q**a**b^{e}l at the end of a sentence or before a consonant followed by a vowel, e.g. q**a**b^{e}l s**ē**^{c}a (*an hour ago*). For further explanation, see Rule 5 below.

A single word may, of course, be marked with more than one number. The numbers $\boxed{2}$ $\boxed{5}$ beside the word š**u**ġl remind us, firstly, that it starts with a sun letter and, secondly, that it behaves like b**i**nt – i.e. firstly that il- becomes iš- (iš-š**u**ġ^{o}l) and secondly that at the end of a sentence it acquires a helping vowel (see Rule 5) and assumes the form š**u**ġ^{e}l // š**u**ġ^{o}l.

These little numbered squares will provide you with valuable information about the idiosyncrasies of each new word you learn and show you how to use them.

The numbers of the rules given inside the squares are identical to the numbers used for the same purpose in the *Olive Tree Dictionary*[1] (pp. 755-763); this means that those of you accustomed to using the dictionary will feel at home here, too. The rules given here have been adapted to suit the contents of this course and the style of transliteration used in it. At this point we have provided only the rules you have already learned: we have no need of rules 9, 11, 12, 15 or 16 at present.

Those of you who find the profusion of signs (e.g., // < > [ ], and, in this book, also # and the numbered squares) a bit much to cope with will perhaps draw some comfort from recalling the infinitely greater number of signs you had to learn to pass your driving test... Here, however, if you miss a signal or two, at least it won't be life-threatening!

---

1. *The Olive Tree Dictionary: A Transliterated Dictionary of Conversational Eastern Arabic (Palestinian)*, J. Elihay, published by Minerva Instruction and Consultation, Jerusalem, 2004.

[1] The definite article is il-. This is the form it takes at the beginning of a sentence: il-w**a**lad (*the boy*). After a word ending in a vowel it shortens to ‿l-: š**u**fna‿l-w**a**lad (*we saw the boy*). The letter -l itself changes before certain consonants, as explained below in Rule 2.

[2] Before a word beginning with the letters d, d̲, ḍ, n, s, š, ṣ, t, ṭ, z, ẓ, r (which are referred to as **sun letters**), the -l of il- is assimilated into the first letter of the word:

the fire = il- + n**ā**r → in-n**ā**r
the cinema = il- + s**i**nama → is-s**i**nama

This assimilation can occur together with the disappearance of the i-, as explained above in Rule 1: ^{c}ala + in-n**ā**r → ^{c}ala‿n-n**ā**r

[3] Before all words that begin with two consonants – apart from the sun letters, i.e. the consonants listed above in Rule 2 – the definite article is l-^{e}, e.g., l-^{e}kt**ā**b (*the book*)

Some speakers use this form before sun letters, too, and so we may hear:

the little boy = il-w**a**lad iz-zġ**ī**r, in accordance with Rule 2
or il-w**a**lad l-^{e}zġ**ī**r, in accordance with Rule 3.

When a word like this, which starts with two consonants, is at the beginning of a sentence, a "helping vowel" (^{e}) may be inserted, e.g.,

^{e}kt**ā**b (*book*), ^{e}mb**ā**reḥ (*yersterday*). See also Rule 4, below.

[4] When a word ending in a consonant (e.g. w**a**lad) is followed by a word that starts with two consonants (e.g. kb**ī**r) a helping vowel similar to that described in Rule 3 is inserted:

w**a**lad + kb**ī**r → w**a**lad‿^{e}kb**ī**r (*a big boy*)

[5] A word that ends in two consonants (e.g. š**u**ġl, q**a**bl), is pronounced

a) With a helping vowel (^{e} / ^{o}) in the following cases:

– At the end of a sentence or before a natural break in the flow of speech:
k**ī**f iš-š**u**ġ^{o}l? (*how's work?*)

– Before a consonant followed by a vowel:
q**a**b^{e}l s**a**ne (*a year ago*)
š**u**ġ^{o}l h**a**yyen (*easy work*)

– Before the attached pronouns in **group B** below (i.e., before a consonant followed by a vowel: -ha, -na, -kom, -hom):

qab^e^l-kom *(before you)*

šuġ^o^l-na *(our work)*

b) Without a helping vowel (ᵉ / ᵒ), when followed by a vowel, i.e., in the following cases:

– Before the attached pronouns -i / -ak / -ek / -o (see **Group A**, below)

šuġli *(my work)*, qablo *(before him)*

– Before a word that begins with two consonants, because Rule [4] applies and actually the word begin with the vowel ᵉ.

qabl‿ᵉsnīn *(years ago)*

bint‿ᵉkbīre *(a big girl)*

šuġl‿ᵉktīr *(a lot of work)*

Summary

– Before a vowel, no helping vowel (ᵉ / ᵒ) is required:

qabl-i – qabl‿id-dars – qabl‿ᵉsnīn

– Before a **single** consonant / at the end of a sentence, a helping vowel intervenes:

qabᵉl s̲ane – qabᵉl-k̲om – 'ana jīt qabᵉl

Attached pronouns

Group A Starts with a vowel		Group B Starts with a consonant	
-i	*my*; (*for*) *me*	-ni	*me* (after a verb)
-ak	*your*; *you*^m sing^ (object)	-ha	*her* (possessive; object)
-ek	*your*; *you*^f sing^ (object)	-na	*our*; *us*
-o	*his*; *him*	-kom (-ku)	*your*; *you*^m/f pl^ (object)
		-hom (-hen)	*their*; *them*^m/f^

[6] In words marked with this number, the final vowel (usually -e)
– drops when a **Group A** (see above) attached pronoun is added;
– is stressed when a **Group B** (see above) attached pronoun is added:

misek *(he caught)* → misko; misek-ha *(he caught him; he caught her)*

ṣāḥeb *(friend)* → ṣāḥbi; ṣāḥeb-na *(my friend; our friend)*

7 A noun that ends in a **consonant** or in -i or -u is usually masculine, unless otherwise indicated. Nouns that denote women, girls or female animals, are, of course, feminine, e.g. ’**i**mm / ’**u**mm (*mother*).

– Words ending in -a, -α and -e are feminine:

m**a**drase (*school*); q**u**ṣṣα (*tale / story*)

– These endings may be added to a participle, an adjective or certain types of noun, to change them from masculine to feminine, e.g.,

mr**a**ttab → mr**a**ttabe (*organized*[m] → *organized*[f]).

The pronunciation of the ending varies in accordance with the preceding consonant, as follows:

-a, -α after

1) the gutturals ᶜ, h, ḥ, ħ ....,	mn**ī**ḥ → mn**ī**ḥa (*good* m → f)
2) the emphatic consonants. ḍ, ṣ, ṭ, ẓ	mαr**ī**ḍ → mαr**ī**ḍα (*ill* m → f)
3) r (with the exception of -**ī**r)	majb**ū**r → majb**ū**rα (*obliged* m → f)

-e is used in all other cases:

makt**ū**b → makt**ū**be (*written* m → f), kb**ī**r → kb**ī**re (*big* m → f)

8 Nouns ending in -a / -α / -e assume a special form when immediately followed by another noun: the final -a / -α / -e become -et, e.g.,

nih**ā**ye	*end*
nih**ā**yet id-d**a**wrα	*the end of the course*
bid**ā**ye	*beginning*
bid**ā**yet il-q**u**ṣṣα	*the beginning of the story*

This form ending in -et is called the ‘construct form’ (often shortened to ‘contruct’). The English equivalents of the construct state are *of* (as in the examples above) and *’s* as in:

ġ**u**rfe	*room*
ġ**u**rfet ’ab**ū**y	*my father’s room*

The construct form of a noun is also used when that noun is followed by an attached pronoun (-i, -ak, -ha, -na...)

ġurf**e**t-na	*our room*

The -e preceding the -t tends either to disappear or to become stressed, in accordance with rule 6 above,

f**a**rše	*bed*
f**a**ršt-i; farš**e**t-ha	*my bed; her bed*

[8*] A word marked like this belongs to the □a□□a□a / □a□□a□e group of nouns, e.g., m**a**drase (*school*), m**ɑ**ṣlɑḥɑ (*interest / benefit*). Words like this obey Rule [8], e.g.,

m**a**draset Mun**ī**r — *Munir's school*

madras**e**t-na — *our school*

However, when an attached pronoun from **Group A** is added (see table above), the stress moves to the **penultimate** syllable:

madr**a**sti — *my school*

mɑṣl**ɑ**ḥto — *his benefit*

[10] This number indicates nouns ending in -**i**yye, e.g., haw**i**yye (*identity; identity card*). Rule [8] applies to these nouns, too, e.g.,

haw**i**yyet ... — *'s identity card*

hawiyy**e**t-ha — *her identity card*

However, when the attached pronouns from **Group A** (see table above) are added to these words, the -**i**yye turns into -**i**yy → -**ī**, e.g.,

haw**ī**tak (haw**i**yytak) — *Your*$^{m\ sing}$ *identity card*

[13] Nouns **in the plural** that denote abstractions or an undefined number of objects require an adjective and verb in the **feminine singular**.

by**ū**t‿^{e}jd**ī**de — *new houses*

kalim**ā**t ^{c}ɑrɑb**i**yye — *Arabic words*

This rule also applies to the pronoun that represents the noun (*I see **them***), as in the phrase:

il-kalim**ā**t illi ba^{c}r**e**f-ha — *the words I know*
<the words that I know them>

Nouns of this type also require a feminine singular verb:

il-jar**ā**yed n**a**šrat il-ђ**ɑ**bɑr — *the newspapers published the news*

The same rule may apply – though this is not obligatory – to verbs describing the actions of groups of people (*human beings, children*), i.e., the verb **may** be put into the feminine singular, especially when it precedes the subject:

'**a**jat in-n**ā**s — *the people came*

This rule also applies to nouns denoting a totality or generality (such as *the streets of the town; books; thoughts*, etc.); however, when the verb / adjective / pronoun qualifies or refers to a noun **defined** by a number or by hal- / hadol (*these / those*), the plural is generally used:

’**a**rbaᶜ‿ᵉby**ū**t j**u**dod	*four new houses*
hal-k**u**tob, baratt**e**b-hom	*I arrange these books* <these books, I arrange them>.

14 The prepositions b- and fi (which indicate place, time and means) are often used interchangeably. With the attached pronouns, however, fi is generally used:

b**a**kteb bil-q**a**lam	*I write with the pen*
b**a**kteb f**ī**ʰ	*I write with it*

17 Long vowels are heard as such only when they are stressed. If the stress moves to another syllable, the long (now unstressed) vowel ā, ī, ū shortens. The shift in stress is indicated in our transcription by the use of **bold** characters, e.g.,

taᶜb**ā**n	*tired*$^{\text{m sing}}$	taᶜbān**ī**n (= taᶜban**ī**n)	*tired*^{pl}
makt**ū**b	*letter*	maktūb**ē**n (= maktub**ē**n)	*two letters*
š**ā**fat	*she saw*	ma šāf**a**t-š (= šaf**a**t-š)	*she didn’t see*

18 In phrases marked with this number the vowel of the verb shortens when an attached pronoun such as -li, -lak -lo (*to me, to you*$^{\text{m sing}}$*, to him*) is added:

q**ā**l *he said*	q**a**l-li *he said to me*
bij**ī**b *he brings*	bij**i**b-lek *he brings to you*$^{\text{f sing}}$

The addition of the negative particle -š may cause a similar shortening:

bij**ī**b *he brings*	ma bij**i**b-š (or m**a** bij**ī**b-ᵉš) *he doesn’t bring*

19 The weather, the seasons of the year, the times of day, darkness and light are attributed to id-dinya (*the world*), which is a feminine noun in Arabic:

id-d**i**nya rab**ī**ᶜ	*it’s spring*	<the world is spring>
ṣ**ū**rat id-d**i**nya l**ē**l	*it’s night-time now*	<the world has become night>